HTML STYLE SHEETS

DESIGN GUIDE

NATANYA PITTS, ED TITTEL,
AND STEPHEN N. JAMES

HTML Style Sheets Design Guide
Copyright © 1998 by The Coriolis Group, Inc.

All rights reserved. This book may not be duplicated in any way without the express written consent of the publisher, except in the form of brief excerpts or quotations for the purposes of review. The information contained herein is for the personal use of the reader and may not be incorporated in any commercial programs, other books, databases, or any kind of software without written consent of the publisher. Making copies of this book or any portion for any purpose other than your own is a violation of United States copyright laws.

Limits of Liability and Disclaimer of Warranty
The author and publisher of this book have used their best efforts in preparing the book and the programs contained in it. These efforts include the development, research, and testing of the theories and programs to determine their effectiveness. The author and publisher make no warranty of any kind, expressed or implied, with regard to these programs or the documentation contained in this book.

The author and publisher shall not be liable in the event of incidental or consequential damages in connection with, or arising out of, the furnishing, performance, or use of the programs, associated instructions, and/or claims of productivity gains.

Trademarks
Trademarked names appear throughout this book. Rather than list the names and entities that own the trademarks or insert a trademark symbol with each mention of the trademarked name, the publisher states that it is using the names for editorial purposes only and to the benefit of the trademark owner, with no intention of infringing upon that trademark.

The Coriolis Group, Inc.
An International Thomson Publishing Company
14455 N. Hayden Road, Suite 220
Scottsdale, Arizona 85260

602/483-0192
FAX 602/483-0193
http://www.coriolis.com

Printed in the United States of America
ISBN 1-57610-211-4
10 9 8 7 6 5 4 3 2 1

Publisher
Keith Weiskamp

Project Editor
Michelle Stroup

Production Coordinator
Kim Eoff

Cover Design
Performance Design

Layout Design
April Nielsen

CD-ROM Development
Robert Clarfield

⊘ CORIOLIS GROUP BOOKS

an International Thomson Publishing company I(T)P®

Albany, NY • Belmont, CA • Bonn • Boston • Cincinnati • Detroit • Johannesburg •
London • Madrid • Melbourne • Mexico City • New York • Paris • Singapore •
Tokyo • Toronto • Washington

ACKNOWLEDGMENTS

We'd like to begin by thanking a few special members of our staff at LANWrights, who helped pull the many pieces of this book together. Starting with Dawn Rader, our project manager and editor extraordinaire, we say "thanks for making our prose as perfect as possible." To Mary Burmeister, Queen of Glossaries, and Chancellor of the Exchequer, thanks not only for helping out with the words that worked for us, but also for keeping things running! You guys are the greatest!

Natanya Pitts
There is a large crowd of people who made this book, and its author's continued sanity, possible. First my loving thanks to Colin, who withstood every storm and stood by me every step of the way. A big thank-you to my co-author, Ed Tittel, a great boss and co-author, for giving me opportunities, wisdom, and guidance I couldn't find anywhere else. Also, thanks to Steve James, my other co-author, for providing strong content and good writing and for helping me hit those tight deadlines!

I too, have special thanks for certain staff at LANWrights. Dawn: What a nice job you did of adding a final polish to each and every page; plus, thanks for being such a great friend. Mary: Not only did you handle the Glossary and other petty details, you oversaw software and screen shot permissions; anyway, how could I be ungrateful to a fellow "Days" fan? Michael: Thanks for listening to me rant when things got tough, and for always providing a level-headed perspective on any problem, no matter how big or how small.

To my parents, Charles and Swanya, for believing in me for all these years. To DJ, who's been there in so many ways for the last ten years. Without you I wouldn't be half the person I am now. I'm so glad you'll be home soon. To Jim, who taught me how to fly on my own. Even though we're not in the same place anymore, we're still somehow always together.

To my two feline familiars, Gandalf and Nada, who always seem to know exactly when to sit on my keyboard and offer a warm purr. And finally, in loving memory to Dusty, the company "yellow dog" who passed away during this project. Walks around the block just aren't the same without you, and nobody else turns a computer off with his tail better than you did! You will be forever part of all of us. Even Dogbert misses you…

Stephen N. James

First and foremost, heartfelt thanks to Natanya Pitts and Ed Tittel, my co-authors on this project, for their inspiration and enthusiasm during this project. As ever, my eternal gratitude to my family, Trisha, Kelly, and Chris, for their understanding and support of my writing habit. Let me encourage our readers to share their feedback with us via email; we learn more from your feedback than any other source of wisdom, and we always try to respond to comments, criticisms, and suggestions for improvement. Look for our email addresses in the introduction.

Ed Tittel

Thanks to both my co-authors for the excellent work they did on this project. I'm especially proud of Natanya, who shouldered most of the responsibility and over half the work. You came through with flying colors! And thanks to you, Steve, once again for bearing with me while we made sure that credit came where it was due. I'd also like to thank the team at Coriolis, especially Keith Weiskamp and Sharijo Hehr, for agreeing to publish a book on this topic so early in its life cycle. We especially enjoyed working with Michelle Stroup, our project editor, and in mustering the pieces necessary to create a color section for the book.

I'd like to close our personal acknowledgments with a fond farewell to my beloved yellow Labrador, Dusty, who passed away in August, 1997. I've never known another dog who was as happy and enthusiastic a friend as you were to me. I'm so very sorry that you suffered so much at the end; I will miss you more than I can ever say. Rest in peace, my pup! There will be other dogs in my life, but none of them can ever replace you.

As a team we'd like to thank the rest of the Coriolis folks who helped bring this book to press, including our redoubtable copy editor, Luanne Rouff, our peerless proofreader Bob LaRoche, and our indefatigable production coordinator, Kim Eoff. We also owe a debt of gratitude to Robert Clarfield, for his outstanding contributions to the CD-ROM that accompanies this book (while we're on the subject, we'd also like to thank the vendors who contributed their software to the CD). Finally, we must thank those unsung heroes in Marketing who launched this book: Josh Mills, Anne Tull, and Donna Ford. We couldn't have done it without you; we're very glad everyone did such a good job!

Austin, Texas
September, 1997

CONTENTS

INTRODUCTION

Welcome to the *HTML Style Sheets Design Guide*! This book is designed to help you understand and master the terminology and notation that underlies what is sometimes called Cascading Style Sheets, Level 1, but more usually referred to as CSS1 in Web designer's lingo. Style sheets offer an unparalleled opportunity for page designers to create and manage consistent, attractive layouts for their Web pages, and to endow them with unique backgrounds, type colors, and element positioning. Style sheets make it much easier for Web designers to customize pages for a particular look and feel. Even better, because a single style sheet can govern the appearance of many Web pages, the work invested in building attractive, compelling styles usually pays for itself many times over.

That's why we've aimed this book not just at explaining and exploring the structure, syntax, and capabilities of HTML style sheets, but also at describing best practices and efficient uses. We've included plenty of do's and don'ts related to the everyday use of style sheets. We've also built a special color section at the center of the book (look for the glossy pages) that incorporates in-depth case studies, plus a full-color chart and lots of named color combinations. It also explores style sheet anatomy in living color, and includes "guided tours" of some pretty stellar style sheets already in use on the World Wide Web. In other words, we've tried to leaven the concepts and theories that drive and inform how style sheets behave, with plenty of practice and examples to give those ideas plenty of form and substance!

Nevertheless, to completely master this method for controlling the look and feel of Web pages, you must build some style sheets of your own. Nothing will help you appreciate their capabilities—and their shortcomings—like modifying existing style sheets for your own purposes, or building your own style sheets from scratch. For that reason, we've included ready-to-run examples of all the style sheets we built for the book on the CD-ROM, along with those examples developed by others whose authors granted us permission to reproduce their work. Either of these ready-made examples can be a source of raw material for your own experiments, and might help save time and energy in bringing the value and control that style sheets offer to your own Web site.

Just remember: When it comes to new tools and technologies, a book like ours can be an essential part of the learning process; but hands-on experience remains the best teacher of all!

About This Book

The *HTML Style Sheets Design Guide* is broken into four parts:

1. Part I: An Introduction To Style Sheets

2. Part II: Using Style Sheets With HTML

3. Style III: Style Sheets And Your Web Pages

4 . *Do It In Color* section: About Color, Using Color, plus Anatomy and Guided Tours

The initial part of the book explains the theory and behavior of style sheets, along with a review of the history that led to their current form and function. It also discusses the drawbacks to plain, unadorned HTML that make style sheets such a welcome addition.

The second part of the book contains the majority of the nitty-gritty details involved in building and tweaking style sheets, including basic structure and syntax, use and format of units of measure, handling position and layout data, plus classifying and managing the elements of style.

The third part includes a discussion of how to use external style sheets in your Web pages, plus a brief overview of something called Dynamic HTML, which permits Web pages to change themselves on the client side without requiring server interaction.

The color section begins with a case study of the *Time Magazine* Web site, which does as good a job of preserving the familiar look and feel of the print publication on a set of Web pages, as any Web site we know. Not surprisingly, style sheets play an important role in their work. Next, we turn our focus to an exposition of the color properties possible on style sheets, with lots of examples in this, the most colorful part of the book. Also included is a comprehensive color chart, with listings (and examples) of a large collection of named colors. Next, the color section dissects both a moderately complex and a highly complex style sheet, to expose and explain what's involved in creating and managing such documents. Finally, the color section concludes with a guided tour of a half-dozen or so of some of the most exciting style sheet-driven Web sites we could find. This concludes the book with a compelling set of examples of what style sheets can do, and how they work.

The *HTML Style Sheets Design Guide* also includes a number of appendices that are worth spending some time with, including:

- A description of how to install and use the CD-ROM that accompanies the book, entitled "About the CD-ROM." This will tell you what you'll find on the CD, how it's laid out, and how to use its contents most effectively.

- Appendix A contains a complete, comprehensive and voluminous list of all the Cascading Style Sheet Level 1 (CSS1) properties discussed throughout the book. Each property includes the syntax, associated values, default value, inheritance state, and a listing of applicable HTML elements.

- Appendix B details the Web pages, sample code, and styled software all available on the CD-ROM enclosed with this book.

- A glossary, that includes definitions for the technical terms we used in the book, plus an expansion for every acronym we could find. Please let us know if we missed anything; we tried really hard to be comprehensive, but we're only human!

Between the contents of the book itself, and its supporting materials, we hope you'll find most of what you need to know to use CSS1 tags and design approaches on your own Web sites. But, because this is a rapidly changing subject, we've also tried to include a plethora of pointers to Web sites, mailing lists, and newsgroups that will help keep you in the vanguard of this leading-edge phenomenon. Please share with us good resources that we've missed, and insights that you think other readers should know: Because we've got the Web site that's related to this book, we can always extend what we tell you to match what all of us can learn and appreciate together. Thanks in advance for your input and information!

How To Use This Book

If you're a newcomer to CSS1 and HTML Style Sheets, we've structured the topics in this book to build upon themselves, so that some topics in later chapters will make more sense if you read the earlier chapters beforehand. That's why we suggest you read it from front to back for your initial pass. If you need to brush up on a topic, or you have to refresh your memory after errors in your work indicate something's missing in your knowledge of syntax or structure, if it's tag-related, consult Appendix A. Otherwise, use the index or table of contents to go straight to the topics and terminology that you need to review. We hope you find the book useful as a reference to all the important aspects of Cascading Style Sheets and their use within HTML documents, or in separate style sheets of their own.

Given all the book's elements, and its focus, we've tried to create a tool that you can use to learn about—and build—style sheets of your own (or perhaps just chunks of style-related markup). Please share your feedback on the book with us, especially if you have ideas about how we could improve it for future readers. We'll consider everything you say carefully, and to respond to all suggestions (if only with a thank-you email). The authors are all available via email at natanya@lanw.com (Natanya), snjames@wetlands.com(stephen), or etittel@lanw.com (Ed). Please remember to include the title of the book in your message; otherwise, we'll be forced to guess which of our many books you're talking about. We don't like to guess—we want to *know*!

Thanks, and enjoy the book!

HTML
STYLE SHEETS
DESIGN GUIDE

PART 1

STYLE
SHEETS
ON THE
WEB

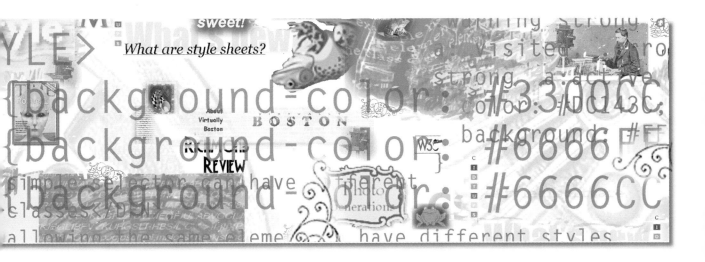

CONCEPTUAL-IZING STYLES AND STYLE SHEETS

1

Style. Flair. Panache. These characteristics are associated with standing out from the crowd, distinguishing unique individuals that have a special knack for doing things. On the Internet, where anyone has a chance to be someone special, it's sometimes necessary to use every trick available in order to make Web pages and resources stand out amidst the teeming masses of online information.

But there's more than one way to build stylish Web pages. This chapter examines a variety of definitions of style, especially in the context of the World Wide Web. After an intellectual perambulation around this fascinating topic, we'll narrow our field to a definition of style that serves as the focus for this book. Next, we'll consider the importance of consistency and control, revisit some traditional HTML implementations of style, and discuss the role that style plays when you're constructing Web pages.

A Definition Of Style

Look in any dictionary: You'll find several column inches, at a minimum, dedicated to the definition of style. Style is used to mean many different things, such as elegance of presentation and definition of character. The same is true of style on the Web. The first Web-based definition of style that comes to mind is one that serves as a measure of how *au courant* you, and your pages, may be. But style also has another, potentially more important, definition—namely, as a method of defining how elements on a page should appear on screen when displayed within a Web browser; our book deals only with this latter definition. But to avoid any confusion or miscommunication, let's begin with a look at both takes on style and the Web.

How Cool Is The Style?

At a look-and-feel level, style operates as a major component of coolness. Style describes how a site presents its content, and may be identified by whatever special characteristics mark the site's information as unique, unusual, or visually arresting. Not everyone's sense of style is the same, and quite frequently, one person scoffs at what another believes to either represent the epitome of what's "in style" or qualify as "stylish." Ultimately, a "cool" style is very much a matter of taste.

Here's a real-world example: Each year a small group of men and women, appropriately known as fashion designers, dictate the clothing styles for the upcoming year. If they combine an orange sleeveless top with lime-green slacks and proclaim it "the thing," that combination may ultimately define what's popular and in demand. If other designers employ similar combinations to create "me-too" ensembles, and "the thing" catches on, people flock to the stores to buy such ensembles, ever-fearful of being out of style (even if they don't really like orange and lime-green).

This phenomenon is not unknown on the Web. In fact, Web styles come and go about as frequently as fashions. In 1995, scrolling ticker-tape-style banners appeared as an early "must do" Web trend. Then, in late 1996, placing background gifs on the left-hand side of the screen to create a colored border became immensely popular. 1997 ushered in black backgrounds and frames. What style will boom next is always hard to predict, but you can be certain it will be recognizable as it spreads like wildfire across the Web.

A Design Tool

At a more elementary level, style is a way to define page layout elements, and to harness their power to focus the layout of a collection of Web pages. Using style guidelines, it's possible to define everything from text colors to the amount of space

between lines (which typographers call *leading*, pronounced like the metal). Style specifics can be defined for most existing HTML markup elements, as well as for customized content elements, such as footnotes, bylines, and more.

According to this definition, style describes how an element should be rendered. Every HTML element already incorporates style information; and as a Web designer, you probably make choices about what markup to use for your information based largely on how that markup appears when rendered within a Web browser. For example, the <B>...</B> tag pair causes the enclosed text to appear as bold, in a font darker and heavier than normal text. Such font specifics are part of the tag's style, and you may choose to use a tag because of those characteristics in order to mark text that needs to stand out against the less compelling appearance of normal text. In many cases, therefore, the style of the element drives its use.

It is this aspect of style—the specific information about how to render markup elements—that we'll discuss in this book. HTML style has changed a great deal during its relatively short life. Also, due to the development of style sheets, style has also become a dominant factor in the evolution of Web pages and their appearance.

The use of style as a descriptor is not new, and takes its inspiration and functionality from style sheets used for traditional print media. Reflecting on how style works to make designing easier and ensure consistency among similar documents makes it easier to understand how style can work within a set of Web pages. Although Web pages do not precisely mimic their print cousins, they do share common attributes and conventions. Thus, the selfsame style sheets that have worked well in print media have become prime targets for adoption on the Web.

The remainder of this chapter is devoted to a description of style sheets, starting with a look at traditional implementations of style sheets B.W. (before the Web), followed by an overview of how style sheets have been renewed and revitalized for Web use.

Style Sheets: The Key To Consistency

Consistency of appearance is important for individuals and organizations, whether on or off the Web. Image is all about wearing a consistent face for the world to see, and associating you with a particular presence. Inconsistent presentation and slipshod communications create an impression of disorganization and a lack of focus.

Organizations and individuals create a physical "look and feel" that applies to everything from logos to publications, from clothes to cars. Image connotes not only ability, flair, and competence, but also establishes how an individual or organization is perceived by an audience. Web site creators must be careful to create and maintain a positive image.

Consistency is not always easy to achieve. This is especially true when different individuals or departments within an entity are responsible for creating materials. Although any group is the sum of its parts, uniformity is not possible if each contributor is permitted to do what he or she thinks best represents

their collective image. In general, the more people that are involved in a Web site, the more important it is to create a specific set of rules describing exactly how information should be presented.

Style sheets and style guides provide one method of encoding such sets of rules. Style sheets (or guides) describe in detail how certain types of information are to be formatted and presented. They aren't limited to printed information, but can also include guidelines for spoken presentations, as well as radio and television advertisements. When developed and used correctly, style guides are simply part of the process of preparing information for dissemination or publication. As the Internet has grown and Web pages have become a standard means of information delivery, style guides have become an integral part of the processes of preparing information for delivery via the World Wide Web.

Style sheets take the guesswork out of creating information presentations. Rather than wasting time trying to figure out if presentation slides are supposed to be in 32- or 34-point type by holding them up to the light and comparing font sizes, a quick look at a style sheet can answer the question. Style sheets are created to make things easier by explicitly specifying formats, so you can focus on creating the unique content that a particular communication medium is supposed to deliver.

Style sheets and guidelines are not meant to be dictatorial. For anyone seeking to present information in a uniform manner—as most Web authors do—style sheets provide a logical way to define style standards and apply them directly to different forms of information and documents.

Traditional Implementations: Style Sheets And Guidelines

We've already hinted at some of the ways in which style sheets have been used to define how information should be presented. Style sheets can also provide an easy way to ensure consistency when disseminating such information. This section takes an in-depth look at traditional implementations of style sheets and related guidelines.

Here, our goal is to show you how style has worked in pre-Web days—to create a consistent look and feel within bodies of information—and to explain the role that style sheets play in facilitating and maintaining such consistency. As you read along, you will notice that many of these issues also apply to the Web.

Style Sheets And Print Media

In the not-so-very-distant past, print publications were put together on light tables using Xacto knives and hot wax. Styles for headings, captions, body text, and other copy had to be defined for any given publication to keep them consistent throughout. These specifications were outlined in the publication's style guide.

As organizations that publish materials grow larger, the number of people who contribute to them grows apace. Style guides are the only way to ensure that everyone's work will look the same. The amount of space text takes up is directly related to its font size; by using established font guidelines, the original authors are able to write to the correct amount of space allotted—no more, no less.

As a Web author, you won't have to break out the Xacto knife and hot wax, but you may have to contend with multiple contributors to a site, or a specific set of pages. By incorporating style sheets into your Web pages, you can be assured that all the information is presented consistently, even when the content varies.

People are more comfortable when they deal with the familiar. If you present them with the same look and feel around different content, they won't be distracted by an unfamiliar environment. This principle is best seen in the magazine industry. All of the same columns and icons appear in each issue, but the content varies. This approach allows readers to concentrate on the information at hand; this is a key concept for Web design. The look and feel should never interfere with the content. Style sheets can make this a snap.

Many publications offer online versions of their printed materials. The fonts, colors, and general layout used closely reflect their print counterparts. With different authors and editors also contributing to online versions, style sheets maintain a consistent look and feel across the individual Web pages that make up the site.

In *Do It In Color* I, we'll examine a full-color, online version of *TIME* magazine. *TIME* has successfully and tastefully ported its look and feel from the print version to the online one. This case study shows how style can transfer from one medium to another, while maintaining a recognizable image and identity. It also illustrates how important it is to create and maintain a consistent environment that users can instantly relate to and recognize.

Style Guidelines Promote Organizational Standards

Every individual or organization has a certain identity, corporate or otherwise, that should be reflected in everything they do—from the products they create to their everyday communications. This identity is intended to reflect the individual's or company's abilities, products, and business culture. It is also designed to be easily recognizable, to create the fond familiarity mentioned in the preceding section. Identity evolves over time, but it must be created, tailored, and refined carefully. Once an identity has been established, you should create guidelines to ensure that all subsequent works and products reflect it accurately and consistently.

Organizational standards and guidelines provide an effective means of ensuring that an identity will be managed carefully and applied rigorously. Traditionally, such standards and guidelines—detailing everything from letterhead to packaging—are handed down in large printed volumes sometimes called the *corporate identity kit.* New products and publications must have a look and feel created for them that not only reflects their individual purpose, but that also marks them as part of that larger identity. Even seemingly unimportant items like notepads, coffee mugs, memos, and pencils cannot escape identity standards. (One wonders why Scott Adams hasn't created an extensive collection of cartoons on the subject. A *Dogbert's Guide to Creating a Corporate Identity* could sell millions.)

No one would deny the role that identity plays in an organization. The only way to maintain an identity is to set down, almost always in writing, a set of style guidelines that cover all facets of information dissemination and communication. Web sites are just as much a part of corporate identity as letterhead, and most organizations demand that Web sites meet the same standards of quality. Because the Web is an entirely new medium, many companies are grappling with how to make their site an extension of the corporate identity while working within the limitations of the medium, and exploiting its potentials. You will discover that the same kind of creativity—but probably more of it—applied to a coffee mug design will have to be applied to Web site design as well.

Of course, the biggest Web hurdle that organizations must face is an inability to establish complete control over the look and feel of their Web pages. Because users can turn graphics on or off and use their own custom backgrounds, font sizes, and link colors, absolute control over appearance is impossible. In this new environment, the real style challenge becomes how to present an identity on the Web without requiring total control. Web style sheets can give designers more control over final page displays, although that control will never be complete. The rest of this book explains how to achieve this laudable goal.

But first, let's revisit some important predecessors to Web style sheets—namely, application style sheets. Integrating style sheets into word processors and page layout programs gave organizations the ability to create customized style guidelines that anyone could use from a desktop PC. In some ways, this makes maintaining a corporate identity simple (once the style sheet has been defined, that is).

Application Style Sheets

We've seen a company style guide dictating that official letters should always:

- Use 12-point Garamond type
- Use 1.5-inch margins on either side of a page, with 1-inch margins at the top and bottom of the page
- Begin with the company logo, followed by 10 blank spaces
- Be written in paragraphs separated by 8-point blocks of white space

Although this sounds good, and is no doubt intended to ensure consistency across all company correspondence, such guidelines are much easier said (or written) than implemented. Someone inevitably forgets the logo, uses Times instead of Garamond, or puts a 10-point block of white space after paragraphs, instead of the mandated eight.

What's the difference between style guidelines and style sheets? Style guidelines enunciate a list of rules, but include no enforcement; style sheets enforce the rules electronically and make them a simple reality. Before the addition of styles to word processing and page layout programs, users had to add paragraph specifics, change fonts, and set margins manually for each individual document. With style sheets, these specifics need to be set only once and may then be used repeatedly. The ability to create style *templates* makes maintaining a consistent corporate look and feel easier—and far more enforceable—than ever before.

A template can be copied many times and widely distributed so that everyone in an organization has ready access to it. Some organizations store templates for all their official documents on a central file server to minimize the chances of corrupted files, and to impose centralized control over the canons of official style.

As you begin to work with Web style sheets, you'll notice a marked resemblance to some application-based predecessors. In the next section, we explore the features that traditional style sheets have in common with new, Webified versions. You'll find that many of the principals and mechanisms are similar. Before you know it, you'll be ready to jump headfirst into a Web style sheet, using your knowledge of application style sheets as a springboard.

Nouveau Style Sheets: Bringing Style To The Web

Figure 1.1 shows a Microsoft Word style definition for a new style called Style1. It specifies a centered paragraph style using 12-point Garamond blue type with a 1-point border on all sides, and 0.5-inch indentation. This Style1 definition was created by working through a series of dialog boxes, as shown in Figures 1.2, 1.3, and 1.4, to specify paragraph, font, and border settings.

The following Cascading Style Sheet (CSS) code defines a style setting almost exactly like the preceding Word style definition:

```
<STYLE>
P.style1 {
  text-align: center;
  font-size: 12pt;
  font-family: garamond, serif;
  color: navy;
  line-height: 8pt;
  text-indent: .5in;
  border: solid 1pt;
}
</STYLE>
```

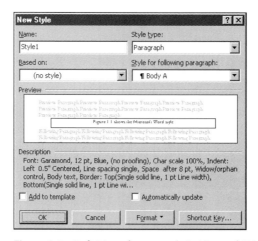

Figure 1.1 Definition of a new style in Microsoft Word.

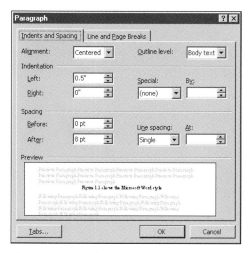

Figure 1.2   Specifying paragraph settings for a Microsoft Word style.

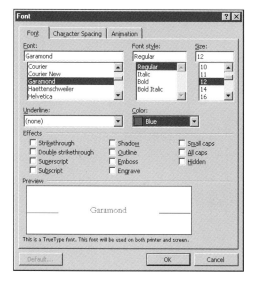

Figure 1.3   Specifying font settings for a Microsoft Word style.

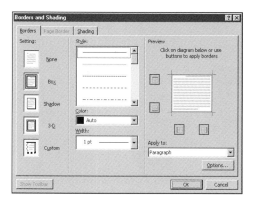

Figure 1.4   Specifying border settings for a Microsoft Word style.

Although the syntax may look a little odd to the uninitiated (don't worry, you'll be an expert by the time you've finished this book), it does make sense. Properties, such as text align, take values such as center. Group them all together for a single element, such as <P>, give it a unique name, such as style1, and you've got a Cascading Style Sheet (CSS) style definition.

For another example, let's look at lists of elements. Figure 1.5 shows the Bullets and Numbering dialog box used to specify what kind of symbol should be used for a bulleted list style that we've named bullet1.

Figure 1.5   Specifying symbol settings for a Microsoft Word bullet style.

The equivalent CSS code looks like the following:

```
.bullet1 {
    list-style-type: square;
}
```

I agree that the syntax looks a little weird, but the effect should be obvious. We've created a new CSS tag named bullet1 that produces square bullets, rather than the standard round bullets, whenever the <LI CLASS=bullet1> tag appears in the Web document. And you thought this was going to be hard....

We've used some new terms, acronyms, and code in this section, and given you your first exposure to style syntax and markup.

Never fear, all of this is explained in detail throughout this book. In fact, Chapter 4 focuses entirely on the rules, a.k.a. syntax, of styles. Although Web style sheets don't support as many style elements as a word processor because the medium of communication and its inherent characteristics are different, the mechanisms behind the creation of styles are similar. This book will show you exactly what you can and can't do with Web style sheets. We think you'll be pleasantly surprised by the possibilities.

Looking Ahead

Now that you've been introduced to the concept of style, it's time to take a step or two back in time to visit the origins and ancestry of style on the Web. Chapter 2 covers the history of style sheets as they were born of necessity, and matured through popular demand. It's an interesting journey, so pack a lunch and come along!

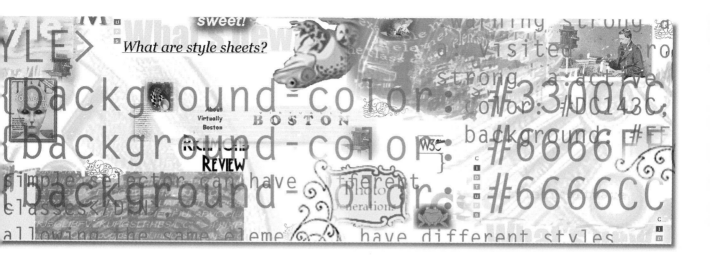

THE HISTORY
OF STYLE
SHEETS FOR
THE WEB

2

In this chapter:

- **Early style sheet concepts**

- **Cascading Style Sheets (CSS) appear**

- **The Document Style Semantics and Specification Language (DSSSL)**

- **The important role of the Standard Generalized Markup Language (SGML)**

- **The CSS1 Specification**

Almost since their inception, the technologies that drive the Web have included concepts of style, especially in the norms that have governed the rendering of individual HTML tags and elements. From the introduction of the HyperText Markup Language (HTML) that defines Web pages, the HyperText Transfer Protocol (HTTP, and the associated MIME types it recognizes) that ferries object requests from browsers to servers, and the corresponding Web text information and other document elements from servers to browsers, style has mattered quite a lot.

In this chapter, you'll investigate the dialogue surrounding Web style. You'll explore how implicit notions within HTML markup itself failed to meet all the requirements for document layout and control. Then, you'll learn about the major ideas, the contributing technologies and their chronology, and some of the high points of the discussions, that led to the promulgation of a draft standard for Cascading Style Sheets (CSS) in October 1994.

We'll also track the events between the introduction of the draft CSS definitions and the publication of a Level 1 Specification for CSS from the World Wide Web Consortium (W3C) in December 1996. Finally, you'll see how today's version of CSS remains a work in progress; and learn how to keep track of that progress and the future developments, specifications, and standards that will inevitably follow publication of this book.

The Original Impetus

In order to understand the significance of style for the Web, we must return to the very beginnings of this technology. This puts us in Geneva, Switzerland, in 1988 and 1989, at the Conseil European pour la Recherche Nucleaire (CERN), a high-energy particle physics laboratory. This is where Tim Berners-Lee and his band of merry researchers undertook the task of providing a simple, text- and graphics-capable information delivery system that researchers at various CERN locations could use to exchange research information findings quickly and easily.

Before the advent of the Web, CERN researchers had to share data the old-fashioned way. This meant going through the following tedious and time-consuming actions anytime something had to be shared with one's colleagues:

1. Locating the required file on a computer, whether local or remote.

2. Establishing a connection to that computer.

3. Downloading the necessary file, which might include copying and translations, should the source and destination machines differ significantly.

Each step in this process might require a separate application, not to mention gaining access to a wide range of machines with dissimilar operating systems.

The fundamental design principle motivating the work that Berners-Lee and his colleagues undertook in creating a system at CERN was uniform access to a broad range of information through a single, common, and consistent user interface. Most essential was easy access to data, to avoid the contortions so often involved in bringing electronic information from "there" to "here" across a network.

This motivation is what spurred the design activity at CERN in 1989 that ultimately led to the widespread introduction of the World Wide Web by 1991. In the interim, the team created and refined a detailed specification for the project, and coding began. By the end of 1990, the CERN team had built and deployed a text-mode browser much like Lynx, and had also built a prototype graphical browser for the then-popular NeXT computer platform.

Throughout 1991, access to the Web and its browsers became commonplace within CERN. The technology was a smash hit with the CERN researchers, and quickly spread beyond CERN into the research and scientific communities that have long been the breeding ground for Internet technologies. The initial implementation let users access simple hypertext Web pages and the contents of several Usenet newsgroups. A powerful appetite for access to information through this interface led to development of interfaces to WAIS, FTP, Telnet, and Gopher by the end of 1991. At that time, the most publicly accessible information on the Internet was even more accessible to those users lucky enough to have access to the Web.

In 1992, CERN began to promote the Web outside those research and academic communities. The impetus that made the Web so useful to researchers and academics proved equally appealing to users of all stripes. Clearly, the Web provided a communications medium with revolutionary possibilities, way beyond its roots in particle physics.

In 1992, CERN also published the source code for its Web servers and browsers, which led to their wholesale proliferation around the globe. That year also witnessed two significant phenomena that catapulted the Web into the forefront of Internet technology:

- Users and organizations everywhere began to create Web pages and make them available to the Internet at large. These pages quickly covered a broad spectrum of interests and subjects of all kinds. This phenomenon has continued unabated to this day.

- Software developers—including Marc Andreesen and the Mosaic team at NCSA (National Center for Supercomputing Applications), and the WinWeb and MacWeb teams at MCC—began work on a second generation of more powerful graphical Web browsers for a variety of computing platforms, including PCs and Macs.

By the end of the following year, you could find Web browsers for many flavors of Unix, X Windows, the Macintosh, and PCs running a plethora of operating systems (but especially Microsoft Windows). By 1993, it was also clear that the Web was not a passing fancy, and that it would change the way individuals and organizations created, deployed, and obtained information of all kinds.

Style Rears Its Head

Early—we're almost tempted to use the adjective "prehistoric"—Web browsers treated text crudely. Monospaced screen fonts ruled the world, and not much special handling for text was possible, nor did it receive too much attention as a consequence. But the introduction and nearly instant preeminence of graphical browsers, starting in 1993, made it obvious to pioneering Web developers (and the typographically sophisticated) that the ways in which text was rendered on screen was important. Because this took the form of bitmapped fonts of many sizes, it also quickly led to a proliferation of proprietary HTML tags—in Mosaic, and then later in Netscape Navigator and Internet Explorer—for that very purpose.

As an example, the folks at Microsoft developed many tags that are only supported by (surprise!) Internet Explorer, such as the **<IFRAME>** tag. **<IFRAME>** defines what is called a floating frame. The problem with using proprietary tags like **<IFRAME>** is that users who are not viewing your site with a particular browser may not get the information you want to disseminate. Rather, users are frustrated when a page doesn't render correctly or is just plain inaccessible. So, if you MUST use browser-specific tags, be sure to also provide another set of materials for users who can't see it the other way.

In the absence of style sheets, it remains true to this day that most of the control over how HTML markup appears within a browser is a matter of tuning and tweaking the browser's interface on the user end of a client/server connection. In other words, the ultimate meaning of style is completely beyond the control of a Web designer, unless he or she forgoes the use of text and markup for some completely graphical or non-HTML form of text delivery. This should help to explain why headlines, marquees, and other strange forms of "image management" recur so frequently on Web sites—they represent a way for designers to impose some control over the look and feel of their Web pages, which users who monkey with the defaults for their Web browsers cannot override easily (unless they forgo graphics altogether, a not uncommon strategy for users with slow connections to the Internet).

Based on the chronology for the introduction of the Web itself covered in the preceding section, it should be no surprise that the dialogue about Web style started in earnest in 1993. In fact, this dialogue commenced just as the implications of popular second-generation Web browsers were beginning to make themselves felt. It's quite clear that the move to a more graphical presentation of text and images is what elevated the discussion of style on the Web from a background concern to a topic of intense interest and scrutiny.

Style's First Formulation

It seems that members of the O'Reilly & Associates (ORA) publication team were the first to air this subject in a significant way. In June 1993, Robert Raisch of ORA posted an email message entitled "Stylesheets for HTML" to the www-talk mailing list. His message touches on future design issues for HTML, and it opened the style debate.

The key points of this message (which may be accessed online at: **http://www.eit.com/ www.lists/www-talk.1993q2/0445.html**) may be paraphrased as follows:

- Today, Web designers create pages to exploit specific features and functions of particular browsers; that is, they use proprietary markup to obtain desired layout and appearance "effects."

- The original intent of the Web was to carry presentation information along with content, but designers are forced to use markup solely for appearance, which is sometimes contrary to content.

- Separate style sheets can be linked to Web documents to provide "suggestions or hints about behavior" as a way to give designers more control over appearance.

Raisch's document goes on to define a set of markup attributes, and associated values, for things such as font families, spacing, stroke weight, font treatment, and leading. It has all the characteristic layout and text controls that would be commonplace in any word processor or page layout program. Thus, from its very beginnings, HTML style has had its roots in familiar paradigms and everyday applications.

During the intervening years between mid-1993 and the present day, this dialogue on style has continued. Along the way, Web designers and developers have held prolonged debates on implementation models, methods, and details. But the basic objectives have remained the same—to provide Web page designers with additional controls over appearance, and to help separate style from substance.

As we investigate some of the alternatives that have been discussed, where some ideas were abandoned and others kept alive, it's interesting to note that ideas about what style *is*—and the role it should play in document rendering—have remained consistent. How style *works,* how style sheets may be applied, and the precise details of how styles are invoked and specified have changed a good deal along the way. But today's prevailing model— which provides the basis for the rest of this book—draws on much of the dialogue that led to its specification. To that end, we present a chronology of the significant proposals and ideas that have led to Cascading Style Sheets (CSS), examining those proposals and ideas for the useful elements that they have contributed to this model.

A Chronology Of HTML Style

Starting in mid-1993, the dialogue on style sheets for Web use commenced in earnest. As shown in Table 2.1, a number of notable proposals and

Table 2.1 A chronology of HTML style discussions and proposals.

Date	Author	Title	Source
06/06/93	Robert Raisch	Stylesheets for HTML	www-talk
11/22/93	Pei Y. Wei	Stylesheet language	www-talk
11/26/93	Steven Heaney	Comments on Wei's Proposal	www-talk
11/01/94	Jon Bosak	HDL Proposal	www-talk
11/10/94	Håkon W. Lie	Cascading Style sheets—A proposal	www-talk
02/05/95	Kevin Hughes	Thinking about Style Sheets	www-talk
03/31/95	Bert Bos	Stream-based Style Sheet Proposal	http://odur.let.rug.nl.~bert/ stylesheets.html
12/13/95	Jon Bosak	DSSSL Online Application Proposal	http://occam.sjf.novell.com:8080/ docs/dss-o/do951212.htm
12/17/96	Lie & Bos	CSS Level 1 Spec	http://www.w3.org/pub/WWW/ TR/REC-CSS1

discussions culminated in a collaboration between Bert Bos and Håkon Lie, which resulted in a draft proposal, and then a formal specification, for Cascading Style Sheets through the W3C HTML working group.

We've already covered the salient points of Raish's ideas; in the sections that follow, we'll examine significant elements of the dialogue that followed. (Note: This chronology is adapted from the W3C's own discussion of style sheets, which may be found under the heading "Historical Style Sheet proposals" on the W3C Web site, at the following URL: **http://www.w3.org/Style/**).

Pei Wei's "Stylesheet Language"

(http://www.eit.com/www.lists/www-talk.1993q4/0264.html)

Here, Wei identifies attributes to accompany normal HTML tags that control how text associated with the tag is to be presented. This includes foreground and background colors, font size, slant controls, and list presentations. It's easy to grasp, easy to use, and easy for browsers to parse. All of these characteristics are desirable for HTML extensions of any kind. Although the idea isn't fully fleshed out, it follows more or less in the same footsteps as Raisch's earlier email, but differs significantly in the details.

Steve Heaney's "Comments On "Wei's Proposal"

(http://www.eit.com/www.lists/www-talk.1993q4/0295.html)

Heaney opens what will be a recurring theme in the dialogue on HTML style sheets—namely, why not exploit the relationship that already exists between HTML and its progenitor, SGML? In this communication, Heaney shows how everything that Wei proposes can be handled using SGML's formidable format-handling capabilities (consult the sidebar entitled "Playing The SGML Card," which appears in the section on DSSSL Online later in this chapter, for further discussion of this topic). The point does not elude his audience, as the ensuing and protracted dialogue inspired by SGML and its many tools and utilities illustrates.

Jon Bosak's "HDL Proposal"

(http://www.ora.com/davenport/HDL/hdl.proposal.html)

HDL (Hypertext Delivery Language) is a version of Hewlett-Packard's Semantic Delivery Language (SDL) tailored specifically for HTML. Like its progenitor SDL, HDL is designed to use only a few elements, to parse and display quickly, and to provide incredibly rich abilities to structure and present platform-independent text within online documents. Bosak argues persuasively that this makes it nearly ideal for use within HTML documents. (Since this message appeared, Bosak has left Novell for Sun Microsystems, but he remains a key player in the working groups that deal with style-related matters for HTML.)

In fact, SDL is yet another instance of an SGML-based system that's presented as relevant to HTML and style-related handling. Unfortunately, Bosak's proposal, although technically sound and quite interesting, was completely blown away less than ten days later by a counterproposal from Håkon Lie.

Håkon Lie's "First Proposal On Cascading Style Sheets"

(http://www.w3.org/People/howcome/p/cascade.html)

In the year that intervened between the Wei-Heaney dialogue and Lie's initial proposal, the merits of SGML-based presentation methods and tools were discussed, and numerous contenders for handling style in Web pages emerged from this camp. One especially strong contender, named Document Style Symantics and Specification Language (DSSSL) Lite (now known as DSSSL Online) was formulated, promoted, discussed, and set aside in favor of Lie's proposal, simply because DSSSL turned out to involve more complexity than the average Web designer wanted to handle (DSSSL Online is covered later in this chapter).

Lie's initial proposal defines what he calls "presentation hints," a simple mapping between HTML elements and rendering techniques. But the real strength of Lie's proposal—and the explanation for its continued support to this day—lies in its understanding that Web designers can only define a possible set of styles when rendering a Web page.

Because the visually impaired must be able to override designs aimed at those who can see and appreciate the original, Lie's proposal allows individuals to accept or replace those "presentation hints" that designers establish through style sheets.

The cascade effect, in fact, allows a strict hierarchy of style sheet application to be enforced, so that it's easy to document and understand how style works for any given user. Most users accept the defaults established by a designer, resulting in a level of control that's acceptable to both designers and ordinary users, but one that leaves room for users with special requirements to change font sizes arbitrarily, or to force text-to-speech or text-to-Braille rendering for those who require other methods of getting intelligible information.

Kevin Hughes's "Thinking About Style Sheets"

(**http://www.w3.org/Style/mail/kh-2-may-95.html**)

Hughes sums up the dialogue in the wake of Lie's original CSS proposal. It not only does an excellent job of recapping the major issues, but also argues eloquently that CSS is technically superior to other proposals and approaches under consideration. Hughes' primary points are as follows:

- CSS is "simple yet flexible." This means that CSS is succinct and compact, which makes it easy for browsers to parse and interpret style information. Nevertheless, CSS is also semantically rich enough to permit plenty of expressive power when defining and assigning styles.

- CSS is "human readable and writable." This strikes at the heart of many objections to

SGML-derived approaches: Although they're rich, powerful, and incredibly expressive, they're also complex, difficult, and hard to learn and understand. Hughes states forcefully that "...the Web will be rewarded a hundredfold by using a format for which it is easy to create tools..."

In this document, Hughes goes on to make some excellent suggestions about how style information could be included within an HTML document, or referenced by a pointer to a style sheet elsewhere; and a number of other useful notions about syntax, wild cards, and other ways to improve on Lie's original proposal. Much of this work will eventually make its way into the final version of the specification. But Hughes's two primary points best explain why CSS will ultimately prevail.

Bert Bos's "Stream-Based Style Sheet Proposal"

(**http://odur.let.rug.nl/~bert/stylesheets.html**)

Here, Bos describes a "simple" style sheet language based on SGML and the syntax used by X resource files from the Unix world. This enables it to draw on existing parsers and token generators available for other such files in use. This proposal also relies on standard dot notation, familiar to object-oriented programmers everywhere, that takes the form "object.attribute" to address attributes for specific markup elements (so that the text-color attribute of the <A> anchor tag, for example, becomes "A.textcolor," which may then be assigned a value). The syntax is straightforward, its intelligibility to computers and humans is more than acceptable, and the notation makes sense.

In fact, Bos does a thorough job of both describing the kinds of attributes that style entails and in managing the assignments of values, variables, and wild cards to such attributes. But the proposal never really takes off, nor does it generate widespread support. Bos's work on the proposal, however, was appreciated, and he became one of the primary authors of the specification for CSS that would emerge at the end of 1996.

Jon Bosak's "DSSSL Online Application Profile"

(**http://occam.sjf.novell.com:8080/docs/dsssl-o/ do951212.htm**)

DSSSL Online began life as a subset of the Document Style Semantics and Specification Language, initially known as DSSSL Lite. Full-blown DSSSL is an International Standard (ISO/IEC 10179:1995) specifying document transformation and formatting, that is intended to be neutral to both the computing platform and the software in use. As Bosak puts it, "DSSSL can be used with any document format for which a property set can be defined according to the Property Set Definition Requirements of ISO/IEC 10744. In particular, it can be used to specify the presentation of documents marked up according to ISO 8879:1986, Standard Generalized Markup Language (SGML)." And therein lies the rub....

In fact, DSSSL offers capabilities not present in CSS, including a systematic transformational ability to specify changes to SGML source files that permits the reordering of lists, the rearrangement of elements, and the automatic generation of indices, tables of contents, and other forms of document

support. DSSSL Online elected to stick with the other main thrust of full-blown DSSSL capabilities—its formal style language, which supports queries about defined styles; and a rich syntax for expressing styles, which governs how they might be rendered by a suitably equipped (SGML-enabled) browser.

In addition to the elements of style—such as headings, paragraphs, text controls, and other individual elements—DSSSL Online also supports various methods for text flow requirements. That is, it defines rules that specify how document elements may follow one another; or it outlines specific requirements, so that element B must follow element A whenever A is present, for instance.

Finally, DSSSL Online includes sequence descriptions for complex collections of elements, such as pages, tables, scrolling regions, links, marginalia, and other complex elements. Likewise, DSSSL Online also includes markup governing all kinds of complex typography, embedded objects, foreign languages (especially for non-Roman alphabets), mathematical notation, and direct SGML support. In short, DSSSL Online encompasses most of the areas of discussion and controversy that Web mavens have been debating for years, in a complete and standardized form.

Unfortunately, when it comes to playing the SGML card, serious professionals separate quickly from dilettantes. Although DSSSL itself, and even DSSSL Online, can convey oodles of style definitions, controls, and information, most mere mortals don't want to mess with learning the underlying syntax and the terminology that goes with it.

PLAYING THE SGML CARD

Technically, HTML is not a programming language; nor is it completely correct to call an HTML document a program. Normally, a program is defined as a set of instructions and operations to be applied to external data, called *input*.

Instead, HTML combines instructions right along with data to tell a display program, called a *browser*, how to recognize and render content that the document contains. Even though it's not a programming language, HTML supplies numerous structuring and layout controls for managing a document's appearance and specifying the linkages necessary to support hypertext capabilities. HTML style sheets are supposed to abstract this structuring and layout information so that it can be referenced in an HTML document, but its appearance can be controlled through separate controls (or as attributes within the document).

As it happens, HTML is defined by a special type of SGML document called a *Document Type Definition,* or *DTD*. This means that any HTML document is also an SGML document. In fact, HTML represents a specific form of expression defined by SGML. This should help explain why SGML appears in so many discussions of HTML and related technologies—it's not a coincidence; it's a deliberate attempt to leverage the powerful and complex engine used to define HTML in the first place.

Generalized Markup Describes Whole Universes of Documents

The Standard Generalized Markup Language (SGML) originated at IBM in the 1960s to help address problems that occur when documents must move among multiple, largely incompatible hardware and software systems. The original version was called *GML*, for General Markup Language, and was intended to give IBM staff a platform-independent way to define and work on documents. In fact, GML represents an early write-once, publish-many-ways strategy for document handling—a concept that's considered state of the art even today.

GML's designers were Charles Goldfarb, Ed Mosher, and Ray Lorie (whose combined initials form another possible interpretation for GML). By the 1970s, they realized that GML would work outside of IBM as well as within Big Blue's hallowed halls. Their work led to the definition and standardization of SGML in the 1980s, a standardization that today forms the basis of the ISO 8879 document standard.

SGML is a powerful, complex tool that can represent documents of almost any kind. In fact, SGML is designed to create document specifications, the DTDs we mentioned earlier, of all kinds. Any DTD, once defined, can be used to describe and construct an infinite number of documents that conform to its requirements. Because HTML represents a family of DTDs, this should explain the relationship between HTML and SGML that's renewed each time HTML is extended, improved, enhanced, or updated.

Defining Document Elements And Structure

SGML defines a formal method for describing the sections, headings, styles, and other elements that make up a document so that references to such elements in any document will be governed by those descriptions. This enables any document that adheres to a particular DTD to be rendered consistently, regardless of the platform it is created or displayed on.

In its most generic form, an SGML document contains three primary parts:

- A description of the legal character set and metacharacters used to distinguish plain text from markup (in HTML, this means the angle brackets used to bracket tags; and the special characters— ampersand— [&]—and semicolon—[;]—used to bracket entities)

- A declaration of the DTD that governs the document, including a list of the legal markup it can contain

- The document itself, which includes references to markup tags, mixed with the document's actual content

Where HTML is concerned, the first two items need not be present, but the version of the DTD that governs the document should be. This is why you'll see strings like <!DOCTYPE HTML PUBLIC "-//IETF// DTD HTML3.2//EN"> at the head of most well-written HTML documents: It identifies the document as conforming to the public, English-language version of the HTML 3.2 DTD.

For HTML, the first item is covered by the ISO Latin-1 character set, which defines character and numeric entities for non-Roman and special ASCII characters, along with the metacharacters used to bracket HTML markup itself. The standard DTD is what covers the second bulleted item. Together, these elements permit HTML to be conveyed by pure ASCII files that follow the conventions established by item 1, and the rules and markup defined by item 2.

When it comes to matters of style, SGML includes an incredible range of expression not fully tapped in any of the standard HTML DTDs. Because of the parental relationship between SGML and HTML, it was only natural that HTML experts who understood the parent's legacy and capability would seek to draw on this relationship for matters of HTML style.

These factors, more than anything else, tilted the balance toward Lie's CSS proposal, because it was judged more palatable to the largely unsophisticated HTML design crowd (unsophisticated at least where SGML knowledge and expertise is concerned, we hasten to add).

Lie & Bos: "Cascading Style Sheets, Level 1" (W3C Recommendation)

(http://www.w3.org/pub/WWW/TR/REC-CSS1)

When the dust settled, the proposal combining simplicity with flexibility, while remaining intelligible to the vast audience of Web designers, is the one that prevailed. Because we're going to cover most of the substance of this specification throughout the remainder of the book, we'll skip the details here. Suffice it to say that after long rumination and much fulmination, the needs of ordinary Webmasters and document designers won. This occurred despite the desires of a powerful, well-connected group of experts who sought what probably was—and still is—the best technical solution available today. It's almost enough to give you hope in the standards-making process.

It is strongly recommended that you download and read this specification at your leisure. It still serves as the ultimate definition of all we discuss in this book. If nothing else, it should make you grateful for the background information, examples, and more lighthearted tone of this book.

The State Of HTML Style Today And Tomorrow

Right now, work continues in many areas related to HTML style, extending and refining the work that

the current CSS recommendation represents. Two important observations apply to this specification:

- It's a recommendation, not a requirement. Like the ongoing work toward the "next version" of HTML—code-named Cougar—this version of CSS is intended primarily to give developers a well-defined notion of what implementing style controls within a browser entails.

- It's a moving target. As prototype implementations appear and a body of experience in defining and using style sheets for HTML accretes, the specification will change to reflect that experience, and to accommodate the inevitable mistaken and missing elements that may currently lurk within (or be lacking from) its contents.

In plain English, it's a good idea to stay on top of the ongoing dialogue and research work on HTML style sheets, just as you must with other aspects of this markup language.

The best place to do that is on the W3C Web site, where the ultimate set of pointers to Style Sheet-related information resides at **http://www.w3.org/Style/**. Check in on this page regularly to see what's new and interesting in this area: As significant developments occur, you'll find them quickly reflected here. You will also find a regular report on style-related activities at the W3C at **http://www.w3.org/Style/Activity/**.

You will also want to investigate the document entitled "HTML and Style Sheets," (W3C Working Draft 24-Mar-97), which explains the relationship between the CSS recommendation and the forthcoming version of HTML (Cougar). You can find this document at: **http://www.w3.org/TR/WD-style**. An important disclaimer in the document identifies it as purely a "work in progress," and it should not be cited or used as the foundation for anything other than speculation or prototype development work. Nevertheless, it's an illuminating look at what HTML style is about, and how it will work in the emerging generation of Web browsers.

Looking Ahead

But it's time to leave the history behind and take a first close look at the CSS specification. That's precisely what we do in the next chapter, as we peel back the covers and look at what's inside the concepts and terminology involved in Cascading Style Sheets.

HTML AND STYLE SHEETS: CSS

The *American Heritage Dictionary* defines style as "a customary manner of presenting printed material, including usage, punctuation, spelling, typography, and arrangement." This definition applies well to Cascading Style Sheets (CSS). The dictionary also defines style as "a quality of imagination and individuality expressed in one's actions and tastes," which certainly applies to Håkon Wium Lie and Bert Bos, the originators of Cascading Style Sheets.

Not-So-Humble Beginnings: The Founders Of CSS

Just as Adobe's PostScript page-description language gave the desktop publishing industry a method of controlling text formatting on complex printed pages in 1985, Lie and Bos' first-level Cascading Style Sheets recommendation (CSS1) has given the World Wide Web a method of describing and controlling the formatting of complex text on Web documents in 1997. And they've done it with an elegant sense of style. CSS1 not only proposes a method for adding style to HTML, it includes a way to establish an order of importance applicable to multiple style sheets.

Who Are These Guys?

Would you believe they are just a couple of regular computer techies who got lucky and were in the right place at the right time? Nah, neither do we. Both Bert and Håkon have been interested in the inner workings of the Internet for some time, and both desired to help move the Web into the next generation of usage. They both knew that plain text and static graphics weren't going to keep users interested for very long. A quick look at TV and computer and video games showed them that without fast, colorful, easily changed text to accompany the graphics and audio, the Web would be dead.

Håkon Wium Lie is a graduate of the MIT Media Lab, which, along with the Institut National de Recherche en Informatique et enAutomatique (INRIA), hosts the World Wide Web Consortium

(W3C). He works for Tim Berners-Lee, head of the W3C and the acknowledged "father of the Web." Håkon is based at the INRIA site in southern France and spends most of his time promoting style sheets. You can find out more about him at: **http:// www.w3.org/People/howcome/**.

Bert Bos studied mathematics in Gröningen from 1982 through 1987. He produced a thesis, "Graphic User Interfaces (1987– 1993)," and worked on an Internet browser and the surrounding infrastructure for the Faculty of Arts in Gröningen. He currently works for the World Wide Web Consortium. You can find out more about him at: **http://www.w3.org/people/bos/**.

What Do They All Want?

Of course, ever since the very first word of text was published on the Web, users and authors have cried for, begged for, and de- manded more formatting power. Simply using a few **<H>** or **<FONT>** tags, or replacing a few bytes of text with a 20,000 byte image to display a large, colored word, wasn't going to appease them. They wanted more, *much* more, *a whole lot* more! Oops, we've gotten ahead of ourselves a bit here; back to our history.

Even before the W3C was formed in 1994 to promote the stan- dardization of nonproprietary HTML and Web specifications, Robert Raisch (O'Reilly and Associates) sent out a request for comments (RFC) regarding style sheets in HTML documents. After numerous proposals and no general consensus, Bert Bos formu- lated and published (May 1995) his goals for a standard for style sheets. Shortly thereafter, Håkon Wium Lie's, "Cascading HTML Style Sheets—A Proposal," was published via the W3C. His method of "cascading" or linking style sheets in an ordered fash- ion, along with rules to govern how they would be interpreted, provided the flexibility that users so desperately craved. The rest is rapidly becoming history as Cascading Style Sheets appear to be on the verge of taking the Web by storm. But where did Bert and Håkon get their ideas for CSS?

Déjà Vu: Conventional Desktop Style Terminology

The style sheet concept is not new. It has been available in word processing and page layout programs for years. In general, a style sheet defines a set of layout parameters for a document to ensure that similar elements in the document appear uniformly. Let's use this book and this paragraph as an example. Pulling down the style list in the trusty Word for Windows word processing program that we're using to type this paragraph will display styles for five levels of headings, a couple of body styles, bulleted list styles, HTML code styles, a chapter title style, and several others. A sample of this pull-down menu is shown in Figure 3.1. The Body A style of the text you are reading right now is composed of the 3Stone Informal, with flush left positioning and double line spacing. Throughout this book, the first paragraph following a major heading will look the same as this paragraph because all use the Body A style. This keeps us from having to set each of the font and paragraph parameters separately for the first paragraph of each section. We simply select

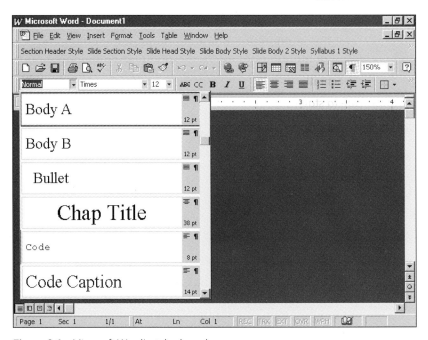

Figure 3.1   Microsoft Word's style drop-down menu.

Body A from the list of styles and type away. Pressing the Enter key at the end of this sentence will automatically switch this style to Body B for the next paragraph in this section because part of the Body A style specification says that a paragraph following Body A will use the Body B style.

The list of properties that can be used in word processing style sheets varies with the word processor program. However, the CSS1 recommendation contains a list of about 50 properties and their values that can be used in Cascading Style Sheets in your HTML documents. These properties and values should display properly on any computer running a CSS1-compliant browser. This cross-platform functionality is one of the great advantages of using style sheets on the Web. And now, on to an example of an HTML style sheet.

A Simple Style Sheet Mechanism

Simple, as in, "not involved or complicated," is a relative term. Using style sheets can greatly simplify the task of producing not-so-simple Web documents. Style sheets can save time by allowing you to specify the style for entire documents—or your entire site—with a single HTML tag, when the single HTML tag links a pre-constructed style sheet to your Web document. Creating a style sheet is actually quite simple. A style sheet consists of at least one rule (a statement concerning the style attributes of one or more HTML elements):

```
H1 { color: gray }
```

The preceding line constitutes a one-rule style sheet. A rule consists of two parts: the *selector* and the *declaration,* separated by a colon. This rule consists of "H1" (the selector) and "{color: gray}" (the declaration). It selects level-one headings and declares that they are to be displayed in gray. When inserted into the proper place in your Web document, this style sheet will cause all **<H1>** text in the Web document to be displayed in gray. To accomplish this with standard HTML tags, you would have to put the following at every place you use the H1 tag:

```
<FONT COLOR= "COCOCO"><H1> Heading text here </H1></FONT>
```

The basic style tags are as simple as the following:

```
<STYLE TYPE="text/css">
<!--H1{color:gray}-->
</STYLE>
```

Placing the preceding tags in the **<HEAD>...</HEAD>** portion of your Web document will cause it to be used by CSS1-aware browsers, such as Microsoft's IE 3.0 and Netscape's Navigator 4.0. The **TYPE="text/css"** attribute is set to **text/css** to tell the browser you are using cascading style sheets. The actual style rule (selector and declaration) is enclosed in the SGML comment tags **<!—...—>** to keep older browsers from displaying it as text. Older browser versions will ignore the **<STYLE>...</STYLE>** tags. Because the STYLE element is declared as "CDATA" in the DTD, CSS1-aware browsers will properly parse the command, rather than treating it as a comment.

Using multiple rules together creates a style sheet in which you can define a series of styles for headings, body text, captions, and so on. The appropriate style will automatically be used by the browser at the proper time. Of course, you must insert the HTML tag that tells the browser about the style sheet in the appropriate place in your Web document. You have four choices for accomplishing this:

The first approach is to type the style information directly into the **<HEAD>...</HEAD>** section at the beginning of each HTML document, as shown in the following example:

```
<HEAD>
<STYLE TYPE="text/css">
<!--H1{color:gray}-->
</STYLE>
</HEAD>
```

Second, you can put all the style information in a separate HTML document and then **<LINK>** the style sheet (which uses the .CSS extension) to each HTML page, using the following tag structure.

This approach is great if you want the styles to affect all of the documents on your site.

```
<LINK REL=STYLESHEET TYPE="text/css" HREF="yourstyle.css" >
```

Third, you may use the CSS @import notation:

```
<STYLE TYPE="text/css">
@import URL (http://yoursite.com/yourstyle.css);
 H1 {color:gray}
</STYLE>
```

The fourth method lets you apply specific styles to sections of your document, even if you've already defined a document-wide style. This option mixes style with content and obviates the advantage of using style sheets to some extent.

```
<P STYLE="color: blue">This tag will cause this
line to display in blue.
```

Some of these methods are not so simple, but they're not theoretical math either. If we can use them, so can you. We'll discuss these methods in much more detail later in this chapter and in subsequent chapters.

Cascading, Linked Style Sheets

Perhaps the most fundamental feature of CSS1 is that style sheets can cascade. (Okay, okay, you thought we'd never get there, but here we are.) A style sheet "cascades" when an author, user, or both, have established an order of precedence that the browser can apply to multiple style sheets. The browser applies the style from whichever style sheet has the highest precedence (detailed in the following section). The general order of precedence (from highest to lowest importance) is: Inline **<STYLE>** declaration, Embedded **<STYLE>** block, then External linked style sheet.

So what in the galaxy does this truly mean? It means that you can attach preferred style sheets to a Web document by supplying definitions for what you want the information to look like. Don't worry, we cover this in detail in the following section.

Cascading Precedence

As previously mentioned, CSS contains a set of rules for resolving style conflicts that arise from applying multiple style sheets to the same Web document. The specifics of the rules of precedence are still recommendations rather than standards and are, therefore, subject to change. However, they undoubtedly depend on the assignment of a numeric weight to represent the relative importance of each style item. Using the suggested method, you assign a value between 1 and 100 to a style element referenced in a style sheet. After all referenced style sheets and their alterations are loaded into memory, style sheet conflicts are resolved by applying the definition with the greatest weight, ignoring all others.

To prevent your settings from completely overriding users' preferences (set in their browser option and preferences dialogs, as shown in Figure 3.2 and 3.3) you should always set your weights to less than the maximum of 100. By using a value lower than 100, you leave the door open for your users to override settings when they deem it necessary. The ability to override some style sheet settings is especially helpful for visually challenged users who may require all characters to be

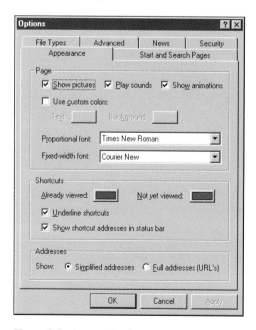

Figure 3.2 Internet Explorer's Options dialog box.

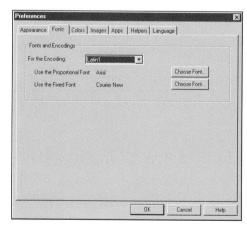

Figure 3.3 Netscape Navigator Preferences dialog box. Users can set their own preferences in either browser.

larger than your font settings, or for users who need special text-to-speech settings. For example, Figure 3.4 shows the W3C home page rendered in large type with the style rules overridden by the browser so that a visually impaired user will be able to see the content without the styles getting in the way.

W3C

Web Style Sheets

(This page uses CSS style sheets)

What's new?

What are style sheets?

Figure 3.4 The W3C page shown in Chapter 1 with user preferences overriding style rules.

For example, assume you create a style for a level-one heading, <H1>, so that it uses the color blue, and you assign it a weight of 85 percent. Also assume that one of your readers has defined a style for <H1>, colored red with a weight of 90 percent. In this case, the user's CSS-enabled browser uses the user's style definition because it has the greater weight. Although this is a simple example of cascading style sheet precedence, it gives you the basic idea that is carried through the entire CSS process.

The Benefits Of Implementing CSS

Several other benefits can be yours by implementing CSS on your Web site:

- **Grouping**—Group multiple, similar style elements or definitions within a single style rule:

```
H1 {font-size: 12pt;
line-height: 14pt;
font-family: helvetica
}
```

- **Inheritance**—Any nested tags inherit the style sheet definitions assigned to the parent tag, unless the same elements are
  explicitly redefined. For example, in the following HTML line:

```
<H1>The Heading <B>is</B> Significant!</H1>
```

  if **<H1>** is defined to display in blue, the text enclosed by **<B>**
  also appears in blue, unless **<B>** is specifically defined to use
  another color.

In a nutshell, you can relatively easily produce complex layout
and formatting with style sheets, but not with regular HTML.
Style sheets go several steps beyond the recent extensions to
HTML that have attempted to control document layout by adding complex border, margin, and spacing controls to most HTML
elements. Using style sheets also extends the capabilities introduced by most of the existing HTML extensions. You can now
assign background colors or images to any HTML element, instead of just the **<BODY>** element. You can also apply borders to
any element, not just to tables.

Style sheets aren't a universal panacea, as they only specify
information that controls display and layout information. You
can't replace style tags that convey the nature of the content
with style sheets, just as hyperlinking and multimedia object
insertion are not a part of style sheet functionality—although
controlling the appearance of these objects *is* part of style sheet
functionality. The CSS1 recommendation attempts to encom-
pass all of the HTML functionality used to control the display
and layout characteristics of Web documents. For more information, see the section on cascading in the CSS1 Specification
or the Index DOT HTML section on the Style Sheet Cascade
process at:

http://www.w3.org/pub/WWW/Style/Welcome.html

Advantages And Disadvantages Of Style Specification Methods

Each method of specifying style information has good points as well as drawbacks. The following factors should be considered when planning your use of Cascading Style Sheets.

Linking To Or Importing External Style Sheets

Advantages

- Controls styles for multiple documents at once.

- Creates classes for use on multiple HTML tag types in many documents.

- All selector grouping methods can be used to apply styles.

Disadvantages

- Downloading is required to import style information for each document.

- The document will not display until the external style sheet is loaded.

- Overly complicated for small quantities of styles.

Document-Level Style Sheets

Advantages

- You can create classes for use on multiple tag types in the document.

- All selector grouping methods can be used to apply styles.

- Downloads are not necessary to receive style information.

Disadvantages

- Cannot control styles for multiple documents simultaneously.

Inline Styles

Advantages

- Useful for small quantities of style definitions.

- Can override other style specification methods at the local level.

Disadvantages

- Does not separate style information from content.

- You cannot create classes of tags to control multiple tag types.

- Cannot control styles for multiple documents at once.

- Selector grouping methods cannot be used to create contextual tag conditions.

Looking Ahead

By now, you are hopefully beginning to understand the basics of Cascading Style Sheets. Once you have the concept fairly clear in your mind, the rest is merely assembling a few selectors and declarations into rules to suit your needs.

Congratulations, you're ready for syntax, the subject of the next chapter. (Hmm, syntax...isn't that the tax levied on...oh, never mind.)

PART 2

USING STYLE SHEETS WITH HTML

THE SYNTAX OF STYLES

4

When we introduced you to your first bit of style sheet code in Chapter 1, we promised a translation in Chapter 4 and we have every intention of keeping our promise. In this chapter, you will take an in-depth look at the syntax of styles: the rules, properties, and values that comprise correct style markup. The ins and outs are pretty straightforward and should fit right in with all you already know about HTML markup. Onward ho!

Playing By The Rules: Style Sheet Syntax

First things first; where exactly do you put style sheets? There are several ways to link style information to your HTML pages, including referencing external style sheets and adding style specifics to tags using attributes. For now, we concentrate on the easiest method: including style information directly within your HTML pages themselves. Include your style information within the <STYLE>... </STYLE> tags. The style definitions you create affect the entire document, so you should include the <STYLE>... </STYLE> tags and their contents within the <HEAD>... </HEAD> tags. The HTML code looks like this:

```
<HTML>
<HEAD>

<TITLE>Style Sheet Samples</TITLE>

<STYLE TYPE="text/css">
... your style information here ...
</STYLE>

</HEAD>

<BODY>
... your HTML content here ...
</BODY>

</HTML>
```

Notice that the <STYLE> tag includes the **TYPE=** attribute. This lets the browser know what kind of style sheet rules you'll be using. In most cases, the attribute's value will be **text/css** to indicate CSS1. Now that you have a place to put your style information, here's a short lesson in style syntax.

The Magic Formula: Selector+Declaration=Style Rule

A basic style sheet rule has two parts:

- **The selector**. This is the HTML markup tag affected by the rule. For example, the selector **P** indicates that the HTML tag **<P>** (paragraph) is the tag affected by the style specifics of that rule.

- **The declaration**. The style specifics are defined in the declaration using sets of properties and values. A property indicates what aspects of a tag's display are affected and the value specifies how it should be affected. The declaration **background-color: white** changes the background of the selector to white. The property is **background-color** and the value is **white**. Declarations are enclosed in curly braces ({ and }), with the property listed first, followed by a color and the value.

The full syntax for a basic style sheet rule is

```
Selector {property: value}
```

A sample rule within the context of an HTML page would look like the following:

```
<HTML>
<HEAD>

<TITLE>Style Sheet Samples</TITLE>

<STYLE TYPE="text/css">
P {background-color: white}
</STYLE>

</HEAD>

<BODY>
</BODY>

</HTML>
```

A FEW QUICK NOTES ON STYLE SHEET SYNTAX

In style sheet rules, as in HTML (excluding file names), case doesn't matter. The rule **P {background-color: white}** means exactly the same thing as **P {BACKGROUND-COLOR: WHITE.**

In style sheet rules, as in HTML, curly quotes do matter. Later, we'll show you how to name your selectors, which involves the use of quotation marks. Curly quotations are not part of the ASCII character set and will render your rules unreadable by a browser.

These are little things, but they can make or break your style rules in a heartbeat.

That's it, style rules in a nutshell. Every tag in the HTML 4.0 specification is fair game for use as a selector and you have 50 different style properties from which to choose. Style sheets are simply collections of style rules that affect a group of HTML tags within a page or pages.

The More The Merrier: Grouping

Because style sheets are a collection of rules, they have the potential to grow long very quickly. The individual rules are short, sweet, and to the point, but start piling them one on top of the other, and things can start to get hairy. To avoid such complications, the concept of *grouping* has been built into style sheets in order to make style rules as abbreviated as possible while still providing complete definition information. Grouping involves combining like selectors, declarations, or both into compact rules. You can create groups in three different ways.

Groups Of Selectors

Often, several selectors share the same declaration. If you want bold, italic, and strongly emphasized text to all be blue, it is cumbersome to list each one separately, as we did here:

```
B: {color: blue}
I: {color: blue}
STRONG: {color: blue}
EM: {color blue}
```

Grouping allows you to combine all four lines of code into the following one line of code:

```
B, I, STRONG, EM: {color: blue}
```

Another quick example: If you want all of your document headings to be in Garamond, the following single line of code does the trick:

```
H1, H2, H3, H4, H5, H6 {font-family: Garamond}
```

Because similar selectors may need to assume similar style aspects, it's much easier to write one line of code. It is also much

easier to change one line of code later on down the line when it
is time to update the style sheet. Always remember to separate
your selectors with commas, or the browser will be looking for a
single tag, like **<H1H2H3H4H5H6>**, instead of a group of tags.

Groups Of Declarations

You will often want to define more than one aspect of an
element's style. It may be that all of your document headings
should not only be in Garamond, but they should also be indented one-half of an inch, red, and in small caps. You could
use individual rules to define each aspect, as does the code that
follows:

```
H1, H2, H3, H4, H5, H6 {font-family: Garamond}
H1, H2, H3, H4, H5, H6 {text-indent: 0.5in}
H1, H2, H3, H4, H5, H6 {color: red}
H1, H2, H3, H4, H5, H6 {font-varient: small-caps}
```

Or, you could group them all together in one rule to save space
and time, as this code does:

```
H1, H2, H3, H4, H5, H6 {
   font-family: Garamond;
   text-indent: 0.5in;
   color: red;
   font-varient: small-caps;
}
```

You'll notice we stuck a couple of new syntax elements into the
preceding code. Semicolons are used to separate multiple declarations, and the format for the rule changed a bit. Although we
could have listed all of the declarations on one line, it would
have become difficult to read, so we kicked each declaration onto
its own line and indented it. We ended the rule with a right curly
brace, as all rules end, but it has its own line as well. This is the
accepted code layout for complex rules that include several declarations. The code is easier to read because individual rules can
be found and changed by simply scanning the list. Checking for
errors, such as missing semicolons and right curly braces, is also
easier when each line is broken out. Ultimately, the browser

GROUPING DEFINED

Grouping is, in essence, a shorthand for style. To ensure proper grouping syntax, remember the special functions of each of these characters:

- , (comma)—Separates selectors in a selector-based grouping

- ; (semicolon)—Separates declarations in a declaration-based grouping

- (space)—Separates values in a family-based grouping

doesn't care if your entire HTML document were on one line, because it ignores line breaks in general.

Special Syntax For Individual Property Families

Many of the property families have their own syntax—especially for creating groups of rules. You may want to specify several font declarations for one paragraph. You can use the declaration grouping method we described previously, as shown in this code:

```
P {font-family: Garamond;
   font-style: italic;
   font-size: 12pt;
}
```

This code can be reduced even further using the special group syntax for the font properties family:

```
P {font: Garamond italic 12pt}
```

Notice that the specific values are separated only by spaces. The rule is comprised of one property; **font**; and three values: **Garamond, italic,** and **12pt. Font** is the property that combines all of the font property families into one. As we discuss each property family in turn, we examine the grouping property specific to the group and the values it takes.

Although basic style rules are very simple, they are just the beginning. Selectors can be defined to create multiple styles for a single HTML element. You can have 30 different paragraph styles and 50 different level-1 headings if you so desire. However, even as selectors and declarations change, the basic style rule remains the same. The remainder of this chapter details the different types of selectors you can create and takes a closer look at property and value specifics.

Broadening The Selector Horizon

If style sheets were limited to the basic rules outlined at the beginning of the chapter, you would only be able to define one style for any given HTML element in any given page because there is no way to define different instances of a tag within a page. Style sheets incorporate three ways of giving unique identities to individual style rules: the ability to assign unique names to multiple versions of a single HTML tag with different style definitions; a method for creating a rule that can be applied to many different elements; and a way to create exceptions to a rule.

Using Class As A Selector

A new addition to the HTML 4.0 specification, the **CLASS** attribute, now gives you a way to create multiple instances of one tag, each with its own unique name and style. This makes it possible, for example, to create one paragraph style with a half-inch indentation and another with a one-inch indention, while both use the **<P>** tag.

You can label different classes within style rules by adding a period and the class name directly after the selector. The syntax looks like this:

```
Selector.class {property: value}
```

Once again, it's that simple. To create the two types of paragraphs we just discussed, use the following code:

```
<HTML>
<HEAD>

<TITLE>Style Sheet Samples</TITLE>

<STYLE TYPE="text/css">
P.onehalf {text-indent: 0.5in}
P.one {text-indent: 1in}
</STYLE>

</HEAD>

<BODY>
</BODY>

</HTML>
```

Now that the class names have been created by the style rules, use the **CLASS="name"** attribute with the <P> tag to apply the styles within an HTML document:

```
<HTML>
<HEAD>

<TITLE>Style Sheet Samples</TITLE>

<STYLE TYPE="text/css">
P.onehalf {text-indent: 0.5in}
P.one {text-indent: 1in}
</STYLE>

</HEAD>

<BODY>

<P CLASS="onehalf">This text has a one-half inch indentation.
<P CLASS="one">But this text has a one-inch indentation.

</BODY>
</HTML>
```

The resulting HTML page is shown in Figure 4.1

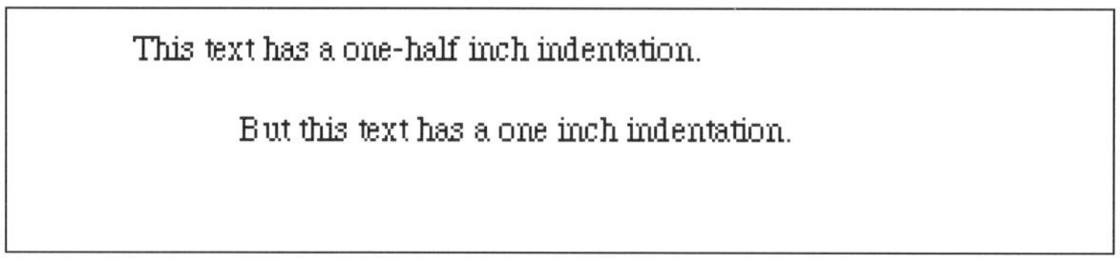

This text has a one-half inch indentation.

But this text has a one inch indentation.

Figure 4.1 Two paragraph styles created using style rules with class specifications.

Classes are very handy for creating a style sheet that is referenced by many HTML pages in order to ensure consistency among the pages. We cover how to store and reference external style sheets fully in Chapter 8. For now, it is enough to know that you can create documents containing nothing but style information, and reference them in multiple documents using the <**LINK**> tag. The rule syntax is the same; it's just saved in a different document.

The World Wide Web Consortium (W3C) Cascading Style Sheet page at **http://www.windows.com/workshop/design/des-gen/ss/css-des.htm** is built using style sheets, and it takes full advantage of classes in several instances.

For example, it uses the following style sheet code to create two classes of the <**SPAN**> tag:

```
SPAN.date { font-size: 0.8em }

SPAN.attribution {
  font-weight: bold
}
```

In the body of the document, it uses this HTML to reference the specific classes of <**SPAN**> and format the enclosed text accordingly:

```
<H2><A NAME="news">What's new?</A></H2>

<UL>

<LI><SPAN CLASS=date>970623:</SPAN>
<A HREF="http://interaction.in-progress.com/cascade">Cascade</A>
is a comprehensive Cascading Style Sheets editor for Mac.

<LI><SPAN CLASS=date>970623:</SPAN>
<A HREF="http://www.astrobyte.com">Astrobyte</A> has announced
<A HREF="http://www.astrobyte.com/About/BeyondPress3.0Release.html">
BeyondPress 3.0</A> which will convert QuarkXPress documents into HTML
and CSS.

<LI><SPAN CLASS=date>970527:</SPAN> Silicon Graphics has an embeddable
web browser used in a number of applications and their desktop, which
supports CSS.

<LI><SPAN CLASS=date>970415:</SPAN> The
<A HREF="http://interaction.inprogress.com"> Interaction</A>
dynamic site management system includes a comprehensive
<A HREF="http://interaction.in-progress.com/components/style">
Macintosh CSS editor</A>.

<LI>><SPAN CLASS=date>970404:</SPAN>
<A HREF="http://www.w3.org/pub/WWW/Style/CSS/Buttons/Menu">CSS
buttons</A> are now available -- put one on your CSS pages!

</UL>
```

Each item in the list takes the date class of the <**SPAN**> tag. If the attribute had been **CLASS=attribution** instead of **CLASS=date**, all of the items would have been formatted using the style defined in the **SPAN.attribution** rule rather than the **SPAN.date** rule.

NAMING SELECTORS

When creating an ID selector naming scheme, we suggest you come up with one that is consistent and will make sense to you later. Also consider adding comments before or after your rules as a future reference for you or anyone else who might work with the pages you've designed.

Using classes, you can create an unlimited number of different rules for any given HTML tag. But wait, classes aren't the only way to create different style rules. ID selectors create rules without using HTML tags as selectors.

Using ID As A Selector

When class is used with a selector, the class is tied directly to a specific HTML element. In the previous W3C example, **.attribution** and **.date** were associated specifically with the <SPAN> tag. If we had tried to use a <P> tag with a **CLASS=date** attribute, the style rule we defined for **SPAN=.date** would not be automatically transferred to the paragraph. Although there are many instances when you want to have different style rules for the same HTML element, there are also times when you want one style rule to be applicable to several different elements. ID to the rescue.

Another new addition to the HTML specification, ID is designed to create a unique rule that can be applied to many different HTML elements in a single page. The rule code looks like the following:

```
#id {property: value}
```

Notice the ID begins with a pound (#) sign and doesn't contain a period or any other notation. The id can contain any combination of alphanumeric characters.

The HTML code that invokes the style rule is similar to the markup we saw for specifying a class:

```
<TAG ID="id"> ... </TAG>
```

Returning to the code behind the W3C's Style Sheet page, we find that it utilizes ID selectors in addition to the CLASS selectors we showed you earlier. It contains an entire set of ID selectors:

```
#s1 {
  color: #DDD;
  font: 100px Impact, sans-serif;
}
```

```
#p1 {
  margin-top: -30px;
  text-align: right;
}

#s2 {
  color: #000;
  font: italic 40px Georgia, serif;
}

#p2 {
  margin-top: -80px;
  margin-left: 5%;
}

#s3 {
  color: #080;
  font: 40px Verdana, sans-serif;
}

#p3 {
  margin-top: 10px;
  text-align: center;
}

#s4 {
  color: #37F;
  font: bold 40px Courier New, monospace;
}

#p4 {
  margin-top: -20px;
  text-align: right;
}

#s5 {
  color: #F73;
  font: bold 60px Verdana, sans-serif;
}

#p5 {
  margin-top: -80px;
  text-align: left;
}

#s6 {
  color: #22A;
  font: bold 25px Verdana, sans-serif;
}
```

```
#p6 {
  text-align: center;
  margin-top: 0px;
}

#s7 {
  color: #088;
  font: italic 20px Verdana, sans-serif;
}

#p7 {
  text-align: right;
  margin-top: -10px;
}

#s8 {
  color: #088;
  font: italic 20px Verdana, sans-serif;
}

#p8 {
  margin-top: -10px;
  margin-left: 3%;
}

#s9 {
  color: #000;
  font: 20px Georgia, serif;
}

#p9 {
  margin-top: -10px;
  margin-left: 30%;
}

#s10 {
  color: #900;
  font: bold 10pt Georgia, serif;
}

#p10 {
  text-align: right;
  margin-top: -10px;
}

#s11 {
  color: #990;
  font: italic 20px Georgia, serif;
}
```

```
#p11 {
  margin-top: 0px;
  margin-left: 20%;
}
```

These selectors create a series of styles that can be applied to any element. There are two different types of rules: the "s" series specifies font color, size, type, and font face; the "p" series defines the top and left margins. Throughout the page the rules are referenced in the markup as they are needed:

```
<P ID=p1><A HREF="#news"><SPAN ID=s1>What's new?</SPAN></A>
<P ID=p2><A HREF="#learn"><SPAN ID=s2>Learning CSS</SPAN></A>
<P ID=p3><A HREF="#browsers"><SPAN ID=s3>CSS Browsers</SPAN></A>
<P ID=p4><A HREF="#editors"><SPAN ID=s4>Authoring Tools</SPAN></A>
<P ID=p5><A HREF="#specs"><SPAN ID=s5>Specs</SPAN></A>
<P ID=p6><A HREF="#history"><SPAN ID=s6>History</SPAN></A>
```

When viewed with a style-enabled browser, as shown in Figure 4.2, the styles have quite an impact on the page's design.

When viewed with a browser that doesn't support style sheets, the results are completely different, and nowhere near as exciting, as shown in Figure 4.3.

Because the ID selectors are not tied to any one HTML element, they can be reused over and over again throughout a page. This allows you to create a set of style rules and apply them whenever and wherever you like, without having to go back and create a new CLASS-based selector for each HTML element.

Figure 4.2 A style sheet-based Web page when viewed with a style-enabled browser.

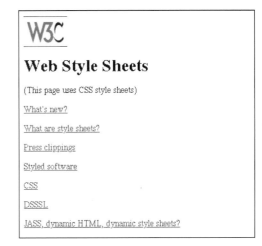

Figure 4.3 A style sheet–based Web page when viewed in a browser that doesn't support style sheets.

Using Context As A Selector

As anyone who reads and writes the English language knows, every rule has at least one exception. The same is true for any given style rule. Most HTML markup elements can contain other markup elements. **<B>** is legal within **<P>**, **<P>** within **<TD>**, and so on. The question is: How do you change the style of one element nested within another element that already has a style rule created for it? What if you only want the style to apply when element A is nested within element B, but not when nested within element C? Here's an example to illustrate. The style code

```
I {color: black}
B {color: teal}
```

turns all the text within **<I>...</I>** tags black, and all text within **<B>...</B>** tags teal. If you nest boldfaced text within italicized text under these style rules, the nested boldfaced text will be teal, as will any other boldfaced text on the page, nested or not. But what if you want only boldfaced text nested within italicized text to be teal and all other instances of boldface to be left alone? *Contextual selectors* are the answer.

A contextual selector is made up of one or more single selectors with spaces (not commas) between them. In order for text to be affected by the style rule, it must be contained within all of the simple selectors listed. For example:

```
I B {color: teal}
```

only affects text within boldfaced markup that is also nested within italicized markup. This HTML:

```
<I>This is some italicized text <B>followed by some boldfaced and
italicized text</B> followed by more italicized text.</I>
```

meets the style rules requirements, whereas this text:

```
<I>This is some italicized text.</I>
<B>This is some boldfaced text.</B>
```

does not meet the requirements because the bold markup is outside of the italics markup, not nested within it. Another, longer example:

```
H1 I B {color: teal}
```

This only affects text within boldfaced markup nested within italicized markup that is, in turn, nested within heading level-1 markup.

Later in the chapter we discuss *inheritance,* or how style rules assigned to one element affect other elements nested within it. For now, we're concerned with the syntax of contextual selectors. A contextual selector can contain basic HTML elements, CLASS attributes, and ID attributes, in any combination. All of the following contextual rules are perfectly legal even though they include three different types of simple selectors:

```
H1 I B #345 STRONG.new {color: teal}
#445 P.byline P.me I {color: teal}
```

Contextual selectors can be grouped just like simple selectors. This rule:

```
H1 I B #345 STRONG.new, #445 P.byline P.me I {color: teal}
```

is equivalent to the two complex selectors you just saw. Remember that white space separates single selectors in a contextual selector, and commas separate selectors in all groups.

You've now seen the different types of selectors, how they're invoked in HTML markup, and how they can be combined to create groups and contextual selectors. The next style sheet concepts to tackle are *pseudo-classes* and *pseudo-elements*.

Pseudo-Classes And Pseudo-Elements

So far, the selectors we have discussed—simple, class-based, ID-based, and contextual—have all focused on applying style rules to page elements in much the same way HTML tags do. Style rules introduce new control and specification mechanisms not previously available in standard markup, but still function in essentially the same way as tags do. However, there are some design conventions that standard markup does not support, such as style changes based on state, and formatting based on a character or line's position within a paragraph. CSS includes two new mechanisms: pseudo-classes and pseudo-elements, which are specifically designed to address this missing functionality.

Pseudo-Classes

When we looked at classes a few sections ago, you added a class to a selector using **.classname** and referenced it in an HTML tag using the **CLASS=** attribute. Pseudo-classes are added to a selector using the same **.classname** syntax. They are invoked in the HTML body by the status of the text enclosed within the element defined by the selector, rather than by using the **CLASS=** attribute. The only HTML element that currently takes pseudo-classes is the anchor (**<A>**) tag. The style of the text enclosed in an anchor tag can be set based on the status of the link. An anchor can have three possible status settings:

- **Link**—The default status for an anchor. The text within the anchor tags is a link but has not been selected yet.

- **Visited**—The user has already viewed the resource to which the anchor points. The length of time all links are considered visited is set by the user in the browser's preferences section.

- **Active**—A link is active in the brief moment when the user selects it, before the linked resource is loaded into the browser window.

An anchor is a link until it has been selected; it is active for a second or so when the user clicks it; and it is visited after the user has viewed the resource the link points to and has returned to the page containing the link.

The HTML doesn't change using pseudo-classes, but the style of an element does when status changes. For obvious reasons, only those elements whose contained text can change status, such as the anchor tag, use pseudo-classes. In future versions of HTML, other elements—such as forms—may also accept pseudo-classes.

The properties and values a pseudo-class can take are generally limited to those that change the appearance of the enclosed text without changing its size, margins, or any other property that would force the browser to reformat the entire document once the status of the link had changed. The exact properties and values that may not be supported by any given browser depend entirely on the browser's implementation of style sheets. It is safe to assume that you can change font color and face, as well as add or remove underlining and bold or italicized formatting.

In addition to other selector classes, the W3C style sheet we've been using as an example throughout this chapter utilizes the anchor pseudo-classes using the following code:

```
A:link { color: #900 }

A:visited, A:active { color: #009 }
```

All active links on the page start out as color #900, and end up as color #009. (We'll provide more information about colors and their numerical equivalents in Chapter 5.) Notice that selectors including pseudo-classes use the syntax

```
Element:pseudo-class {property: value}
```

A colon takes the place of the period we used when creating class selectors. The second selector in the W3C example is a grouping of two simple selectors that take pseudo-classes, and is created using the same syntax as groupings of other selector types.

Pseudo-Elements

When a style is applied to text within an HTML element, all of the text is affected. There will be times when you want to affect only a part of the text contained within an element. Enter pseudo-elements. Only two pseudo-elements are currently available:

- **First-letter**—The style rule only affects the first letter of the contained text.

- **First-line**—The style rule only affects the first line of the contained text.

These pseudo-elements only work with block-level elements, such as <P>, <SPAN>, and <DIV>, that affect logical groups of text.

The syntax for creating rules with pseudo-elements is

```
Element.class:pseudo-element {value: property}
```

A sample pseudo-element rule looks like the following:

```
P.init1:first-letter {color: blue}
```

This code creates a rule, based on the <P> element with a class name **init1**, that takes the pseudo-element **first letter**. The first letter of the first word of any text contained in the tag <P CLASS=init1> will be blue. This rule combines the class naming technique we saw in CLASS selectors with pseudo-elements. Using this notation, you could have several instances of the HTML paragraph element, each with a different class name and initial letter color.

Add the following rule into the fray:

```
P.init1:first-line {color: red; font-variant: small-caps}
```

The result is a paragraph whose first letter, if begun with the tag <P CLASS=init1>, is blue, with all other characters on the first line rendered in small caps and red text.

The majority of the properties and values covered in the next several chapters can be applied to first letters and first lines.

WHAT YOU SEE ISN'T ALWAYS WHAT THEY GET

Keep in mind that users can set their browsers to display pages using pre-defined settings for fonts, link colors, and backgrounds. These settings override any equivalent properties or attributes and their values that you may assign to text using style sheets or HTML tags. Even though style sheets give you more control over the display of your Web pages, the user has final say-so for many common display options.

DROP THAT CAP!

Use a pseudo-element to create a drop cap initial letter. First, create a rule that enlarges the initial letter of a paragraph using the code P.init1:first-letter {font-size: 250%}. This makes the first letter 250 percent larger than the rest of the text in the paragraph. To force the now large capital letter to drop down into the text, add the float: left declaration to the rule. This forces the text up and to the left of the large capital letter, creating the drop-cap format frequently used in printing. An example is shown in Figure 4.4. The final rule looks like this:

```
code P.init1:first-letter
     {font-size: 250% float:
     left}
```

Figure 4.4 Sample drop cap.

As with pseudo-classes, the pseudo-elements supported by particular browsers may differ. If a browser doesn't support a pseudo-class or pseudo-element, it ignores the related style rule and formats any affected text as if it were regular text.

Who Gets What: Inheritance

In the world of HTML and style sheets, inheritance refers to the passing of style properties from one element to text contained in elements nested within the first element. For example, consider a set of style rules that read as follows:

```
<STYLE>
H1 {font-family: Courier}
B {font-style: italic; font-size: xx-large}
</STYLE>
```

This HTML

```
<H1>This is the <B>title</B> of my document.</H1>
```

produces the output shown in Figure 4.5.

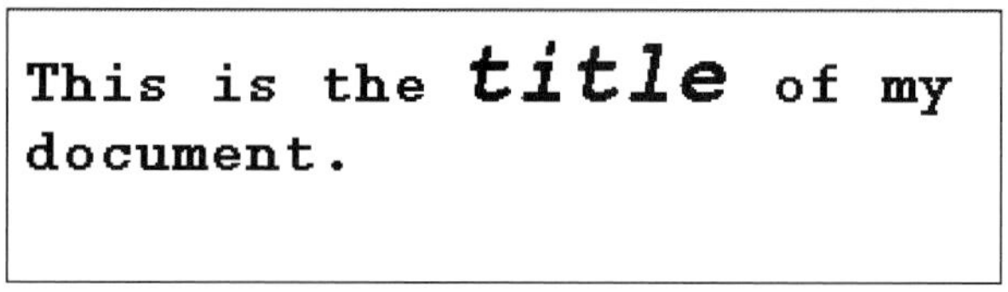

This is the *title* of my document.

Figure 4.5 One HTML element inherits the style properties and values of the element it is nested within.

The preceding style rules specify that all heading level-1 text should be displayed in Courier, and that any boldfaced type should appear extra-large and italicized. When <B>...</B> is nested within <H1>...</H1> the text within the bold tags appears extra-large and italicized but is also in Courier because it inherited that style from the heading level-1 tags that also surround it.

This inheritance of style is based on the idea that all HTML documents follow a tree structure. Figure 4.6 shows the tree structure

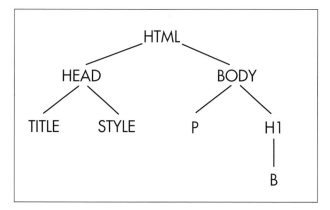

Figure 4.6 The tree structure of a basic HTML document.

for a typical HTML document, including the <H1>...</H1> and <B>...</B> tags we just referenced.

The bold tag pair is a descendent, or child, of the parent heading level-1 tag pair, so it exhibits the style properties defined for its parent, as well as its own style properties. In this code

```
<H1>This is the</H1> <B>title</B> <H1> of my document.</H1>
```

the bold tag pair is not a child of the level-1 heading pairs because the first <H1>...</H1> tag pair opens and closes before the <B>...</B> begins. Figure 4.7 shows the difference in rendering when the bold tags are not related to the level-1 heading tags.

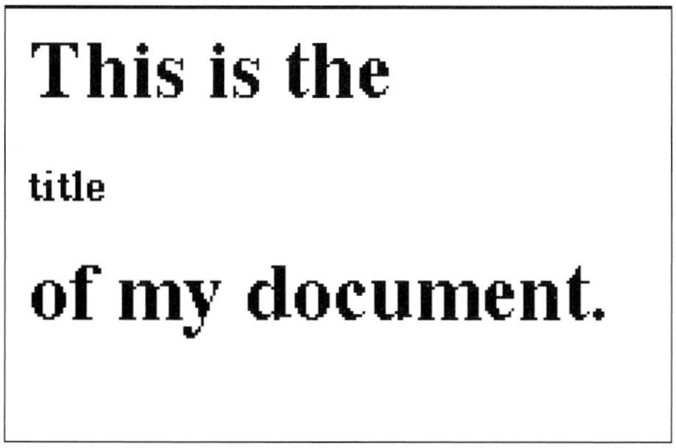

This is the

title

# of my document.

Figure 4.7 When tags are not nested, styles are not inherited.

The principle of inheritance makes it easy to apply style rules to a large portion of text by setting the rule on the element's common ancestor. For example, if you want all of the text in your document to be teal, you could add the **color: teal** property and value to a style rule for each element you use. Instead, it makes more sense to set the rule once in the <**BODY**> element because it is the parent of every other element in the document.

The question then becomes: How do you force a child's style rule to override the styles established for its parent? It's actually pretty simple. The more specific style rule overrides the more general. For example, if we set the color of the body text to teal, using the rule

```
BODY {color: teal}
```

we can override the color selection for a specific paragraph using the rule

```
P.byline {color: black}
```

This happens because the second style rule, the one for a paragraph element class byline, is more specific than the body rule, as it only affects the text within the byline paragraph, not the entire body. This method of resolving inheritances makes it possible to define a general rule that affects the majority of the document, and then create rules for use in specific instances. Some properties, such as **BACKGROUND**, do not inherit from parent to child. We will alert you to these as we discuss each individual property family.

The Rules Rule

There you have it—a complete rundown on the syntax of style sheets. Rules are made up of selectors and declarations, which are a combination of properties and values. There are two different ways to create a unique identity for a selector—by class or ID—and context can determine whether a rule applies or not. Pseudo-classes and pseudo-elements bring functionality to selectors that is missing from HTML markup. Any selector can have more than one property defined for it and all selectors can be combined to create a selector group.

Looking Ahead

Whew! That's quite a bit to remember, but the more style rules you create, the more the rules and regulations will become second nature; sort of like driving a car (but fortunately we don't have style police). The next few chapters, as well as *Do It In Color Sections* II, III, and IV, cover in depth each of the property families and their associated values. The first such family, the unit properties, await us in Chapter 5.

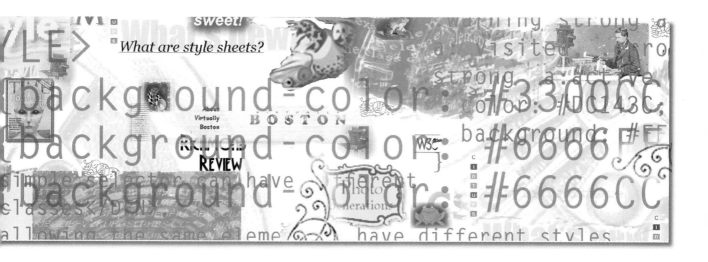

UNDERSTAND-
ING 5 AND
USING UNIT
PROPERTIES

In this chapter:

- **Methods (and units) of measurement**

- **Positioning elements precisely**

- **Length and display units**

- **The roles of absolute and relative measures**

- **Specifying colors and Web addresses**

As you've already learned, one of the distinct advantages that CSS confers upon its users is more precise control over the layout of document elements, along with significant improvements in control over margins, leading, and other forms of white space. Precise positioning requires specifying either a location or distance information for document elements or white space, which must be expressed in units of measure.

In this chapter, we'll investigate those units of measure that work with CSS and how they're expressed. We also cover the profound differences between absolute and relative units of measure, and explain which type of unit makes the most sense when designing an electronic document.

Measuring Methods

In the CSS environment, many properties accept numeric values, which represent a certain number of units of a particular measure. Any numeric value can be a whole number (0, 1, 2, etc.), or a decimal fraction (0.3, 1.56, 2.33, etc.). In CSS, negative numbers are also permitted, and may either be negative values (-1, -2, etc.) or negative decimal fractions (-0.3, -1.56, -2.33, etc.).

When a property's value describes a length, a unit of measure is appended directly after the number with no intervening spaces. For CSS, all units of measure take two-letter abbreviations, with no period at the end of a value string. Valid examples of such expressions include 22px, 1.14cm, and 7pc. The various units of measure allowed for length values in CSS are shown in Table 5.1, with conversion factors to millimeters.

Note the presence of three "not applicable" (N/A) entries in the conversion factor column. These units cannot be arbitrarily converted to millimeters because their exact millimeter values depend on the font (em and ex) or the resolution of the display device (px) in use. Whereas all the other units can be predictably converted into or out of millimeters and are, therefore, absolute, these units of measure must be considered in light of specific

Table 5.1   CSS legal units of measure.

Name	Abbreviation	Type	Conversion Factor
centimeter	cm	absolute	10
em	em	relative	N/A: point size for current font
ex	ex	relative	N/A: x-height for current font
inch	in	absolute	0.039370079
millimeter	mm	absolute	1
pica	pc	absolute	0.00656168
pixel	px	device-dependent	N/A: depends on display in use
point	pt	absolute	0.000556807

values based on designer choices or hardware that cannot be calculated in advance.

Thus, em, ex, and px units of measure are "relative," in that they must be expressed in terms of an underlying font choice or device resolution before they can be completely converted into absolute terms. The CSS1 specification, however, distinguishes that ex and em are relative to font size, and types them explicitly as "relative." Because pixels have an absolute size, but that size is completely device-dependent, the CSS1 specification types px as "device-dependent." Finally, although percentages and keywords are not units of measure *per se*, both represent relative methods of specifying values for style properties (this distinction is discussed further in the next section).

Unit Properties

Given the basic definitions for values stated in the previous section, we can now describe how units of measure (and relative values) may be associated with CSS-related properties. Properties may restrict the acceptable range of numbers and lengths. As an obvious example, the font-size property cannot be set to a negative value because all font sizes must be greater than or equal to zero. By convention, all CSS properties that accept lengths will accept a value of 0 as legal without requiring a units designator (zero equals zero whether it's measured in inches or centimeters).

Absolute units of measure specify a fixed numeric value, such as 0.25 in, 6 pt, or 12 mm. Because absolute values cannot be scaled—that is, multiplied or divided to match some arbitrary conversion factor—absolute values are often of limited use in style sheets. Where absolute units are concerned, it's important to understand that once they are converted for rendering on screen, absolute values can only be matched as closely as a display device permits (that is, small differences may be indiscernible).

Relative units of measure specify one value relative to some other value, usually the font size of the element itself. Relative units have a distinct advantage over absolute units: they scale automatically—that is, by changing the basis upon which a value rests, the value changes along with it. Thus, by changing the size or selection of a base font, all units expressed in terms of ex or em measurements change proportionally.

Device-dependent units of measure depend on the monitor (display device) on which the measure is applied. Currently, the pixel is the only such unit defined in CSS1. (See the sidebar "Of Screens And Pixels" for more information on this common and versatile unit of measure.) Because so many computer displays have relatively low resolutions, it's not safe to assume that small differences in point size will scale precisely; on the other hand, because pixels are device-dependent, small differences in pixel counts do scale precisely. Thus, two pixels are twice as wide as one, and a four-pixel square is twice as wide and high as a single pixel, as illustrated in Figure 5.1.

Length Units

Length units designate absolute or relative sizes associated with CSS properties. All of the units of measure mentioned in Table 5.1 may be used as valid length units when assigning values to CSS properties that can take such values. (Be sure to observe whatever restrictions a property may impose on numeric values, however.)

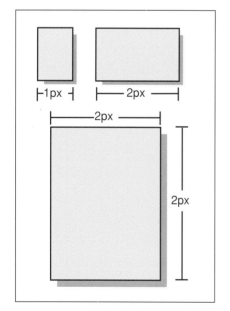

Figure 5.1 Pixels scale precisely as the count goes up, based on the resolution of the user's display.

OF SCREENS AND PIXELS

Most computer display devices—such as cathode-ray terminals (CRTs) and liquid crystal displays (LCDs), among others—are designed to be directly addressable in terms of the horizontal and vertical location of individual display elements. This permits precise control over graphics displayed on screen, as individual locations can be updated independently (which significantly speeds screen refresh, with only a small portion of the display area needing to be updated, rather than the whole thing). Each individually addressable display element is called a *picture element*, commonly abbreviated as *pixel*. In the crudest of possible terms, a pixel corresponds to a single dot on a CRT or an LCD display.

Different display devices have pixels of different sizes. Typical CRTs employ pixels between 0.25mm and 0.38mm in size; LCDs—especially smaller displays like those found in camera or camcorder viewfinders—use pixels between 0.22mm and 0.35mm. Pixels provide a useful form of measurement because a difference of one pixel is guaranteed to be visible on any display.

But because differences in size may only be displayed in terms of an absolute number of pixels, small gradations in image or font size may not be discernible when displayed. In other words, if size changes amount to less than one pixel after calculation for display on a particular device, such changes will be either invisible or irritating (that is, they'll accumulate until a jump in image values occurs, resulting in a phenomenon sometimes called the *jaggies*).

Pixels are among the various units of measure that CSS1 supports. Because pixel size and position—and even color handling capabilities—are device-dependent, working with pixels requires making certain assumptions about display devices. Fortunately, pixel sizes are fairly consistent on most computer displays, and high-resolution devices are commonly configured to treat a group of physical pixels as a single logical pixel for display purposes. This helps explain why output on a 600 dpi laser printer (which has between six and eight times as many pixels per inch as most CRTs) uses a 4x4 square of pixels to emulate a single pixel on screen.

Ultimately, working in pixels provides the most direct method for controlling what a user sees on his or her display, that is, if the underlying assumptions make sense.

IT'S ABSOLUTELY PIXELATING!

When using pixel measurements, it's wise to make some assumptions about how much real estate is available. It's common for page designers to lay out elements on a 640x480 grid, because this represents typical PC VGA resolution. Even though using a smaller grid means that users with higher-resolution devices won't be able to display as much information on their screens, this approach guarantees that VGA users won't be forced to scroll every screen that appears. Such assumptions are critical when designing framed HTML pages, or when assigning widths to tables and other document elements. Such assumptions will also guide decisions about how much room to allocate for text, and for the white space around the text that gives it room to breathe.

Percentage Units

Many properties that accept a number or a length as a value, also accept percentages as well. Examples include 25%, 75%, and 95% (the percent sign, %, is required). Even though percentages don't represent units of measure *per se*, they are similar to relative units of measure in that they scale automatically as the size of the display area changes.

What a percentage value represents—that is, what its value is relative to—depends on the particular property to which the value is assigned. Most frequently, it's a percentage of the value that the property occupies within its parent element. For example, if an HTML tag such as <P> (paragraph) is assigned a font size of 75%, the font size for the text within the paragraph will be three-quarters the size of the parent tag, which is probably the <**BODY**> tag in most HTML documents.

One exception to this rule is the line-height property, which indicates how lines within a paragraph are to be spaced by specifying a minimum separation of the baselines between adjacent lines of text. As always, length values may be absolute, relative, or device-dependent. Line height, number, percentage, and length behave similarly when measured, but differ in how they handle inheritance.

Remember the significance of inheritance: An element's parent defines the basis for relative calculations. Where line height is concerned, percentage values are relative to the font size of the parent element (so that 60% of 10 pt becomes 6 pt, and 120% of 5 pt becomes 6 pt, and so on). Likewise, an em value is interpreted relative to the parent's font size (so that the equivalent values would be 0.6 em on 10 pt to produce 6 pt, and 1.2 em on 5 pt to produce 6 pt, and so on).

A line height specified as a number value is computed for the parent and for each of its children as they're encountered. But a line height specified as a percentage or an em is computed only once, and the exact result of that computation is inherited by all

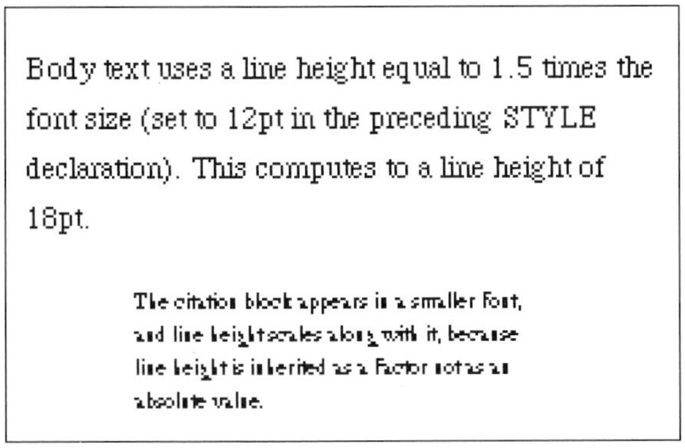

Body text uses a line height equal to 1.5 times the font size (set to 12pt in the preceding STYLE declaration). This computes to a line height of 18pt.

> The citation block appears in a smaller font, and line height scales along with it, because line height is inherited as a factor not as an absolute value.

Figure 5.2 Setting line height as a number makes line spacing scale.

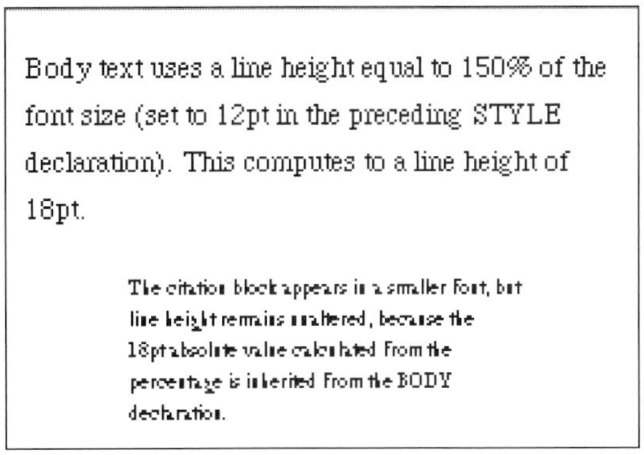

Body text uses a line height equal to 150% of the font size (set to 12pt in the preceding STYLE declaration). This computes to a line height of 18pt.

> The citation block appears in a smaller font, but line height remains unaltered, because the 18pt absolute value calculated from the percentage is inherited from the BODY declaration.

Figure 5.3 Setting line height as a percentage maintains the line spacing of the parent object.

children. (In fact, this is true for all properties that permit values to be specified as percentages or em values.)

This means that the results of scaling behave as expected when line height is specified as a number, but not when specified as a percentage or an em value. Figures 5.2 and 5.3 illustrate the difference between number and percentage values for line height based on a **<BLOCKQUOTE>** contained in a **<P>** (paragraph): Using a percentage (and by extension, an em value) maintains the same line height even when type size decreases, but using a number decreases line height in proportion to the font size. (See the underlying code in Listings 5.1 and 5.2.)

Listing 5.1   Setting line height as a number.

```
<STYLE TYPE="text/css">
  BODY { font-size: 10pt; line-height: 1.2 }
  BLOCKQUOTE {font-size: 8pt }
</STYLE>
<BODY>
<P>Body text uses a line height equal to 1.2 times the font size
(set to 10pt in the preceding STYLE declaration). This computes
to a line height of 12pt.
<BLOCKQUOTE>
<P>The citation block appears in a smaller font, and line height
scales along with it, because line height is inherited as a factor
not as an absolute value.
</BLOCKQUOTE>
</BODY>
```

Listing 5.2   Setting line height as a percentage value.

```
<STYLE TYPE="text/css">
  BODY { font-size: 10pt; line-height: 120% }
  BLOCKQUOTE {font-size: 8pt }
</STYLE>
<BODY>
<P>Body text uses a line height equal to 120% of the font size
(set to 10pt in the preceding STYLE declaration). This computes
to a line height of 12pt.
<BLOCKQUOTE>
<P>The citation block appears in a smaller font, but line height
remains unaltered, because the 12pt absolute value calculated from
the percentage is inherited from the BODY declaration.
</BLOCKQUOTE>
</BODY>
```

Keywords Values

The distinction between these settings may seem odd at first. But numerous properties understand how to interpret and apply keyword values such as "large" and "larger," or "small" and "smaller." Thus, keywords can control sizing and spacing information based on what's already known about the current parent element. Even for "ultimate parents" such as the **<BODY>** tag, a well-defined set of defaults exists to provide a baseline from which to calculate relative, keyword-set values.

Color Values

Most ordinary computer monitors use a red, green, blue (RGB) color scheme. Essentially, this means that colors are described by a trio of values, where the first value represents a setting for red, the second a setting for green, and the third a value for blue. When displayed on a monitor, these three colors are mixed according to the values provided in the trio, and represent specific color combinations.

CSS1 supports three methods that may be used to specify color values:

- **By percentage**—Each element of the RGB trio must be between 0 and 100%. Such trios take the form of (100%,0%,0%), which happens to represent pure red.

- **By number**—Each element of the RGB trio must be between 0 and 255, and a computer's innate capability to deal with binary values maps the range between 0 and 100% into 256 discrete values. Such trios take the form of (255,0,0), which also represents pure red.

- **By name**—16-color names are predefined in the specification, as shown in Table 5.2. The actual colors are depicted elsewhere in this book, in Color Project 2: *Working With Color And Background Properties*. Please note that this named set of colors represents a varying of the values for each element of the trio from 0%, to 50%, to 100%. Note also that one of the primary colors (green) occupies a nonintuitive location in this matrix of values (it's the only primary color that uses a 50% value instead of a 100% value for its exclusive setting).

A NOTE ON NOTATION

Although all three forms of notation are acceptable in CSS1 style descriptors, hexadecimal values are by far the most commonly used. As you examine source code for HTML style sheets and ordinary documents, you will observe a preponderance of this notation compared to other legal forms.

URLs

As you examine any legal Uniform Resource Locator (URL) in HTML source code, you'll find a text string that looks something like Figure 5.4.

Table 5.2 The predefined CSS1 color names.

Name	RGB Percentages	RGB Byte Value	RGB Hex Value
Aqua	(0%,100%,100%)	(0,255,255)	#00FFFF
Black	(0%,0%,0%)	(0,0,0)	#000000
Blue	(0%,0%,100%)	(0,0,255)	#0000FF
Fuchsia	(100%,0%,100%)	(255,0,255)	#FF00FF
Gray	(50%,50%,50%)	(127,127,127)	#808080
Green	(0%,50%,0%)	(0,127,0)	#008000
Lime	(0%,100%,0%)	(0,255,0)	#00FF00
Maroon	(50%,0%,0%)	(127,0,0)	#800000
Navy	(0%,0%,50%)	(0,0,127)	#000080
Olive	(50%,50%,0%)	(127,127,0)	#808000
Purple	(50%,0%,50%)	(127,0,127)	#800080
Red	(100%,0%,0%)	(255,0,0)	#FF0000
Silver	(75%,75%,75%)	(192,192,1920	#C0C0C0
Teal	(0%,50%,50%)	(0,127,127)	#008080
White	(100%,100%,100%)	(255,255,255)	#FFFFFF
Yellow	(100%,100%,0%)	(255,255,0)	#FFFF00

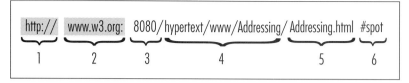

Figure 5.4 Parts of an URL.

As you can see, an URL consists of six parts, each of which may be explained as follows:

1. **Protocol/data source**: For networked resources, this is usually the name of the application-level protocol used to access whatever data resides at the "other end" of the address. The syntax for this part of the name is as follows:

   - **ftp://** Points to a file accessible using the File Transfer Protocol.

   - **gopher://** Points to a file system or document collection accessible using the Gopher protocol.

   - **http://** Points to a hypertext document (typically an HTML or graphics file) accessible using the HyperText Transfer Protocol (HTTP).

   - **mailto:** Links to an applications that permits data to be sent in the form of an email message to a predefined address. (Note that the slashes are absent in this address.)

   - **news://** Points to a Usenet newsgroup, and uses the Network News Transfer Protocol (NNTP) to access the information.

   - **telnet://** Links to a remote login on some other Internet, host using the Telnet protocol, typically to permit selection from a predefined set of choices or options.

   - **WAIS://** Points to a Wide Area Information Server on the Internet, thereby providing access to a system of indexed databases.

     When reading files from one's own desktop through a Web browser, the required URL syntax varies, but usually looks something like the following: **file://** or **file:///c|** This indicates that it's a local file, not some publicly accessible Web document (or other protocol resource).

The "c|" in the second example names a PC's C: drive; a vertical bar replaces the typical colon, which is reserved for use after the protocol designator.

2. **Domain name:** The fully qualified domain name for the Web (or other) server where the desired Web page (or other resource) is located.

3. **Port address:** In most cases, the port address is absent; in that case, the default value is ":80". The only time you'll see a value here is when, for whatever reason, an alternate port address is in use. If such an address occurs in an URL, it's a good idea to leave it there (even if it's the default value).

4. **Directory path:** This specifies the location of a file or document in the server's file system. Regardless of whether or not the underlying operating system uses forward slashes to separate directory or folder names, URL syntax requires the use of such slashes.

5. **Object name:** The actual name of the HTML file for the desired Web page; the name of the graphics file for the image; or the name of whatever other resource may be required.

6. **Spot:** This element is optional in an URL; its job is to identify specific locations within an HTML document so that an URL can drop users off there, as well as at the document's head. By preceding the name of an HTML anchor with a pound sign (#), it's possible to direct users to a precise location within a document.

When an URL appears within a CSS1 style sheet, it must be preceded by the string "url(", and followed by the string ")"; optionally, any URL may be bracketed by either single or double quotes. For example, both url('http://www.w3.org') and url("http://www.w3.org") are legal URL designators in style definitions, but url(http://www.w3.org) is also legal.

In order to permit "illegal" characters to appear within URLs (as they sometimes must for queries and other forms of URLs

OF FONTS, AND FONT MEASUREMENT

Typographic fonts are complex beasts, enough so to have spawned their own terminology and some specific metrics. As depicted in Figure 5.5, the x-height measures the vertical dimension of the lowercase letter "x" and the em-width the horizontal dimension of the lowercase letter "m." These two letters form the basis for measuring fonts in both dimensions, but it's the em-width that typically designates a font's size. Thus, 10 point Times Roman indicates a version of that font whose m is precisely 10 points wide. Other common terms associated with fonts include

- The ascender height, which measures the distance from the top of the lowercase x to the tops of those letters that ascend above the x-height, whether lower- or uppercase.

- The descender depth, which measure the distance from the bottom of the lowercase x, and the bottoms of those letters that descend below it. Typically, these are lowercase characters like g, j, p, q, and y.

- The baseline establishes a line upon which all characters rest (except those that include descender portions), and defines the reference point from which all other heights and depths are measured.

intended to deliver specific information to search engines or other applications), a special form of quotation called *URL-encoding* must be used. Such illegal characters include parentheses; commas; white-space characters; single and double quotes; and ampersands; and they must be escaped by preceding them with a backslash (for example, "\(", "\,", and '\"' are legal; notice that single quotes surround the escaped double quote, to improve readability).

Using Units Effectively

Because scalability of page layout is so desirable, it's important to use relative units when sizing type or white space properties. This permits users to select different fonts or document sizes, while preserving as much of the original page designer's intent as possible. It's especially important to be cognizant of the role of inheritance when using percentage or em units. These sometimes fail to scale, due to the calculation of absolute values from such units based on the font size for an element's parent in an HTML document. Using number values maintains scalability in these circumstances and, for that reason, represents the best approach.

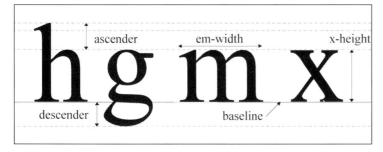

Figure 5.5   The various metrics for measuring fonts include x-height, em-width, descender depth, and ascender height.

Looking Ahead

Now that we've told you how to control the layout of document elements, let's move on to discuss the use of classification properties to control the basic way that browsers display HTML. Proper assignment of classification properties gives you the power to decide how your pages are displayed. They define the controls that give style, whether HTML or otherwise, its true meaning.

HANDLING BOX PROPERTIES

6

In this chapter:

- **Boxing up pages**

- **Pixel properties**

- **Managing margins**

A page—be it on the Web or in print—can be easily divided into "boxes" of information. The basic page is a single box in which other, smaller boxes of information relative to the page and one another are arranged. CSS box properties are based on this page design model and allow you to define borders, margins, and other rules for boxed areas of text and graphics.

In this chapter, we'll explain how a page and its information can be boxed up (is it Christmas yet?); show you how to incorporate the box model into your Web page design; and give you a complete rundown on the style sheet box properties you can use to affect the look and feel of your Web pages. Box properties are some of the most powerful elements style sheets have to offer because they give you the power to create margins and borders in your document without having to use complicated table and nested <**BLOCKQUOTE**> tags.

Boxing Up Web Pages

We tend to think of a page of information, electronic or otherwise, as a collection of words and pictures that flow one after the other in a linear manner. Considering that we read a page from top to bottom, this makes sense. However, if you think about the way information can be laid out on a page, you'll see that it isn't just arranged vertically, but horizontally as well. Text and graphics can be horizontally aligned to the right, left, or center. Text can be wrapped around either side of an image, or placed in multiple columns within a page. Margins and borders can be added to an entire page or to select portions of the page. These layout devices add the horizontal aspect to a page, making it possible to arrange textual and graphical elements in a wider variety of ways.

The LANWrights, Inc., home page, shown in Figure 6.1, incorporates both horizontal and vertical elements in its design.

The initial graphic and text on the page are centered, but the content flows from top to bottom. The three bottom graphics are

Network-Oriented Writing and Consulting

LANWrights, Inc., is an Austin, TX, company that specializes in network-oriented writing, training, and consulting. Our projects cover a broad range of subjects, including those listed in the table below. LANWrights' goal is to provide accurate, timely information on cutting edge technology and useful services. We are as glad to be of assistance to computer novices as to professional systems and network managers.

Please browse our pages; we hope you'll find something of interest! Thank you for visiting.

        LANWrights
Online
Resources

        Site
Outline

        Wayfinding
Tool Kit

Shows a menu of what's on   An index of   Explains how to find your
this site.   what's on our site.   way around our site.

Figure 6.1   The LANWrights, Inc., home page utilizes vertical and horizontal design elements.

evenly spaced horizontally across the page, using a table, as is the text below each one describing the resource to which the graphic links. If we remove the pictures and text, we can create a box-based model of the page like the one shown in Figure 6.2.

This box-based model reduces the page to a collection of elements arranged both horizontally and vertically. However, the final layout of the elements is based both on their content and functionality within the page, as well as their size and relationship to the overall design of the page. Although the design of the page might look just fine if we switch the company logo with the series of alternating images and text boxes from the bottom of the page, it wouldn't make much content sense. The box model provides a useful method for both visualizing the elements in a page and separating them so style effects can be applied to each

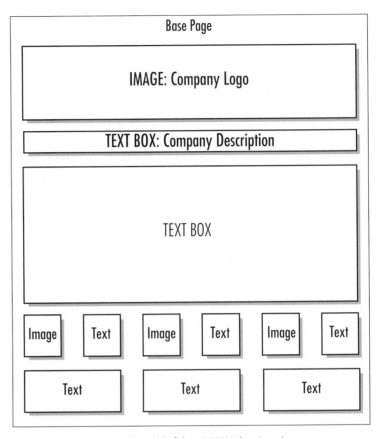

Figure 6.2 A box-based model of the LANWrights, Inc., home page.

individually; it also works directly with the content of the actual elements themselves to drive page design.

Creating The Horizontal Aspect Of A Web Page

Horizontal page layout elements have been available to print page layout designers for many years, and software packages such as Adobe PageMaker and QuarkXPress include tools that make implementing and manipulating these elements quick and simple. When HTML was first created, it was an inherently vertical markup. There were no mechanisms for aligning text horizontally, creating margins, or adding borders.

Tables: The First To Go Horizontal

The introduction of table markup and improved image markup brought the first horizontal elements to HTML. By dividing entire pages into grids, a Web designer was able to gain better control over the placement of objects, both horizontally and vertically. An empty table row with no border can be used to create much needed white space, as shown in Figure 6.3.

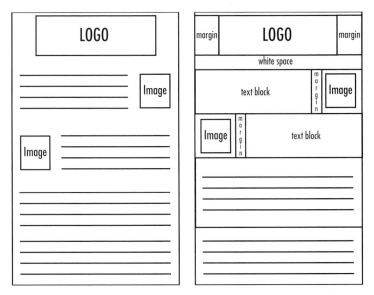

Figure 6.3 This shows the difference in the usual linear approach (left) and the grid approach (right).

While the page content has not changed, the way it is visualized has. The white space in the linear example will be determined by the browser. In the grid, it will be determined by measurements supplied in the table markup. Table markup also allows multiple images to be set next to text and arranged horizontally across the page, a technique used on the LANWrights, Inc., home page previously shown in Figure 6.1. However, tables are complicated creatures that can easily become unruly and difficult to modify, as the following code illustrates:

```
<TABLE CELLPADDING=8 WIDTH="100%">

  <TR ALIGN="CENTER" VALIGN="TOP">
```

```
<TD>
  <A HREF="menu.htm">
  <IMG BORDER=0 SRC="graphics/menu.gif" ALT="Menu"
   ALIGN="middle" WIDTH="54" HEIGHT="54">
  </A>
  <BR>
</TD>

<TD>
  <A HREF="menu.htm">LANWrights Online Resources</A>
  <BR>
</TD>

<TD>
  <A HREF="outline.htm"><IMG SRC="graphics/outlinebtn.gif"
   ALIGN="MIDDLE" WIDTH="35" HEIGHT="36" BORDER="0">
  </A>
  <BR>
</TD>

<TD>
  <A HREF="outline.htm">Site Outline</A>
  <BR>
</TD>

<TD>
  <A HREF="navigate.htm"><IMG ALIGN="MIDDLE" BORDER="0"
  SRC="graphics/tool.gif">
  </A>
  <BR>
</TD>

<TD>
  <A HREF="navigate.htm">Wayfinding Tool Kit</A>
  <BR>
</TD>

</TR>

<TR ALIGN="CENTER" VALIGN="TOP">

<TD COLSPAN=2>
  Shows a menu of what's on this site.
  <BR>
</TD>

<TD COLSPAN=2>
  An index of what's on our site.
  <BR>
</TD>
```

```
<TD COLSPAN=2>
  Explains how to find your way around our site.
  <BR>
</TD>

</TR>

</TABLE>
```

Although this code works to create a table, there is an easier way to produce this type of layout, which we describe in the following section.

The Next Level: Style Sheets And Box Properties

The combination of style sheets and the box-model approach to page design empowers Web designers with a new kind of control that is designed to affect and control box elements within a page. The CSS box properties are the most extensive family of properties and include margin, border, size, and float properties. In the next section, we'll describe each property and its associated values, and then take a look at the effect it has on elements within a Web page.

Box Properties And Their Values

Box properties allow you to define the margins; padding; border size and type; size; and float values for any given element's box. Because boxes have four sides, you can use style rules to create any combination of individual sides. Many of the properties, such as **margin-left**, **margin-right**, **margin-top**, and **margin-bottom** work in exactly the same way and take the same values, but each acts individually on only one side of the box. So don't be daunted by the sheer number of box properties—many are necessary duplicates.

Margin Properties

Margins help you create white space around elements on an HTML page and are one of the elements most underused by Web page designers. In regard to CSS, the margin is the space between an element's boundary (the border of the box) and the boundary of any bordering element. The exact placement of the margin is also directly affected by the presence of a border or padding. Figure 6.4 illustrates three different margin-border-padding combinations. The amount of physical space the element takes up doesn't change, but the padding and border bleed into the margin, making it appear smaller.

The margin properties include:

- margin-left

- margin-right

- margin-top

- margin-bottom

- margin

Each individual **margin-side** property affects a single side, but the general **margin** property is a shorthand property that allows

Figure 6.4 The combination of margins, borders, and padding affects the overall size and display of an element.

you to set all four margins at one time. All of the margin properties take **length** or **percentage** values to define their size. These
values can be either positive or negative numbers. The **margin-
left** and **margin-right** properties also have an **auto** value that
sets the margin to zero for inline and floating elements, but sets
the margin to as large as possible for block elements. (We'll provide more information on inline, floating, and block elements in
Chapter 7.) The margin properties affect all of the text and images within an element, so this code

```
P.indent {left-margin: .5in}
```

would indent everything within the paragraph one-half of an inch.

Figure 6.5 shows how a browser renders several different style
rules that use margins.

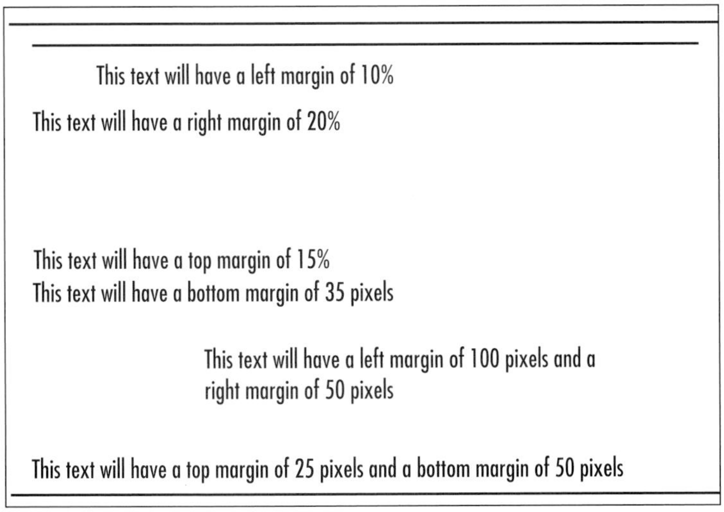

This text will have a left margin of 10%
This text will have a right margin of 20%

This text will have a top margin of 15%
This text will have a bottom margin of 35 pixels

This text will have a left margin of 100 pixels and a
right margin of 50 pixels

This text will have a top margin of 25 pixels and a bottom margin of 50 pixels

Figure 6.5   A bevy of different margin settings can be used within a single
HTML page.

The style rules behind the Web page pictured in Figure 6.5 are
fairly straightforward:

```
<HTML>
<HEAD>
<STYLE>
```

```
DIV.sample1 {margin-left: 10%}

DIV.sample2 {margin-right: 20%}

DIV.sample3 {margin-top: 15%}

DIV.sample4 {margin-bottom: 35px}

DIV.sample5 {margin-left: 100px;
             margin-right: 50px;
             }

DIV.sample6 {margin-top: 25px;
             margin-bottom: 100px;
             }

</STYLE>

<BODY>
<HR>
<DIV CLASS="sample1">This text will have a
left margin of 10%</DIV>

<DIV CLASS="sample2">This text will have a
right margin of 20%</DIV>

<DIV CLASS="sample3">This text will have a
top margin of 15%</DIV>

<DIV CLASS="sample4">This text will have a
bottom margin of 35 pixels    </DIV>

<DIV CLASS="sample5">This text will have a
left margin of 100 pixels
and a right margin of 50 pixels</DIV>

<DIV CLASS="sample6">This text will have a
top margin of 25 pixels and a bottom
margin of 50 pixels </DIV>

<HR>
</BODY>
</HTML>
```

The all-inclusive **margin** tag has a few rules that govern the way it is interpreted. The exact syntax for a margin rule is:

```
p.margin {margin: 1 2 3 4}
```

You can use up to four values (represented by **1**, **2**, **3**, and **4** in the syntax) to represent margin specifics for different sides of the element's box. If you only include one value, it applies to all four sides. This rule:

```
p.margin {margin: 10%}
```

sets the margins on all four sides of the element to 10%, as shown in Figure 6.6.

One value applies the first setting to both the top and bottom margins, while the second value determines the size of the left and right margins. The code

```
p.margin {margin: 10% 20%}
```

creates an element with top and bottom margins of 10% and left and right margins of 20%, as shown in Figure 6.7.

If three values are present, the first sets the top margin; the second sets the right and left margins; and the third sets the bottom margin. So, this rule

```
p.margin {margin: 10% 20% 30%}
```

sets the top margin at 10%, the left and right margins at 20%, and the bottom margin at 30%, as shown in Figure 6.8.

Finally, if you use all four values, each applies to its own individual side in the order top, right, bottom, left. For example, this code

```
p.margin {margin: 10%, 20%, 30%, 40%}
```

creates a top margin of 10%, a right margin of 20%, a bottom margin of 30%, and a left margin of 40%, as shown in Figure 6.9.

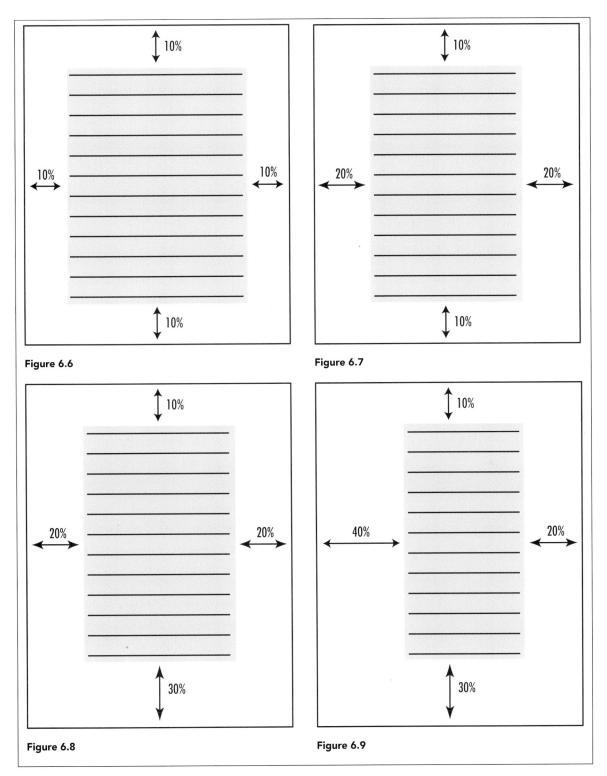

Figure 6.6

Figure 6.7

Figure 6.8

Figure 6.9

The margin property affects different combinations of an element's margins, depending on the number of values you include.

The **margin** property was designed to save you time and take up less space within a style sheet. If you know how the different combinations of four values are interpreted, you can create one line of code instead of four.

Padding Properties

Padding is the amount of space between an element and its margin or its border. The padding properties, much like the margin properties, are used to specify on which sides you would like padding and how thick the padding should be. You will recognize the padding rules and properties because they are almost exactly like the margin rules and properties.

Padding properties include:

- padding-left

- padding-right

- padding-top

- padding-bottom

- padding

Just as with margins, the individual **padding-side** properties affect the width of the padding only on the designated side, while the general **padding** property affects all four sides using one to four values. Padding, like margins, is transparent. If you have included a background on your page, it will show through the padding and surround the object completely.

This style code for the Web page pictured in Figure 6.10, uses margin and padding properties to create a **DIV** selector of **CLASS padding**:

```
<STYLE>
DIV.padding {margin: .5in;
        padding: .5in .25in;
        }
</STYLE>
```

This rule defines a half-inch margin all the way around the text enclosed in the division; sets a top and bottom padding of half

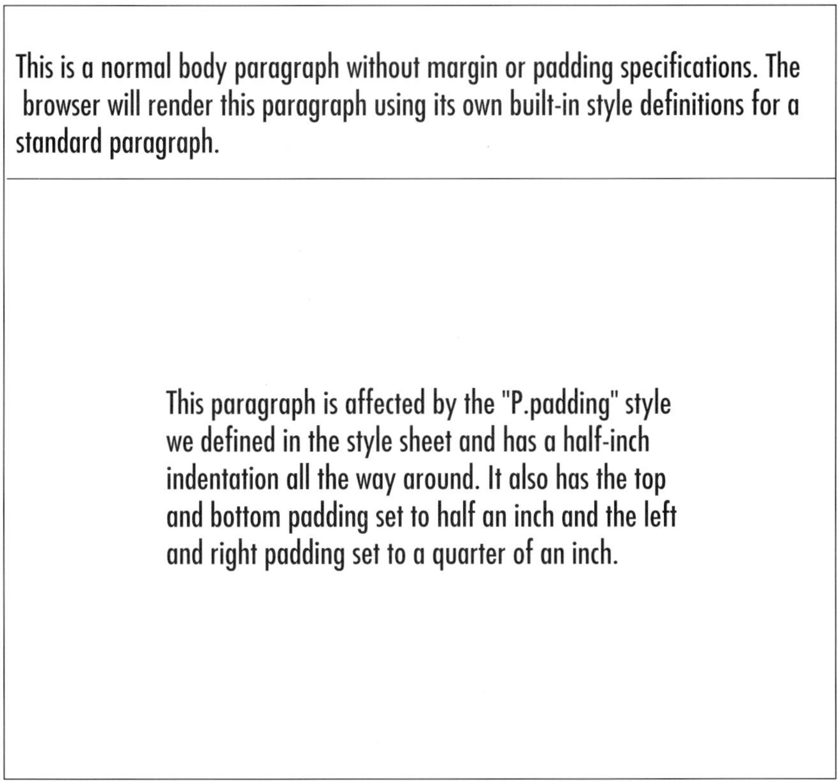

This is a normal body paragraph without margin or padding specifications. The browser will render this paragraph using its own built-in style definitions for a standard paragraph.

This paragraph is affected by the "P.padding" style we defined in the style sheet and has a half-inch indentation all the way around. It also has the top and bottom padding set to half an inch and the left and right padding set to a quarter of an inch.

Figure 6.10 Padding and margin properties can be used within an HTML page to set text apart.

an inch; and sets a left and right padding of a quarter-inch. This HTML markup invokes the style rule:

```
<BODY>
This is a normal body paragraph without margin or padding
specifications. The browser will render this paragraph
using its own built-in style definitions for a standard
paragraph.

<DIV CLASS="padding">This paragraph is affected by the
"P.padding" style we defined in the style sheet and has
a half-inch indentation all the way around. It also has
the top and bottom padding set to half an inch and the
left and right padding set to a quarter of an inch.
</BODY>
```

Padding is best used with the border properties to create space between an element and the border you put around it. Without padding, the border will sit right next to your element, possibly crowding it.

Border Properties

The border properties not only provide you with a mechanism for creating a border around any element, but also allow you to specify the border's width, color, and style. Three different short-hand properties make it possible to define all three for any given side or for all four sides at once. The border properties include:

- border-top-width
- border-right-width
- border-bottom-width
- border-left-width
- border-width
- border-color
- border-style
- border-top
- border-right
- border-bottom
- border-left
- border

Setting Border Width

You will recognize the **border-side-width** properties because they closely resemble both the **margin-side** and **padding-side** properties. The **border-side-width** properties each take one of four values to define the width of the border on any given side. **Thin**, **medium**, and **thick** are all relative thickness measurements, and the final display depends largely on the browser. However, these relative thickness widths remain consistent throughout a document, so all **thick** borders will be the same width, and larger than **medium** or **thin** borders. You may also exactly define the width of any given side's border using a specific **length**, such as 10 px or .01 in.

The **border-width** property can be used in the same way as **margin** and **padding** to set the border width for any combination of

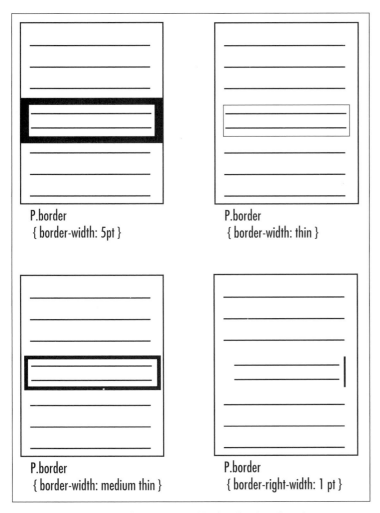

Figure 6.11 You can define border widths for all sides of an element, just one side, or any combination of four sides using the border-width properties.

an element's borders, depending on the number of values you include. One value sets all four margins; two values set the top/bottom and left/right borders; three values set the top, left/right, and bottom borders; and four values set each individual side's border. Figure 6.11 shows how a collection of **border-side-width** properties are rendered.

Defining Border Style

CSS includes many different border style choices. Using the **border-style** property and one of nine possible border values, you can define the style for all four sides of an element's border.

To set different styles for different sides, you must use the **border-side** shorthand notation discussed later. The nine border styles include:

- **None.** The border is invisible, even if you've set a border width.

- **Dotted.** Creates a dotted line that appears on top of the element's background.

- **Dashed.** Creates a dashed line that appears on top of the element's background.

- **Solid.** Creates a solid line that appears on top of the element's background.

- **Double.** Creates a double-line border. The border width is split evenly among the two lines and the space between them.

- **Groove.** Creates a colored, 3D groove. The color is determined by the **border-side** color value.

- **Ridge.** Creates a colored, 3D ridge. The color is determined by the **border-side** color value.

- **Inset.** Creates a fully inset, colored box. The color is determined by the **border-side** color value.

- **Outset.** Creates a raised, colored box. The color is determined by the **border-side** color value.

The actual presentation of each of these border styles ultimately depends on which browser views your document. This sample style rule creates a double border of 20 pixels around an element:

```
P.border {border-width: 20px;
          border-style: double;
          }
```

Adding Color To Borders

As we mentioned in the previous list of border styles, you can also specify the color of an element's border. The value must be one of the 16 accepted color values or in #RRGGBB hexadecimal color notation, as described in Chapter 5. As with **border-style**, the **border-color** property sets the color for all sides. Use the **color** value with the **border-side** properties (coming up) to set colors for individual sides of a border. This code creates a solid teal border that is 20 pixels wide around the entire element <P CLASS="tealborder">:

```
P.tealborder {border-width: 20px;
              border-style: solid;
              border-color: teal;
              }
```

Specifying Width, Style, And Color For Individual Sides Of A Border

The **border-top**, **border-right**, **border-bottom**, and **border-left** properties provide a shorthand method for defining the width, style, and color of any individual border side. This shorthand notation is a bit different than other shorthand we've seen in that it doesn't apply to all four sides at once, but is designed to combine several aspects of a single side's appearance. The **border-side** property can take the **border-side-width**, **border-style**, and **border-color** properties. To create the element <P CLASS="multi"> with four completely different border side formats we use this code:

```
P.multi {border-top: thin dotted;
         border-bottom: thin dashed;
         border-right: thick solid red;
         border-left: thick groove teal;
         }
```

Although we can't vouch for the attractiveness of this layout, it can easily be created using the **border-side** properties and values.

Specifying Width, Style, And Color For An Entire Border

Just as the **border-side** shorthand property sets the width, style, and color for each individual side of a border, the **border** property defines them for the entire border. This shorthand differs from the **margin** and **padding** shorthand in that it doesn't use a combination of four values to set the specifics for each side. The **border-side** shorthand we just discussed does that. Use the **border** property with **border-width**, **border-color**, and **border-style** to set uniform values for the whole border.

This sample code creates a five-pixel-wide, blue inset border around element **<P CLASS=border1>**:

```
P.border1 {border: 5px blue inset}
```

It really is as simple as that. You have a whole collection of border properties and values that allow you to manipulate any single border or any combination of borders using any width, color, or style variety you might choose. This is a good time to remind you, the designer, that just because you can do something doesn't mean you should. Garish borders can easily distract users and detract from your content.

Size Properties

If you have worked with the **<IMG>** tag in HTML, you are probably accustomed to using the **WIDTH** and **HEIGHT** attributes to size your image or define the exact area an image will occupy. The **WIDTH** and **HEIGHT** attributes do much the same thing for the box size of any HTML element. If you use these properties with an image, and they are different from the actual size of the image, the browser will automatically resize the image to fit the specified dimensions. If you use them with text and there is more text than space, a scroll bar will be automatically inserted to allow users to move through the box and read all of your content. Height and width are measured as a percentage of the parent element or in exact lengths.

The following code creates a **<DIV CLASS=menu>** element that is 600 pixels wide by 200 pixels high:

```
DIV.menu {width: 600px;
          height: 200px}
```

Any child elements you might create for this logical division, such as **<SPAN>** elements, will inherit these measurements and must fit within the 600×200 box we created. If you use percentages for defining the child elements' margins or sizes, they will be a percentage of the 600×200 box, not a percentage of the entire page.

The Float And Clear Properties

Floating an image to the far left or far right of the parent element makes it possible for text and other elements to flow around the object. For example, this code

```
P.floatl {float:left}
```

creates an element **<P CLASS=floatl>** that will sit on the far left side of its parent, most likely the screen. However, this code

```
P.floatr {float:right}
```

creates an element **<P CLASS=floatr>** that will sit on the far right side of its parent, most likely the screen. If the value of **float** is **none**, the element will be positioned on the screen based on the browser's built-in specifications and the location of other elements within the HTML document. The default value for **float** is **none**.

The **clear** property works directly with the **float** property to determine whether or not other elements can flow next to a floating element and, if so, on what side. This code

```
P.floatl {float: left;
          clear: right;
          }
```

creates a floating element that will be left-justified and allow other HTML elements to flow directly next to it on the right. The code

```
P.floatr {float: right;
          clear: left;
          }
```

creates a floating element that will be right-justified and allow other HTML elements to flow directly next to it on the left. If the value of **clear** is none, other HTML elements will not be allowed to flow next to the element at all.

Box Properties: Quite A Collection

Box properties present quite a collection of useful placement, margin, border, size, and floating tools that make positioning text and graphics on an HTML page more precise. Before we say good-bye to the box properties, let's walk through an example that converts the HTML table we introduced you to at the beginning of the chapter into a series of style rules that produce the same effect.

A Real-Life Example: Replacing A Table With Style Rules

We originally used a table to create the Web page layout for the LANWrights, Inc., site resources section of the home page we discussed earlier, as shown in Figure 6.12.

 LANWrights Online Resources Site Outline Wayfinding Tool Kit

Shows a menu of what's on this site. | An index of what's on our site. | Explains how to find your way around our site.

Figure 6.12   The LANWrights, Inc., home page site resources section was created using table markup.

A well-planned style sheet can be used to create the same layout. A series of style rules will create nine separate selectors (one for each image and resource name, and three for the resource descriptions that appear under each image/name combination) that, in combination, renders the same effect as the table. To do this, we refer to the box model we created earlier to determine the size and spacing of the nine boxes. Each image is a different size, but the boxes that enclose the images must all be the same size so that the images are distributed evenly across the page. The same is true for the text boxes on the first row. The largest amount of screen real estate we can expect to have on a 15-inch monitor is 640 pixels wide by 480 pixels high. Typically, people reserve a small space on the left or right of their screen for desktop icons, so we conservatively create a page canvas that is 600×480. The height doesn't matter as much as the width because most users expect to scroll vertically, not horizontally.

Keeping this in mind, we have 600 pixels of width to work with and as much height as we need. Because the bottom resource descriptions span the top image/name combination, we'll determine the size of these first. We'll need to include three text boxes with some space between them. If we include 45 pixels of white space on either side of the center box, we are left with three boxes each 170 pixels wide. A little over half that, 90 pixels, should provide enough height. After playing with the numbers some more, we determine that the six boxes where the three

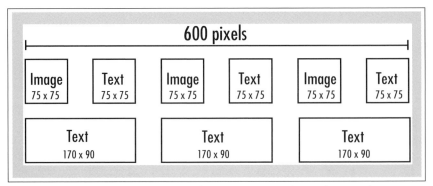

Figure 6.13 A box model of a portion of a Web page provides a reference when creating the necessary style sheet rules.

MARGIN RULES

Also, remember that margins are set relative to adjacent elements, so a left margin of 20px is 20 pixels from the closest element to the left, not 20 pixels from the left side of the page.

images and three resource names will go (above the boxes we just sized) should be 75 pixels by 75 pixels. This leaves 20 pixels of space between each image/name combination. The box model of this portion of our page, with numbered measurements included for reference, is shown in Figure 6.13.

Once we determine text size and spacing, it's time to write the style rules. These style rules will create a single division style blocked out area where the images and text will go as well as nine separate span styles—one for each element block—using class-based selectors and the margin, padding, float, and clear properties, with the required values. We chose not to use paragraph styles because a full line-break is automatically added by all browsers at the end of a paragraph, and many of these elements need to be on the same line. To maintain consistency throughout the rules, all measurements are in pixels.

```
<HEAD>
<STYLE>
DIV.resources {margin-right: 600px}
/* Creates a 600 pixel-wide area for the resource
images, names, and descriptions.*/
SPAN.image1 {margin-right: 75px;
        margin-bottom: 95px;;
        padding-bottom: 20px
        float: left;
        clear: none;
        }
```

```
/* Defines a blocked area 75 X 95 pixels, with a
20 pixel padding on the bottom. This creates a 75 X 75 pixel space
that is left justified with 20 pixels of white space to the bottom.
The float left property aligns the element to the
left and forces all other floating elements to the right. */

SPAN.text1  {margin-left: 20px;
         margin-right: 75px;
         margin-bottom: 95px;
         padding-bottom: 20px;
         float: left;
         clear: none;
         }
/* The left margin takes into account the 20 pixels we
allotted for the space between the resource image and name. */

SPAN.image2 {margin-left: 45px;
         margin-right: 75px;
         margin-bottom: 95px;
         padding-bottom: 20px;
         float: left;
         clear: none;
         }

SPAN.text2 {margin-left: 20px;
         margin-right: 75px;
         margin-bottom: 95px;
         padding-bottom: 20px;
         float: left;
         clear: none;
         }

SPAN.image3 {margin-left: 45px;
         margin-right: 75px;
         margin-bottom: 95px;
         padding-bottom: 20px;
         float: left;
         clear: none;
         }
SPAN.text3 {margin-left: 20px;
         margin-right: 75px;
         margin-bottom: 95px;
         padding-bottom: 20px;
         float: left;
         clear: none;
         }

SPAN.description1 {margin-right: 170px;
              margin-bottom: 110px;
```

```
                            padding-bottom: 20px;
                            float: left;
                            clear: none;
                            }
/* Defines a blocked area 170 x 90 pixels, with a
20 pixel padding  on the bottom. This creates
a 170X90 pixel space that is left justified. The
float left property aligns the element to the left
and forces all other floating elements to the right. */

SPAN.description2 {margin-left: 45px;
                   margin-right: 170px;
                   margin-bottom: 110px;
                   padding-bottom: 20px;
                   float: left;
                   clar: none;
                   }

SPAN.description3 {margin-left: 45px;
                   margin-right: 170px;
                   margin-bottom: 110px;
                   padding-bottom: 20px;
                   float: left;
                   clear: none;
                   }

</STYLE>
```

The most difficult part of writing this particular set of style rules is the calculations, but after you've got those figured out, the rest is easy repetition. The HTML that invokes the style rules and creates a layout like the one we previously used table markup with is very straightforward:

```
<DIV CLASS="resources">
<SPAN CLASS="image1">
  <A HREF="menu.htm">
  <IMG BORDER=0 SRC="graphics/menu.gif" ALT="Menu"
  ALIGN="middle" WIDTH="54" HEIGHT="54">
  </A>
</SPAN>

<SPAN CLASS="text1">
  <A HREF="menu.htm">LANWrights Online Resources</A>
</SPAN>

<SPAN CLASS="image2">
  <A HREF="outline.htm"><IMG SRC="graphics/outlinebtn.gif"
```

```
     ALIGN="MIDDLE" WIDTH="35" HEIGHT="36" BORDER="0">
   </A>
</SPAN>

<SPAN CLASS="text2">
   <A HREF="outline.htm">Site Outline</A>
</SPAN>

<SPAN CLASS="image3">
   <A HREF="navigate.htm"><IMG ALIGN="MIDDLE" BORDER="0"
   SRC="graphics/tool.gif">
   </A>
</SPAN>

<SPAN CLASS="text3">
   <A HREF="navigate.htm">Wayfinding Tool Kit</A>
</SPAN>

<P>

<!-- Creates the line break that positions the description blocks
under the image/name combination blocks -->

<SPAN CLASS="description1">
   Shows a menu of what's on this site.
</SPAN>

<SPAN CLASS="description2">
   An index of what's on our site.
</SPAN>

<SPAN CLASS="description2">
   Explains how to find your way around our site.
</SPAN>
</DIV>
```

Granted, the style rules took a little while to create, but they can be easily modified and, more important, reused on other pages. Keep in mind that you can use text-level markup with the boxes, as we did above with the anchor (<B>) tags. The HTML is simple and clean, and easy to read and modify. The style sheet box properties provide you, the Web page designer, with a new and versatile set of tools that make exact placement of text blocks and images possible. This is one of our favorite property families because of the edge it brings to page design. Once you have spent some time experimenting with these properties, we're sure you'll come to love them as much as we do.

Looking Ahead

In Chapter 7, we describe those elements that allow you to specify styles for white space, list numbers and bullets, and how an HTML page is displayed. Rules created with these properties and values allow you to define how white space is rendered, substitute images for text bullets in lists, and more.

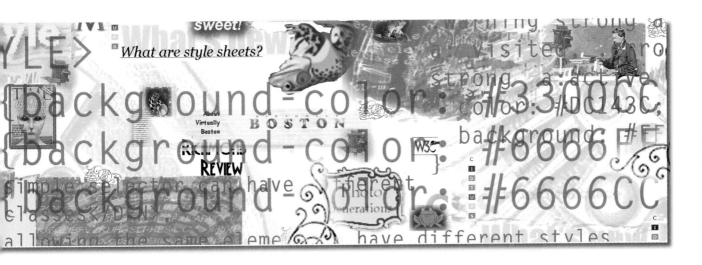

CORNERING
CLASSIFICATION
PROPERTIES

7

In this chapter:

- **Specifying display properties**

- **Controlling white space**

- **Manipulating list bullets, numbering, and display**

Classification properties control the basic way in which browsers display HTML. In general, the majority of HTML tags are either block-structuring elements or character-level elements. Browsers collapse all multiple spaces and line breaks unless they are contained within a <PRE> section. This means that, until the arrival of the classification properties of CSS1, you had very little control over spacing and list displays. Now, with the three basic classification properties, you can change the underlying HTML characteristics for most tags. You no longer need to use a specific tag to create interesting spacing and list characteristics. Be careful, however, using these properties or you may change more than you expect.

The classification properties are comprised of the display property, the white space property, and the four list properties (list-style-type, list-style-image, list-style-position, and list-style). The display property determines whether an element is to be displayed as a block, inline, as a list item, or not displayed at all. The white space property tells the browser to ignore or collapse white space (blank space) inside an element; to leave it; or to wrap it at <BR> tags. The four list properties determine the appearance and shape of the list-item marker; the use of an image for a list-item marker; the position of the list-item marker; and the use of a "shorthand" notation for the first three list properties. Each is discussed in detail in the following sections.

Display Property

The display property controls the fundamental nature of the HTML tag to which you attach it. You can use the display property for each HTML tag to override the default values taken from the HTML specifications. This property allows an element to be treated as a block element, a list-item element, or an inline element. An additional option, none, turns off the display of the element, all child elements, and even the box structure around the elements. This very powerful property can change much more than you may expect, so use it with caution and carefully double-check your HTML with several browsers.

Use the display property to define an element with one of the following four values:

- **Block**—a line break before and after the element
- **Inline**—no line break before and after the element
- **List-item**—same as block except a list-item marker is added
- **None**—not displayed

The default value is block. The display property is not inherited. Each value is discussed further in the following sections.

Block

The block value sets the element to be displayed in the same manner as other block-level elements, such as <H1>, <BLOCKQUOTE>, and <P>. Set the display value to block when you want the element to start on a new line with a line break before and after the element. Think of it as the element blocking off the area for itself.

The general format of the display property using the block value is

```
<P STYLE="display: block">text</P>
```

Inline

The inline value sets the element to be displayed like other inline elements (inline values are also called phrase markup or character formatting), such as <EM>, <B>, and <FONT>. Set the display value to inline when you want the element to start on the same line as the previous element, without a line break before or after the element (see Figure 7.1).

The general format of the display property using the inline value is:

```
<P STYLE="display: inline">text</P>
```

Here is an example:

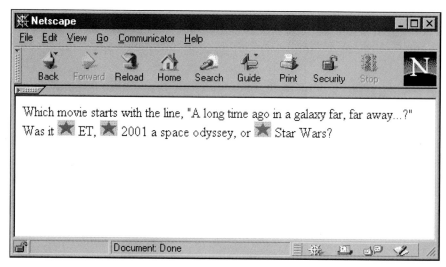

Figure 7.1 Netscape view of the inline value of the display property.

```
<HTML>
<HEAD>
<STYLE TYPE="text/css">
IMG {display:inline}
</STYLE>
</HEAD>
<BODY>
<P>
Which movie starts with the line,
"A long time ago in a galaxy far, far away...?"
  Was it <IMG SRC="redstar.gif" > ET,
  <IMG SRC="redstar.gif"> 2001 a space odyssey, or
  <IMG SRC="redstar.gif"> Star Wars?
</P>

</BODY>
</HTML>
```

By simply changing the display value for the images from inline to block, you get a list-like display without even using the list structure (see Figure 7.2).

List-item

The list-item value sets the display characteristics of the list element to which it is attached. Use it with elements such as <**LI**> and <**DD**>. Use the list-item value to display the element in a separate block with a list-item marker next to it. You may use either the ordered list <**OL**> or unnumbered list <**UL**>, depending on whether you want a marker. Using the UL with the display

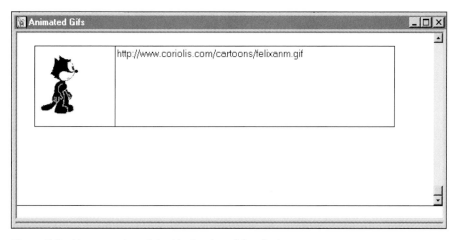

Figure 7.2 Netscape view of the block value of the display property.

property value set to list-item for the **<LI>** element is the quickest way to standardize your bulleted lists.

The general format of the display property using the list-item value is:

```
OL { display: list-item}
```

None

Using the none value turns off the display of the current element, its virtual display box, and its associated child elements. This is very useful for displaying alternating versions of a similar list or for hiding the correct answers to questions until the user's answers are entered. Set the display value to none *only* if you want to turn off display of the element to which it is assigned and, in addition, turn off display in all of its child elements and the box structures around the elements.

The general format of the display property using the none value is:

```
OL { display: none}
```

The following HTML document contains an example of the use of the display and list-style-type (covered later in the chapter) properties with ordered and unordered lists. This style sheet places square list-markers on the unordered list and creates a block style with uppercase, roman-numeral markers in the ordered list:

```
<HTML>
<HEAD>

<STYLE TYPE="text/css">

UL { display: list-item; list-style-type: square }
OL { display: block; list-style-type: upper-roman }

</STYLE>

</HEAD>
<BODY>

<UL>
<LI><P>item A
<LI><P>item B
<LI><P>item C
<LI><P>item E
</UL>

<OL>
<LI><P>item 1
<LI><P>item 2
<LI><P>item 3
<LI><P>item 4
</OL>

</BODY>
</HTML>
```

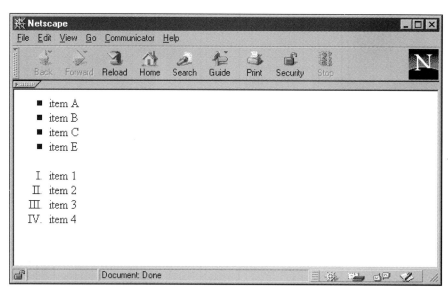

Figure 7.3 Netscape view of unordered list with square markers; and ordered list with uppercase, Roman numerals.

White Space

The white space property determines how tabs, spaces, and line breaks (collectively called white space) within an element in your HTML documents will be handled by the browser. Most browsers automatically ignore or collapse all extraneous white space into a single blank space before wrapping the text to the size of your browser window. You may use the HTML **<PRE>** tag to tell the browser to display a block of text "as is." However, the **<PRE>** tag usually only displays in Courier or another nonproportional font, and you must put each block of text in a **<PRE>** tag throughout your document. The white space property gives you a much better way to control your text throughout the document.

The white space property has three values (normal, pre, and nowrap), which tell the browser to either ignore or collapse white space (blank spaces) inside an element; to leave it, as in the **<PRE>** element of HTML; or to wrap text, and so on, only at **
** elements. The default is normal, which collapses white space. The white space property applies to block-level elements, and is inherited.

Normal

The normal value creates the standard behavior of most HTML tags, in which carriage returns, linefeeds, and multiple spaces are collapsed into a single space. Line wrapping is controlled by the browser. The general format of the white space property using the normal value is

```
<P STYLE="white space: normal">text</P>
```

Pre

The pre value makes text behave like the HTML **<PRE>** tag, in which line-wrapping control is removed from the browser's control and all spaces, carriage returns, and linefeeds in the document are preserved and displayed "as is," but without imposing the font type. The pre value does not collapse multiple spaces. This is a "What-you-type-is-what-you-get" value.

The pre value also contains a formula for displaying tabs. Each tab character is displayed as one through eight spaces, with the last space in any tab landing on a multiple of eight from the left margin of the window. As with the **<PRE>** tag, you will probably want to use the pre value with a nonproportional font only, so it will align properly. However, you can choose the font, or at least suggest one, to be used by the browser. The general format of the white space property using the pre value is

```
<P STYLE="white space: PRE">text</P>
```

The following example shows what you can achieve using the pre value for the white space property. Shown first is the original HTML document, followed by the browser image of what the HTML produces (see Figure 7.4):

```
<HTML>
<HEAD>

<STYLE TYPE="text/css">
</STYLE>

</HEAD>
<BODY>

<P STYLE="white space: normal">
Which movie starts     with the line,
"A long time ago in a galaxy far, far away...?"
  Was it ET,
  2001 a space odyssey, or
  Star Wars?
</P>

<P STYLE="white space: pre">
Which movie starts     with the line,
"A long time ago in a galaxy far, far away...?"
  Was it ET,
  2001 a space odyssey, or
  Star Wars?
</P>

<P STYLE="white space: nowrap">
Which movie starts     with the line,
"A long time ago in a galaxy far, far away...?"
  Was it ET,
```

```
   2001 a space odyssey, or
   Star Wars?
</P>

</BODY>
</HTML>
```

Nowrap

Sections characterized by the nowrap value display carriage returns, linefeeds, and multiple spaces as a single space. However, line breaks are not controlled by the browser, but are instead controlled solely by the HTML BR element. The general format of the white space property using the nowrap value is

```
<P STYLE="white space: nowrap">text</P>
```

List-Style-Type

Use the list-style-type property when you want to change the default appearance of list markers in HTML list structures. The list-style-type property specifies the shape or appearance of the

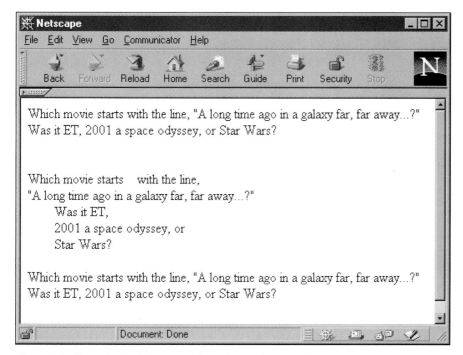

Figure 7.4   Example of white space values of normal, pre, and nowrap.

list-item marker. This is the character (dot, square, number, or letter) normally used next to each item in the list. It is used when the list-style-image has a value of none or if image loading is turned off.

You can set the list-style-type to any of the following values: disc, circle, square, decimal, lower-roman, upper-roman, lower-alpha, upper-alpha, or none. If a list-style-*image* property is also given and it has a value of none or the URL cannot be loaded, the list-style-type property value will be used in its place. Therefore, in case the URL in list-style-image cannot be loaded, you should always specify a list-style-type. This property applies to elements with the display value of list-item. The default value is disc. List-style-type is inherited. You can see an example of list-style-type in the example for list-style-image in the next section.

List-Style-Image

The list-style-image property designates a graphic to be used for list markers in the list structure. This overrides the default appearance of list markers in the current HTML list structure. If a list-style-image is given a value of none or the URL cannot be loaded, the list-style-type will be used in its place. The list-style-type should always be specified in the event that the URL pointed to in list-style-image cannot be loaded.

The list-style-image property specifies that an image will be used as a list-item marker when image loading is turned on, thereby replacing the marker specified in the list-style-type property. You may use an absolute or relative URL to locate an image, or choose none as a value. The default value is none. This property applies to elements with the display value of list-item, and is inherited.

For an external link or document, use a line in your HTML document similar to the following line and in the subsequent document example:

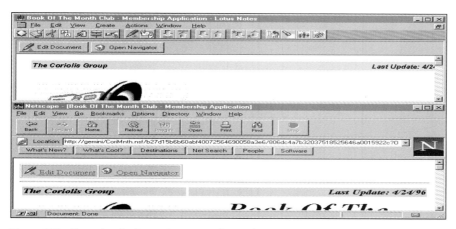

Figure 7.5 Example of using an image as a list marker.

```
{list-style-image:
URL(http://www.yoursite.com/imagename.gif)}
<HTML>
<HEAD>

<STYLE TYPE ="text/css">

UL { display: list-item; list-style-image:
 url(redstar.gif); list-style-type: square}
</STYLE>

</HEAD>
<BODY>

<UL>
<LI><P>item A
<LI><P>item B
<LI><P>item C
<LI><P>item E
</UL>

</BODY>
</HTML>
```

List-Style-Position

The list-style-position property determines where the list marker
is placed in relation to the list item. Use the list-style-position
property with either *inside* or *outside* as a value. Outside is the
default value. If the value inside is used, the lines will wrap under the marker instead of being indented. This property applies

to elements with the display value of list-item, and is inherited.

Outside rendering puts the list marker outside the margins of the list:

```
• List item 1
   Second line of the outside list item
```

Inside rendering sets the margins of the list equal to the list marker:

```
  • List item 1
Second line of  the inside list item
```

List-Style

Use the list-style property to quickly and easily change the default display characteristics of list markers in HTML list structures. You can set the list-style-type, list-style-image, and list-style-position properties in a single line in your style sheet. Use this method to create nested lists with different list-item markers or images for each level. You should also include a standard marker value with each image **<URL>** in case the image is not available or the user's browser can't display it. This property applies to elements with the display value of list-item. It is inherited and has no default value.

You can specify within the same line of HTML code the location of the marker; and a graphic or standard set of symbols to be used. You may use the property values in any order, but you may not use multiple values to control the same property. The general format for the list-style is

```
element { list-style: [marker-type]
[position] [URL] }
```

Using the classification properties in your style sheets will clearly increase the appeal of your Web site as well as decrease your initial development time and later maintenance. Some browsers don't completely or properly implement the CSS1 standard for the classification properties but it is hoped that they will in the near future. They may even be working before the HTML 4.0 draft, with its increased control over the classification properties, becomes a true standard. Only time will tell.

Looking Ahead

Now that you've learned how to ensure that your pages are displayed the way you want by using classification properties, let's move on to learn how to specify the font properties for the text users see in your Web pages.

DO IT IN COLOR!

This *Do It In Color* section brings you the color-related capabilities of style sheets in—you guessed it—full color. Style sheets provide Web designers with a variety of ways to add color to Web pages. Not only can you display text in all the colors of the rainbow, but with style sheet rules you can stripe your pages with different background colors—a capability not available through conventional HTML markup. Background images take on a whole new flavor when included using style rules. You can specify a different background image for each HTML element without resorting to complex table markup. Once you've set your backgrounds, you can control how they tile: horizontally, vertically, both, or not at all. And who says a background has to scroll with the page? Style sheets certainly don't.

The *Do It In Color* sections cover all the necessary components for creating color and background-related style sheet rules. In addition, they take advantage of the full-color layout to look at how style can be carried from one media to the next, explore the inner workings of both simple and complex style sheets, and take you on a brief tour of some of the Web's best examples of style sheet-based sites. Here's what you'll find in the five *Do It In Color* sections:

Do It In Color I
From Print To The Web: Maintaining Style Across Different Media

Here we take a step away from CSS-specific styles to look at how *TIME* magazine's familiar look and feel is carried over from its print magazine to its online alter-ego. This *Do It In Color* section includes a discussion of color and layout techniques, and how they can be used in different media for similar information. The section also focuses on how TIME.com utilizes familiar styles in its implementation of Web-specific technologies such as daily news summaries and threaded discussion. This consistency of style from one media to the next makes users comfortable in their environment and ensures that Web visitors always know whose site they are at.

Do It In Color II
Working With Color And Background Properties

Images and colors can add spice and variety to Web pages while adding value to their content. The individual properties and their associated values used to create style rules that bring color and background images to Web pages are covered in depth in this color section. In addition to a full discussion of how each property functions and the values it can take, a collection of colorful examples shows you what to expect when you begin to add color to your pages via style sheets. A valuable addition to the section is a full color display of the 216 browser-safe colors, with corresponding RGB hexadecimal color codes.

Do It In Color III
Anatomy Of A Simple Style Sheet

As with all things Web, there are two levels of style sheets: simple and complex. What separates the two is not the number of style rules they contain, but rather, the kinds of properties used to create those rules. Color and font properties make up the bulk of the rules in a simple style sheet. This *Do It In Color* section also includes a step-by-step guide to building a style sheet from the ground up.

Do It In Color IV
Anatomy Of A Complex Style Sheet

Building on the discussion of simple style sheets in the preceding section, this *Do It In Color* section focuses on those properties—box, margin, and classification—that make a style sheet complex. Simple style sheets can easily graduate to complex once you begin mixing and matching inline and external style sheets and including inheritance as a factor in how the styles are interpreted by the browser. This section clearly illustrates some of the problems created by inheritance and includes a discussion of the correct way to leverage simple style sheets to create more advanced, complex style sheets.

Do It In Color V
Guided Tour Of The Seven Style Sheet Wonders

Seven real life examples of style sheets at work provide a testimonial to the positive effects a well thought-out style sheet can have on a Web site. This tour highlights the fact that style sheets are not limited to a specific kind of Web content. Screen shots and snippets of style sheet code are included for each site.

One of the most significant aspects of style sheets is their ability to add color to Web pages. In these *Do It In Color* sections, not only can you see the code and the practical implementation of color-related style rules, but you can see the colors too!

FROM PRINT TO THE WEB: MAINTAINING STYLE ACROSS DIFFERENT MEDIA

Many print publications have developed online versions of their materials whose styles very closely reflect their print counterparts. Just as in print, many different authors and editors contribute to these online versions, and style sheets are necessary to maintain a consistent look and feel across the individual Web pages that make up the site. In most cases, the online versions reflect the overall design and style of the print publication, providing users with a familiar environment in which to browse the online content.

TIME Online

The online version of *TIME* magazine provides all of the same content as the print version, as well as hyperlinks to other Web resources related to story topics. The site also takes advantage of the unique capabilities of the Web's media to provide daily news updates and chat rooms. Although the online version contains additional resources and a slightly different format, there is no question that the content is from *TIME*. The TIME.com home page (housed on the Pathfinder site at **http://www. pathfinder.com**/), shown in Figure 1, has been created in true *TIME* style.

The *TIME* logo, graphics style, print cover, fonts, and coloring are all taken directly from *TIME*'s signature style. As you browse the site, notice that these elements are used over and over again, so you always know that you're reading *TIME* material, just as if you had the magazine in your hands.

Figure 1 The TIME.com home page.

A comparison of two articles from the June 23, 1997 online version of *TIME* shows that the same layout and text styles are applied to each article, even though the authors and topics are different.

The article pictured in Figure 2 is the *TIME* cover story for the week of June 23, 1997. It details the fame brought to Roswell, New Mexico, after alien spacecraft allegedly crash-landed there decades ago. The article pictured in Figure 3 focuses on the steps American corporations are taking to eliminate discrimination in the workforce. These two articles, concerning very different topics, are formatted in exactly the same style. The *TIME* logo, issue data and volume number, topic font and size, article title font and size, bylines, and copy text are identical. If we turned the article words to dummy text-groups of random letters with no meaning, there would be no way to tell the two stories apart. Looking at the print version of the June 23, 1997 issue of *TIME*, we can make the same comparisons.

Other *TIME* Web Services

Looking at other sections of the *TIME* Web site, it is easy to see how *TIME* has very carefully designed those areas to fit seamlessly with the publication look and feel, even though the content and services offered are different.

TIME

JUNE 23, 1997 VOL. 149 NO. 25

SOCIETY

ROSWELL OR BUST

A TOWN DISCOVERS MANNA CRASHING FROM HEAVEN AND BECOMES THE CAPITAL OF AMERICA'S ALIEN NATION

BY BRUCE HANDY/ROSWELL

The city of Roswell, N.M. (pop. 49,000), is the birthplace of Demi Moore. It is also home to the nation's largest mozzarella plant. On warm spring nights, visitors deplaning onto the tarmac at the local airport may be struck, in a not necessarily unpleasant way, by the rich, manurelike odor rolling in from the surrounding ranchlands. But none of these things is what Roswell is most famous for.

Figure 2 A TIME.com article about extraterrestrial landings.

TIME

JUNE 23, 1997 VOL. 149 NO. 25

NATION/RACE IN AMERICA

ON THE JOB: EQUALITY PAYS

CORPORATE AMERICA HAS ITS OWN REASON TO WEED OUT DISCRIMINATION--THE BOTTOM LINE

BY GEORGE J. CHURCH

In boardrooms, racism in the workplace, like everything else, is primarily an issue of dollars and cents--as in the case of the $176 million that Texaco will pay out to settle a class-action discrimination claim, or the $500 million being demanded from Bell Atlantic in a suit filed by African-American employees last month. Their complaint, which so far incorporates the charges of 126 workers, runs the entire gamut of possible racial bias on the job, from the

Figure 3 A TIME.com article about discrimination in America's workforce.

The Science and Technology Chat Area

The Science and Technology chat area, shown in Figure 4, incorporates the now-familiar red, white, and blue color scheme. The fonts and hard rule inclusions are very similar to those found in the online and print articles, and the blue "Add New Message" button closely resembles all other navigation buttons found on the site. Finally, just in case all other visual clues aren't enough, the *TIME* banner can be found right at the top of the page.

TIME Daily

TIME Daily provides a frequently updated rundown of the day's top stories. It includes links to the other areas of the site as well as a field for searching for additional information. The best keyword for searching for additional information on an article's topic is even included in the search field. The content of these daily stories is inherently different from that found in the *TIME* online magazine stories. It is more up-to-date, dynamic, and immediate. Although the format of the online daily stories does not match the magazine format exactly, many of the same elements can be found, as shown in Figure 5.

Figure 4   The *TIME* Science and Technology chat area includes style elements that closely follow the print and online magazine designs.

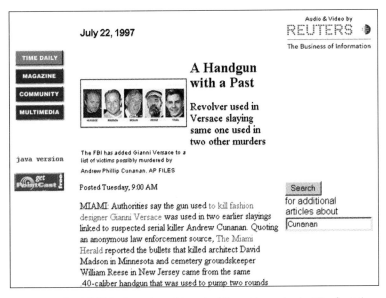

Figure 5 The *TIME Daily* stories, although different in content, still reflect the overall *TIME* look and feel.

Colors, fonts, general layout, and the inevitable *TIME* banner all proclaim very firmly that this is part of *TIME*'s online presence.

TIME Services

Another major part of the *TIME* Web site is the Services area. Here you find information about—and links to—the wide variety of offerings *TIME* has as part of both its print and electronic information distribution. The initial Services page includes links to more information about subscriptions, reprints, *TIME* digital, and other available services. This page, pictured in Figure 6, utilizes many of the stylistic elements you have come to identify with *TIME*.

The descriptive heading for each service is in the same sans-serif font found in other areas of the site, and it is in the easily identifiable *TIME* red. The links to more information about each service are blue, and of course, the page itself is white. The familiar navigation buttons live on the left side of the page and the cover of the current issue is predominantly placed in the center. The TIME.com banner sits at the top left, but leaves no room for doubt about where exactly this information originated.

Figure 6   The Services section of *TIME*'s online presence utilizes many familiar *TIME* style elements.

A Seamless Integration Of Style

Each area of the TIME.com site provides a different type of information or service, while maintaining a consistent style. Once you begin your travels through the site, you never have to wonder if you've linked to an external link or if you're still within the confines of the site. The designers of TIME.com have adapted their famous print magazine's look and feel to both an online version of the magazine and other new, nontraditional, Web-specific services.

We've taken this time to highlight and analyze the use of style on the TIME.com site to illustrate some of the simple mechanisms you can use to maintain consistent style throughout a Web site that contains different content and services. TIME.com is not only an excellent content resource, it is also an excellent example of how to do Web style the right way.

Looking Ahead

In *Do it In Color II*, we'll return to our discussion of style rules and property families. Almost every Web page out there makes some use of color and backgrounds. These properties give you more options and better control over the elements you include in your Web pages.

WORKING WITH COLOR AND BACKGROUND PROPERTIES

Adding color to HTML elements is by far the easiest and quickest way to add a little pizzazz to your Web pages. You don't incur the additional download time associated with color graphics, and your users get a little extra zing in their surfing experience. When HTML was first introduced, one of the most obvious omissions was a mechanism for changing the color of the page and text, as well as adding image-based backgrounds. Later versions included attributes such as **BGCOLOR**, **TEXT**, and **BACKGROUND** to the **<BODY>** tag to supply color-specific information for a page. However, these attributes affect the entire document—you can't add a shade just behind a certain block of text, for example. The **<FONT>** tag provided some relief by allowing developers to manipulate the font size of individual selections of text within a page.

These additions to HTML just weren't enough. Web designers want the same color options for HTML that they have in page layout programs. Once again, style sheets save the day. In this chapter, we'll look at how color is included and interpreted on the Web by expanding on the discussion of color units from Chapter 5. We will then examine each of the color and background properties, their associated values, and the style rules you can create for using them. Color is an exciting and valuable tool for enhancing your Web pages. However, especially because style sheets make including color so easy, always remember that just because you can do something doesn't necessarily mean you should.

Color And The Web

There is as wide a variety of computer color palettes as there are operating systems. The operating system, monitor, and video card all affect the way colors are rendered by a computer. Some monitors support millions of colors, while others are limited to 256 or even 16 colors. What is beige on a Macintosh may be tan on one PC and ivory on another. To create some semblance of consistency among colors on the Web, a "safe" palette—based on the standard 256-color palette, but containing only 216 colors—was created. Although the final rendering of each color may still be affected by individual operating systems, monitors, and video cards, the safe Web color palette levels the color playing field as much as possible. This gives Web designers the opportunity to use color within their pages without worrying about what colors their users' computers will support.

As described in the Color Values section of Chapter 5, there are three different ways to define colors on the Web. All are based on the Red-Green-Blue (RGB) color-naming scheme. The first, a percentage-based system, uses percentages of red, green, and blue to define a color. This method is the least frequently used of the three. The second, the hexadecimal color notation system, assigns hexadecimal codes to all the colors in the Web color palette. In the next section, we'll examine the inner workings of this system and provide you with a complete color reference to help you select the scheme for your pages. The third system uses the actual names of colors, rather than a notation system, to specify colors for Web pages. In "Taking A Cue From Crayons," we'll provide yet another color reference, so you'll know what teal really looks like (in a browser, anyway).

RGB: Color Coding For The Web

Literally millions of colors are available for use on the Web, both for inline graphics and for HTML element color definitions. The slightest variance in shade or hue changes a color in an instant. However, although the actual representation of these colors changes from computer to computer, you can use the safe palette of 216 colors with relative certainty on the Web. This palette was created by blending the standard 256-color palettes for both the Macintosh and Windows operating systems. Of those two palettes, 216 colors are alike; the other 40 are platform-specific. Using palettes is most important when designing graphics for the Web, and it is the best practice to limit your HTML element color specifications to the safe 216 as well. That way, you won't have any nasty color-rendering surprises when you look at your pages on a different platform.

As we searched the Web for more information about color, it became very clear to us why the hexadecimal color-naming system is the best way to go. We couldn't find two color-naming schemes that were alike. What was aquamarine to one person was turquoise to another. Using hexadecimal values is the only way to be precise. There were Web sites with hundreds of colors and their associated hexadecimal values, and some with less than 50. Although we *could* show you the hexadecimal notation for every shade of every color possible, that would take a few more pages than we have. Instead, we've concentrated on bringing you a visual representation of the safe color palette and the RGB hexadecimal codes for each of the 216 colors.

To use any of the colors presented in the next few pages in your style sheet rules, simply include the appropriate hexadecimal code, formatted #RRGGBB, in the rule. For example, to create a <P> element of CLASS=COLOR that turns all the text within the paragraph to red, use this code:

```
P.color {color: #FF0000}
```

It's that simple. Make sure you don't forget the "#" sign. Some browsers may be forgiving and display your color without it, but it's best to do things right.

We've split the palette up by color to make it easier for you to find the particular shade you want. Of course, naming a color and the perception of that color are subjective, so our categories aren't set in stone. Also, please note that because these colors are in the RGB spectrum, they will necessarily appear slightly changed on screen. We recommend you test your pages on more than one computer and with more than one browser. Even the safe colors can be rendered a little differently from machine to machine and browser to browser. Other style rules may be variously interpreted by different browsers, and you want to make sure that what looks good on one computer isn't an absolute disaster on another. That said, let the palette parade begin.

Table 1 Reds and pinks, with their hexadecimal codes.

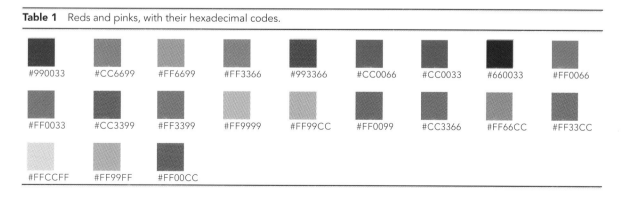

#990033	#CC6699	#FF6699	#FF3366	#993366	#CC0066	#CC0033	#660033	#FF0066
#FF0033	#CC3399	#FF3399	#FF9999	#FF99CC	#FF0099	#CC3366	#FF66CC	#FF33CC
#FFCCFF	#FF99FF	#FF00CC						

Table 2 Purples, with their hexadecimal codes.

#FF66FF	#CC33CC	#CC00FF	#FF3FF	#CC99FF	#9900CC	#FF00FF	#CC66FF	#990099
#CC0099	#CC33FF	#CC99CC	#990066	#993399	#996699	#CC66CC	#CC00CC	#663366

Table 3 Blues, with their hexadecimal codes.

#660099	#6666FF	#0000CC	#9933CC	#666699	#336699	#660066	#333366	#0066CC
#9900FF	#333399	#99CCFF	#9933FF	#330099	#6699FF	#9966CC	#3300CC	#003366
#330033	#3300FF	#6699CC	#663399	#3333FF	#006699	#6633CC	#3333CC	#3399CC
#6600CC	#0066FF	#0099CC	#9966FF	#0033FF	#66CCFF	#330066	#3366FF	#3399FF
#6600FF	#3366CC	#003399	#6633FF	#000066	#0099FF	#CCCCFF	#000033	#33CCFF
#9999FF	#0000FF	#00CCFF	#9999CC	#000099	#6666CC	#0033CC		

Table 4 Greens, with their hexadecimal codes.

#99FFFF	#33CCCC	#00CC99	#99FF99	#009966	#33FF33	#33FF00	#99CC33	#CCC33
#66FFFF	#66CCCC	#66FFCC	#66FF66	#009933	#00CC33	#66FF00	#336600	#33300
#33FFFF	#339999	#99FFCC	#339933	#33FF66	#33CC33	#99FF00	#669900	#666600
#00FFFF	#336666	#00FF99	#99CC99	#00FF66	#66FF33	#66CC00	#99CC00	#999933
#00CCCC	#006666	#339966	#66FF99	CCFFCC	#00FF00	#00CC00	#CCFF66	#CCCC66

(continued)

Table 4 Greens, with their hexadecimal codes (continued).

#009999	#003333	#006633	#33FF99	#CCFF99	#66CC33	#33CC00	#CCFF33	#666633
#669999	#00FFCC	#336633	#33CC66	#99FF66	#006600	#339900	#CCFF00	#999966
#99CCCC	#33FFCC	#669966	#00CC66	#99FF33	#003300	#99CC66	#999900	#CCCC99
#CCFFFF	#33CC99	#66CC66	#66CC99	#00FF33	#009900	#669933	#CCCC00	

Table 5 Yellows, browns, roses, and oranges, with their hexadecimal codes.

#FFFFCC	#FFCC00	#CC99090	#663300	#FF6600	#663333	#CC6666	#FF6666	#FF0000
#FFFF99	#FFCC66	#FF9900	#FF9966	#CC3300	#996666	#FFCCCC	#660000	#FF3300
#FFFF66	#FFCC33	#CC6600	#FF6633	#996633	#CC9999	#FF3333	#990000	#CC9966
#FFFF33	#CC9933	#993300	#FF9933	#330000	#993333	#CC3333	#CC0000	#FFCC99
#FFFF00	#996600	#CC6633						

Table 6 White, grays, and blacks, with their hexadecimal codes.

#FFFFFF	#CCCCCC	#999999	#666666	#333333	#000000

Taking A Cue From Crayons: Named Colors

Hexadecimal color codes are not the easiest things in the world to remember. A missing or additional "F" in the code can create white or lime-green. Not a pretty site. However, as we mentioned earlier, everyone has a different color naming scheme and no two versions of aquamarine are the same. Although it wasn't practical to try to develop a universal naming scheme beyond the hexadecimal coding, there are 16 colors whose names can be used in lieu of their hexadecimal codes. However, because browser interpretations may vary, Microsoft's teal and Netscape's teal may not look exactly alike, nor will they necessarily look alike on Macintoshes and PC. This is because, as Table 7 shows, some of the 16 colors are not part of the standard color palette. They'll be close enough for horseshoes and hand grenades though. Without further ado, we once again present a palette parade, albeit much shorter than the previous one.

Colorizing Pages With Color And Background Properties

You have six different color and background properties and their associated values at your disposal for creating color-related style rules. You can specify text and background colors for individual HTML elements. You can also include background images and manipulate the way they repeat, whether or not they scroll, and their position. These properties take your Web pages beyond the single background colors and simple tiling HTML allows for, to a multicolored realm with a wide variety of tiling, scrolling, and positioning options. Hold on to your hats; the color ride is about to begin.

Table 7 The 16 colors, with their hexadecimal codes.

Aqua #00FFFF	Black #000000	Blue #0000FF	Fuchsia #FF00FF	Gray #8000000	Green #008000	Lime #00FF00	Maroon #800000	Navy #000080
Olive #808000	Purple #800080	Red #FF0000	Silver #C0C0C0	Teal #008080	White #FFFFFF	Yellow #FFFF00		

The Color Property

HTML 3.2 and 4.0 both include the **<FONT>** tag for localized text formatting, including specifying the color of the contained text (see Figure 1). The following example uses the **<FONT>** tag to render text in teal:

```
<FONT COLOR=teal>This text is teal</FONT>
```

Figure 1 shows how this text is rendered in a browser.

<FONT> tags can be nested within one another to create multiple colors of text within the same paragraph. The following code nests teal text within red text, and Figure 2 shows how it appears in a browser:

```
<FONT COLOR=red> This text is red <FONT COLOR=teal>but
    this text is teal</FONT> and this text is red again.
    </FONT>
```

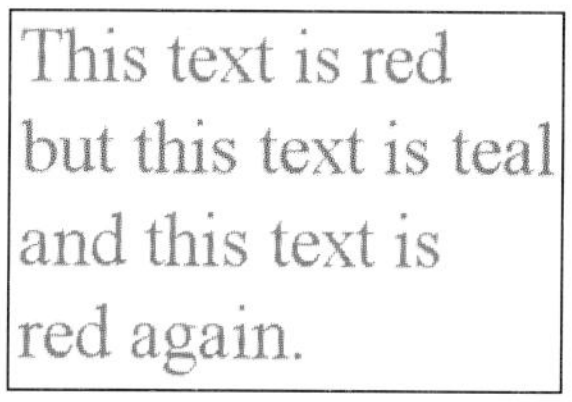

The same kind of effects can be achieved using the **color** property and a hexadecimal or name color value. The syntax is very straightforward:

```
selector {color: #RRGGBB/name}
```

Using our first example, we can create a style rule for **FONT CLASS=teal** that accomplishes the same thing:

```
<STYLE>
font.teal {color: teal}
</STYLE>
```

To invoke this style rule we use this HTML:

```
<FONT CLASS=teal> This text is teal</FONT>
```

Figure 3 shows the results.

You can also duplicate the embedded font trick we used in the second example by using multiple style rules and embedded HTML tags, as shown in the following code:

Figure 1   The <FONT> tag can be used to change the color of text within a Web page.

Figure 2   Nested font tags render multi-colored text within the same paragraph.

Figure 3   A style rule can be used to accomplish the same formatting as the HTML <FONT> tag.

```
<HEAD>
<STYLE>
div.red {color: red}
span.teal {color: teal}
</STYLE>
</HEAD>

<BODY>
<DIV CLASS=red> This text is red <SPAN CLASS=teal>but
this text is teal</SPAN> and this text is red again.</
DIV>
</BODY>
```

This text is red but this text is teal and this text is red again.

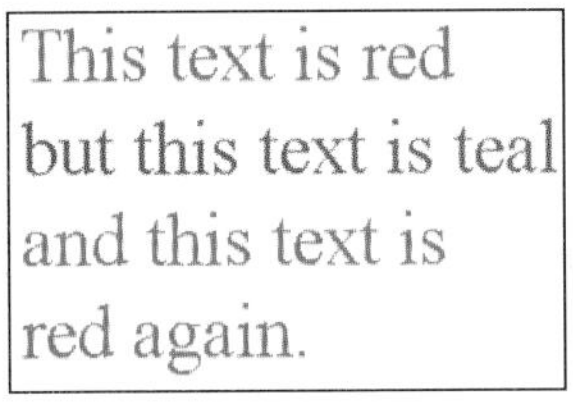

Figure 4 Style rules in combination with embedded HTML tags can render multi-colored text within the same paragraph.

The results are shown in Figure 4.

Notice that we substituted **<DIV>** and **<SPAN>** tags for the two font tags. If we had created rules for two classes of **<FONT>** and then embedded them as we did in the HTML-only example, the rules of inheritance make the entire sentence red. The teal portion of the sentence, regardless of the teal style rule, is red because its parent, the red portion of the sentence, has a color style rule already associated with it. Using **<DIV>** and **<SPAN>**, tags specifically created for embedding, the problem of inheritance is overcome. **<DIV>** applies a style rule to the entire sentence, but **<SPAN>** is intended to apply localized formatting that overrides any rules already in effect.

The HTML-only and style rule/HTML methods for creating teal text within red text are very similar, and neither method is easier than the other. Both require HTML to invoke the style changes, and the style rule/HTML method requires that the rules be created before the HTML is used. So, why use the style rule method when the HTML method is just as effective? The previous examples don't better represent one approach over the other. But in the following scenario, style rules definitely have the advantage.

We need a style rule that combines several different types of properties and will be used several times throughout a document. The selector will be "P" and the class "headline." The text this formatting applies to needs to be red, 16-point Verdana, bold, and centered. To do this with plain HTML we would need to combine at least three different sets of tags, as shown in this code:

```
<FONT COLOR=red FACE=verdana SIZE=+4><BOLD><CENTER>
Headline text </CENTER></BOLD></FONT>
```

This tag combination produces the desired effect, except the font size, +4, assumes that the average user views his or her pages with 12-point text. This is not always the case, but the **<FONT>** tag does not allow you to specify exact text size. The major drawback in using this HTML-only method to create the "headline" style is that we would have to retype, or cut and paste, each and every time we need to create a headline. It would be much easier to use one tag to apply all these different formatting options. A style rule composed of many properties and values, including the color property, does the trick. The necessary style rule is defined in the following code:

```
P.headline {color: red;
        font: 16pt Verdana 700;
            \* uses the font property shorthand to
            specify font size (16pt) font-family
            (Veranda) and font weight (700=bold)*\
        text-align: center;
        }
```

The following single line of HTML invokes the style rule, and the results as seen by the browser are shown in Figure 5.

```
<P CLASS=headline>Headline text </P>
```

That single HTML tag, **<P CLASS=headline>**, in conjunction with the style rule that only has to be written once, creates the same effect as three different HTML tags. So, although using the color property on its own may not seem very effective when the **<FONT COLOR=>** tag works just as well, it has a decided advantage when it is part of a complex style rule.

Headline text

Figure 5   A single style rule takes the place of three HTML tags to create "headline" text.

The Background-Color Property

You are used to setting the background color of an entire document using the <**BODY BGCOLOR=**> tag and attribute combination. Although this HTML convention allows you to get away from the old gray background that is the browser default, it limits you to one, and only one, background color. What if you could have multiple background colors on a page, each one tied to a different HTML element? Each heading level could not only be a different size, font, and color, but also have its own background. The possibilities are endless. The **background-color** property makes this possible. As with the color property, the rule syntax is very straightforward:

```
selector {background-color: #RRGGBB/name}
```

Using this syntax, we generated the following style rule that defines a different background color, each a shade of blue, for each of the six heading levels:

```
<STYLE>
H1 {background-color: #3300CC}
H2 {background-color: #6666FF}
H3 {background-color: #6666CC}
H4 {background-color: #0099FF}
H5 {background-color: #99CCFF}
H6 {background-color: #6699CC}
</STYLE>
```

To invoke these style rules we used this HTML code:

```
<H1> Heading level 1</H1>
<H2> Heading level 2</H2>
<H3> Heading level 3</H3>
<H4> Heading level 4</H4>
<H5> Heading level 5</H5>
<H6> Heading level 6</H6>
```

The resulting Web page is shown in Figure 6.

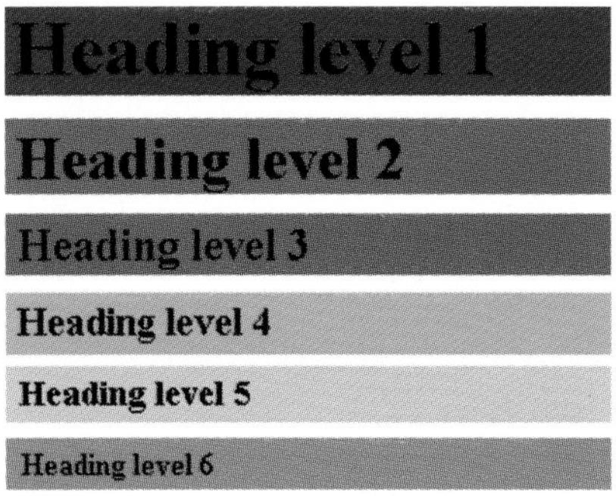

Background colors can be nested within each other just as text colors were. Using our red and teal example, we can create red and teal backgrounds for our text using these style rules and HTML markup:

Heading level 1

Heading level 2

Heading level 3

Heading level 4

Heading level 5

Heading level 6

Figure 6 The background-color property allows multiple background colors to be included on one Web page by linking the backgrounds to individual HTML elements.

```
<HEAD>
<STYLE>
div.red {background-color: red}
span.teal {background-color: teal}
</STYLE>
</HEAD>

<BODY>
<DIV CLASS=red> This text is red <SPAN CLASS=teal>but
this text is teal</SPAN> and this text is red again.</
DIV>
</BODY>
```

Figure 7 shows the results as seen by a browser. Now, instead of the text being alternating colors of red and teal, the backgrounds are.

As with many other style rule properties, the background-color property provides you with an opportunity to litter your Web pages with color. Although this may be fun for learning and experimentation purposes, remember not to let it come between your readers and your content. Use this tool wisely.

> This background is red but this background is teal and this background is red again.

Figure 7   The background-color property allows you to combine different background colors in the same paragraph.

The Background-Image Property

You've probably noticed that the color and background color properties take their cue from existing HTML tags. However, they take color and backgrounds to another level, as the background-image properties, illustrate. The **background-image** property is used just like the **<BODY BACKGROUND=>** tag and attribute combination, to define an image that will serve as the background, or wallpaper, for an HTML element. The syntax for specifying a background image is

```
selector {background-image: url(filename.gif)}
```

To link the graphics file blueback.gif, shown in Figure 8, to a paragraph of class "main" we use this single style rule:

```
P.main {background-image: url(blueback.gif)}
```

If you thought being able to assign different background images to different HTML elements was cool, just wait; there's even more.

Figure 8   Using style rules, you can link a background image to a single HTML element, rather than the entire body of a document.

The next three background properties give you more control over the background image than you ever thought possible.

The Background-Repeat Property

Now that you've selected and included a background image for an entire HTML document or just one specific element, how do you want it to tile? The **background-repeat** property and its associated values allow you to choose how an image tiles across the screen. You have four choices:

- **repeat**—the image tiles both horizontally and vertically, as is customary for standard Web-page backgrounds.

- **repeat-x**—the image repeats from left to right in a single row.

- **repeat y**—the image repeats from top to bottom in a single column.

- **no-repeat**—the image appears once but does not repeat in any direction.

Figures 9 through 12 show how each different **background-repeat** property and value combination affects the placement of the background image.

The Background-Attachment Property

Standard tiled backgrounds on a Web page become part of the page itself. As you scroll down the page, the background scrolls as well. But what if you wanted a background, such as a company logo or decorative top-border, to stay put and not scroll? The **background-attachment** property gives you the flexibility to glue a border to an element (the default) or float it on the screen independently of the element and its contents.

There are two values for the **background-attachment** property:

- **scroll**—glues the image to its element and forces it to scroll with the element.

- **fixed**—allows the image to float behind the page because its position is fixed relative to the canvas. The element may scroll by, but the image won't.

Figure 9 Background-repeat: repeat.

Figure 10 Background-repeat: repeat-x.

Figure 11 Background-repeat: repeat-y.

Figure 12 Background-repeat: no-repeat.

The following code shows the difference between scrolling and fixed background-attachment rules:

```
H1 {background-image: url(blueback.gif);
    background-attach: fixed;
    }
```

Because this property is not yet supported by any of the available browsers, we can't show you any real-life examples of how it works. You'll just have to trust us on this one. As browsers are updated and CSS1 becomes more fully implemented, you will be able to use it on your pages.

The Background-Position Property

Until now, all background images were attached to some HTML element, whether it was the body or an individual paragraph. The initial position of the graphic is determined, by default, by the element. Using the **background-position** property, you can set the initial position of any background image, overriding the default.

You can set the background position of an image using any of the following three methods:

- **percentage**—defines the position of the image by percentage in relation to the element.

- **length**—defines the position of the image in exact measurements in relation to the element.

- **keywords**—uses a set of nine different keywords to set the position of the image in relation to the element.

Notice that all three of the positioning mechanisms are related to the position of the image. Let's take a closer look at each to see how they really work.

Positioning An Image By Percentage

The percentage method of placing an image uses one or two percentage values to determine the placement of the image in relation to the element it is attached to. If you use one value, it defines the horizontal position of the image and the image will be centered vertically. Percentage calculations take into account both the element and the image. This style rule:

```
H1 {background-image: url(blueback.gif);
    background-position: 30%;
    }
```

finds the point within the image that is 30 percent across the image and 50 percent down, and aligns it with the point in the element that is 30 percent down and 50 percent across, as illustrated in Figures 13 through 15. The dots in Figures 13 and 14 represent the points in the background image and element box, respectively, that are 30 percent across and 50 percent down. Figure 16 shows the results when the two are aligned at these points. If you want to make things even simpler, the property **background-position: 50%** aligns the centers of both the image and the element.

Two percentage values define the horizontal and vertical points for both the image and the element, and position the image relative to the element. So the property **background-position: 40% 40%** first finds the point within the element that is 40 percent across and 40 percent down; then finds the point in the image that is 40 percent across and 40 percent down; and then aligns them.

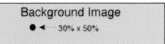

Figure 13 The 30 percent by 50 percent point in the background image.

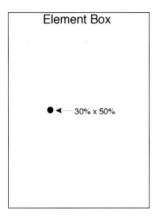

Figure 14 The 30 percent by 50 percent point in the element image.

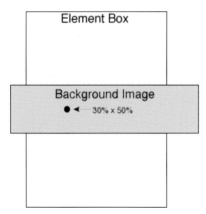

Figure 15 The background and elements aligned.

Once again, this property is not yet fully supported, so we can't show you any examples.

Positioning An Image By Length

The length method of positioning an image works in exactly the same way as the percentage method does, except absolute values are used in place of percentages. The style rule **background-position: 50pt** finds the position in the element that is 50 points across and vertically centered; then locates the point within the image that is 50 points across and vertically centered; and then aligns them. If the property is **background-position: 60pt 60pt**, the points that are 60 points across and 60 points down within both the element and the image are determined and aligned.

Positioning An Image By Keyword

A set of nine keywords can be used to specify the location of an image in relation to its linked elements. All of the keywords have equivalent percentage values. For example, **background-position: center center** is equivalent to **background-property: 50% 50%**. The horizontal and vertical centers are both located 50 percent in from the top and side, respectively. Table 8 lists the keywords and their equivalent percentage positions, and Figure 16 illustrates them.

Positioning And Fixed Images

If you set your background image to "fixed" by using the **background-attachment** property, all of your positioning will be relative to the browser window, rather than to the element the image is attached to. This is a subtle, but important, difference. If a user resizes the browser, the positioning of a fixed image will change. This is a reminder that although style sheets give you greater control over the appearance of your Web pages, the user is the unknown variable that prevents you from having total control.

Table 8 The background-position keywords and their equivalent percentage combinations.

left top 0% 0%	left center 0% 50%	left bottom 0% 100%
center top 50% 0%	center center 50% 50%	center bottom 50% 100%
right top 100% 0%	right center 100% 50%	right bottom 100% 100%

The Background Property

By now you should be no stranger to the shorthand properties, such as font and margin, that combine several like properties into a single property. The **background** property provides the shorthand for all of the background-related properties we have just discussed. Its syntax looks like this:

```
selector {background: <background-image>
<background-repeat>
<background-attachment> <background-position>
```

This collection of style background style rules:

```
<STYLE>
P.story {background-image: url(blueback.gif);
        background-repeat: repeat-y;
        background-attachment: fixed;
        background-position: left center;
        }
</STYLE>
```

can be expressed using this single rule:

```
<STYLE>
P.story {background: url(blueback.gif) repeat-y fixed
left center}
</STYLE>
```

It's usually best to set all the properties and values for any given background image all at once. Because they are all interrelated, forgetting one may yield strange results.

Looking Ahead

The color and background properties give Web designers a great set of tools for taking Web pages beyond black and gray into a world of images and color. Not only do they add visual elements, they also give designers a great deal of control over their display as well. In Color Section 3, we'll explore the inner workings of a real-life style sheet to see how rules are used and applied, and to discuss the Web designer's goals.

left top 0% 0%	center top 50% 0%	right top 100% 0%
left center 0% 50%	center center 50% 50%	right center 100% 50%
left bottom 0% 100%	center bottom 50% 100%	right bottom 100% 100%

Figure 16 The background-position keywords and their equivalent percentage combinations illustrated.

ANATOMY OF A SIMPLE STYLE SHEET

III

In the previous chapters and *Do It In Color* sections, we've presented all the style properties and values; discussed the ins and outs of using them to create style rules; and provided you with three mechanisms for linking to or including style rules in your Web documents. However, simply providing you with these style sheet components would be somewhat akin to giving you lumber, nails, pipes, and paint, and telling you to build a house—without telling you how. So in this chapter, we'll focus on how to combine the parts of CSS to create a style sheet. Then, we take you on a rule-by-rule tour of Jacob Nielsen's Alertbox site to show you how a moderate style sheet is implemented "IRL" (in real life).

Common Style Sheet Components

There are several dozen style sheet properties that, when combined with their potential values, can be used to create literally hundreds of style rules. However, a number of property value rules are found in most style sheets simply because they affect the most common elements on any HTML page. In general, the most common style sheet components are:

- Font color
- Font size
- Font style
- Font family
- Text alignment
- Margins

Although these are only five of the many available style sheet properties, they control the most basic aspects of a page and the text within it. Style rules made up of a combination of these properties, and their associated values can be used to create a unique and colorful page similar to the W3C Style Sheets site we've turned to time and again in this book as an exceptional example of style sheets in action.

Build A Simple Style Sheet, Step-By-Step

Building a simple style sheet from scratch involves more than just combining properties and values to create style rules. Before you type your first "{", consider these two questions:

- Who is your audience?
- What are your objectives?

The answers to these questions should drive everything about your page, not just the style rules you create, and should be answered before you even open a new text file to begin editing your HTML.

Some style-specific issues associated with both of these questions deserve exploration. Once you've answered these two important questions and considered the style ramifications associated with both, you can then collect the pieces of your page and put them all together.

Who Is Your Audience?

All the writing classes we've ever taken have taught us that the first question to ask yourself before putting a single word on paper is: Who is my audience? The audience drives your objectives, and your objectives drive your content. The same is true for Web pages. You create Web pages, probably, because you have information to share with others—your audience—so it makes sense to consider your audience before crafting the information you have for them. Your audience affects your Web document's style in many ways. Font types and sizes, colors, images, and white space are just a few style elements that will vary depending on your audience.

If you are creating a set of Web pages about frogs and their natural habitats for a third-grade science class, you will most likely use large fonts, a wide variety of colors and illustrations, and a great deal of white space. Figure 1 shows an example of what the viewers might see. You will probably break up your content into several pages, with each focusing on a single idea or topic. The basic style rule for these pages might look something like this:

Figure 1   A header with a large, green, friendly frog and a title like "Frogs and Their Homes" may be found at the top of every page so the kids know they are still dealing with frogs.

```
BODY {background: white url(smilyfrog.gif);
            no-repeat;
            }
/* creates a document with a white background and
includes a smiling frog background image that does not
repeat to create the "Frogs and Their Homes" header on
every page in the frog document collection.*/
H1.green {color: green;
        font: 700 small-caps;
        }
/* creates a heading level 1 in green.*/

H1.white {color: white;
        font: 700 small-caps;
        background-color: green
        }
/* creates a heading level 1 in white with a green
background. This provides for alternating strips of green
and white with opposite heading colors.*/
```

However, if you were creating a Web presentation for a college biology class, you would not want to use the same styles. See Figure 2 for an example more suited to this audience. The frog on the banner might still be smiling, but the banner text might be changed to "An In-depth Study of Frog Habitats." Alternating strips of green and white would most definitely not be appropriate; the language would be different, as would the illustrations; and more information, written at the college level, of course, would be contained on a single page. It is appropriate to include multiple citations in a college-level document, so a citation style would be in order. When we include these changes in the style sheet just shown, the HTML now looks like this:

Figure 2 This presentation is suited to a more sophisticated audience.

```
BODY {background: white url(smilyfrog.gif);

              no-repeat;
              }
/* creates a document with a white
background and includes a smiling frog
background image that does not repeat to
create the "An In-Depth Study of Frog
Habitats" header on every page in the
document collection.*/

H1   {font: 700 small-caps}

/* makes all instances of heading level 1
bold and in small caps.*/

CITE  {color: green}
/* adds a bit of color to the page by making
citations green.*/
```

The college presentation style sheet is noticeably more subdued than the elementary-level style sheet, but both use the font and color properties to add meaning to text as well as enhance page design.

What Are Your Objectives?

Your documents' objectives are directly driven by your audience. Why is your audience accessing your Web documents? You may be providing information they are interested in. Or, you may be trying to persuade them to take up your side of a specific cause. You may have incredible images or enticing poetry. Your pages may be the biggest and best repository of a specific kind of software. If you are providing information, your page design should be well-organized, easy to navigate, and cleanly presented. If your pages are meant to be persuasive, they will use text effects to draw attention to key phrases and important groups of information. An image collection should be the focus of the page, which should be styled to create

that focus. Poetry can have new meaning added by simply changing the color or text decoration of a single word. If you have a large software repository, you will want to use organization and navigation styles similar to that of a purely information-oriented site.

In the two previous frog examples, objectives played just as much a role in the page design as the audience did. When creating the style rules for the elementary version of the style sheet, the main objectives were to keep kids interested and provide them with fun tidbits of information about where frogs live. Vibrant strips of color were included to catch and keep their attention, while the smiling frog reminded them they were still learning about frogs even when a new Web page was loaded. Colors and text decoration played a large role in attempting to keep the kids interested, as well as in conveying information.

In the college version of the style sheet, the main objective was to provide information. Stylistically, very little was done to maintain students' attention. Green coloring was added to highlight citations of other interesting resources, and because green is commonly associated with frogs, it was associated with the content as well. Although the information in the two documents is similar, the style sheets were changed to reflect the different objectives of the Web pages.

Collecting The Pieces And Putting Them Together

Now that you've thought your way carefully through your audience and objectives and understand how they will affect all aspects of your Web document, the next step is to collect the pieces of the document. These include:

- Page content
- A basic outline
- A basic page layout

Before you can begin writing style rules, you need to know what they will affect (the content); how they will work together to convey the information (the outline); and what the basic look and feel of the page will be (the layout). You can approach this gathering of information in one of two ways:

- On paper. You can use a yellow legal pad, grid paper, index cards, a white board, or any other medium to assemble your pieces. Divide the content into individual pieces—paragraphs, lists, images, and so forth—and then identify where each fits in the overall outline of the page and how it should be styled. This process helps you create groups of like information that should have similar style characteristics. For example, all summary paragraphs should be in 12-point teal Times, while all introductory paragraphs should be in 14-point navy Garamond. As the pieces of your content begin to form a page outline, the associated styles will fall into place. The entire process is interwoven because the content, outline, and style components are interlinked.

  We are the first to admit that this method of creating page layout and style rules is a bit cumbersome, but we will also guarantee that your pages will reflect the time and energy you put into their creation. The result will be a noticeable cohesiveness to the information, with none of the randomness that sometimes accompanies Web pages. All that's left to do after you've mapped out the organization of your page components is to create the relevant style rules and write the HTML code. Because you will have copious notes and a general plan to draw from, this will be the easy part. Happy coding!

- In an HTML page. If the thought of pages and pages of paper, or stacks and stacks of index cards, is more than you're willing to deal with, you can begin directly within a text or HTML editor. The collection process is still much the same, but the elements will be contained directly within the HTML page you are working with. Once you have all your content in the page, with line- and page-breaks judiciously added as needed, display the document and then consider how the information you are viewing is related to the other information on the page. Do you need to rearrange information? Should the page be broken into multiple documents? How should similar elements be formatted? Add HTML markup and create style rules, checking the results regularly to see how they look with the other content, markup, and style rules you created.

This process is different from the first option because here you design as you go, rather than designing from a whole-page or site view. It allows you to create content, HTML, and style rules all at one time, but it can cause your pages to lose some cohesiveness if you aren't careful. If you use this method, review your pages thoroughly. Then, take a break from them for a day or so and return to them later to see if your markup and style still make sense.

A Simple "IRL" Style Sheet: Jacob Nielsen's Alertbox

Jacob Nielsen, an engineer at SunSoft, the software division of Sun, Inc., maintains a series of compelling articles about the usability of Web technologies on his "Alertbox" site, at **http://www.useit.com/**. The site contains many articles, each on a different topic, that reference the same style sheet. At the top of every article page, the following code references the external style sheet that governs the entire site:

```
<LINK TITLE="Useit House Style"
REL=STYLESHEET
HREF="/useit_style.css" TYPE="text/css">
```

Every page on the site has the same basic style, even though the content differs. This basic style is due in large part to the set of style rules that make up the **useit_style.css** style sheet document:

```
BODY        {font-family: "Times New Roman",
            Georgia, Times, "New York", serif;

            background: white;
            color: black;
            }

CODE        {font-family: "Courier New",
            Courier, Monaco, monospace;}

SMALL       {font-family: Verdana, "Lucida
            Sans", Arial, Helvetica, Geneva,
            sans-serif ; }

HR {color: gray ; }

.navbar     {font-size: 100%;
            font-family: Verdana, "Lucida
            Sans", Arial, Helvetica, Geneva,
            sans-serif;
            background: #FFFF66 ; }

.notrecommended {color: #666666 ; }
```

```
.deemphasized {color: #666666 ; }

TABLE       {font-size: 90% ;
            font-family: Verdana, "Lucida
            Sans", Arial, Helvetica, Geneva,
            sans-serif ; }

TABLE.densetable {font-size: 80% ; }

TR.summaryrow {font-size: 90%;
            background: #00FFFF ; }

CAPTION     {font-size: 100% ; }

.embeddedfloat {float: right;
            margin-left: 3em}

H1, H2, H3, H4, H5, H6
            {font-family: Verdana, "Lucida
            Sans", Arial, Helvetica, Geneva,
            sans-serif; }

UL.referencelist, .footnote
            {margin-left: 4em;
            text-indent: -4em;
            font-size: 83%;
            font-family: Verdana, "Lucida
            Sans", Arial, Helvetica, Geneva,
            sans-serif;
            list-style: none; }

A:link, .simulatedlink {color: blue ; }

A:visited   {color: purple ; }

A:active    {color: aqua ; }

A.notrecommended:link {color: #6666FF ; }

A.notrecommended:visited {color: #CC66CC ; }

A.deemphasized:link {color: #6666FF ; }

A.deemphasized:visited {color: #CC66CC ; }

.overline   {font-family: Verdana, "Lucida
            Sans", Arial, Helvetica, Geneva,
            sans-serif; margin-bottom: -2ex ;
            }
```

```
.updatecomment {font-size: 100%; background: #00FFFF ; }

.outsidecomment {font-size: 100%; background: #E9E9E9 ; }
```

This style sheet may look complicated and imposing at first glance, but it really isn't. It has several style rules, true, but the majority are made up of the common properties we listed earlier: font color, font size, font style, font family, text alignment, and margins. To help make heads and tails of this style sheet, let's look at it in action.

To show you how the previous style sheet applies to an actual Web document, we've chosen Nielsen's article from July 1, 1997, titled—coincidentally no doubt—"Effective Use of Style Sheets," shown in Figure 3 and found at http://www. useit.com/alertbox/ 9707a.html.

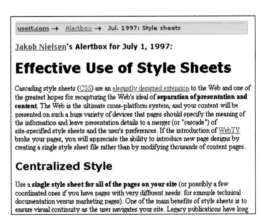

Figure 3 Jacob Nielsen's style sheet article uses a site-wide standard style sheet.

As Figure 3 shows, the Web document accurately reflects the first style rule defined in the site's style sheet:

```
BODY        {font-family: "Times New Roman",
            Georgia, Times, "New York", serif;
            background: white;
            color: black;
            }
```

The background is indeed white with black text, and the displayed font is Times, even though the browser the page was displayed with for the screen shot is configured to use Garamond as the default font. Because the "Always Use My Styles" box wasn't checked in the browser, the style sheet fonts were allowed to show through.

The following style rule

```
.navbar      {font-size: 100%;
             font-family: Verdana, "Lucida
             Sans", Arial, Helvetica, Geneva,
             sans-serif;
             background: #FFFF66 ; }
```

was used in conjunction with the following line of HTML to create the yellow navigation bar across the top of the screen:

```
<TABLE BGCOLOR="#FFFF66" BORDER=1 COLS=1
WIDTH="100%" CLASS=navbar>
<TR>
<TD>
<FONT FACE="Verdana, Lucida Sans, Arial, Helvetica,
Geneva, sans-serif">
<SMALL>
<A HREF="/"><STRONG>useit.com</STRONG>
</A>
<IMG SRC="/images/arrow_yellow.gif" WIDTH=13 HEIGHT=9
ALIGN=bottom ALT="-&gt;">
<A HREF="/">Alertbox</A> <IMG SRC="/images/
arrow_yellow.gif"
WIDTH=13 HEIGHT=9 ALIGN=bottom ALT="-&gt;">
Jul. 1997: Style Sheets
</SMALL>
</FONT>
</TD></TR>
</TABLE>
```

The style rule for small:

```
SMALL        {font-family: Verdana, "Lucida
             Sans", Arial, Helvetica, Geneva,
             sans-serif ; }
```

was also used to create the navigation bar.

Notice that the HTML repeats much of the same style information using tag attributes and the <**FONT**> tag that the style rules do. Why this redundancy? It may seem to be a waste of time to create style rules and then duplicate them in HTML, but this helps ensure that users with browsers that don't support style sheets will still be able to see as much of the style formatting as HTML will allow. Figure 4 shows the same Web page viewed with a style sheets-challenged browser.

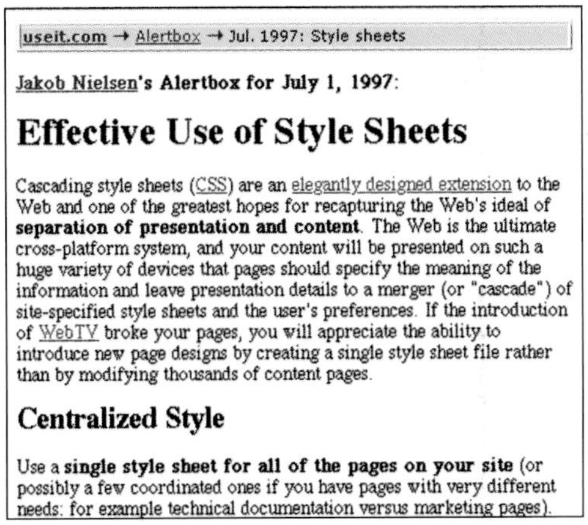
useit.com → Alertbox → Jul. 1997: Style sheets

Jakob Nielsen's **Alertbox for July 1, 1997**:

Effective Use of Style Sheets

Cascading style sheets (CSS) are an elegantly designed extension to the Web and one of the greatest hopes for recapturing the Web's ideal of **separation of presentation and content**. The Web is the ultimate cross-platform system, and your content will be presented on such a huge variety of devices that pages should specify the meaning of the information and leave presentation details to a merger (or "cascade") of site-specified style sheets and the user's preferences. If the introduction of WebTV broke your pages, you will appreciate the ability to introduce new page designs by creating a single style sheet file rather than by modifying thousands of content pages.

Centralized Style

Use a **single style sheet for all of the pages on your site** (or possibly a few coordinated ones if you have pages with very different needs: for example technical documentation versus marketing pages).

Figure 4 When viewed using browsers that don't support style sheets, style markup helps create effects similar to those of style rules.

The two are not identical, but a large majority of the formatting is carried over, which is better than none at all. For a while, as users and developers make the transition from style tags to style sheets, it is important to take the extra time to include style-related HTML markup around those page elements affected by style rules in order to help bridge the gap between the two.

At the end of the document, the **updatecomment** style rule:

```
.updatecomment {font-size: 100%; background: #00FFFF ; }
```

is used in conjunction with this HTML:

```
<P CLASS=updatecomment>
<STRONG>Data nugget:</STRONG>
During the first two weeks of July, the ratio between the
referral commissions earned from Amazon.com for books
ordered through the above link and the number of readers
```

```
of this column comes to a value of <STRONG>4.5 cents per
page view</STRONG>. Not enough to get rich (and I
recommend the book because I like it; not to earn a few
measly cents), but proof that micropayment mechanisms can
be more valuable than advertising (which typically pays
1-2 cents per page view).
</P>
```

to create text with an aqua background, as shown in Figure 5.

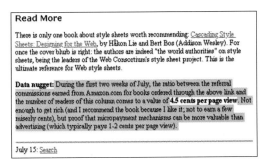

Figure 5 The background of text can be changed in the middle of a sentence using a style rule.

This is a nice way to highlight important text that contains content different from the article's subject matter. Figure 5 also shows the gray hard rule, as defined by this style rule:

```
HR {color: gray ; }
```

The rest of the article is straightforward in its style implementation. Some of the site's style rules are not needed, but it's nice to know they are there.

Having seen the style sheet at work, and having taken a closer look at its innards, you can see it is a simple mechanism that makes all the difference in display. Font family, size, and color are the layout elements most frequently modified. Background colors are changed to a set of navigation and special notes within the body of the page. The style sheet has many tools built into it that the designer can use any time during page creation to ensure that a new page fits well within the established site, and maintains the same style conventions.

Looking Ahead

Simple style sheets are the most common type of style sheet found on the Web today. "Simple" is not defined by a limited number of style rules or by a limited number of property/value combinations in any given rule. Instead, *simple* refers to the six most commonly modified elements of any page (font color, font size, font style, font family, text alignment, and margins). All these elements have an HTML tag equivalent that produces a similar effect. Although users and developers are moving from style markup to style sheets, it is a good idea to include both style rules and their HTML equivalents to ensure that users viewing pages with browsers that don't support style sheets can see style designs. In *Do It In Color IV*, we'll take a step up from simple style sheets to complex style sheets, discussing what makes a style sheet complex; how to decide when to use more complex style sheets; and how to leverage simple style sheets when creating complex ones. Finally, we'll take another "IRL" tour of a site that uses a complex style sheet.

ANATOMY OF A COMPLEX STYLE SHEET IV

In *Do It In Color III,* we took a close look at the components of simple style sheets and then went on to demonstrate a real-world example of a simple style sheet in use. Simple style sheets focus on a few basic document elements such as color and font properties. Sites that use simple style sheets usually apply a single set of rules to several pages. They may have a few specialized inline style rules as well, but in general, these sites like to keep their styles clean and crisp. However, there are times when more complex style sheets are in order. In this chapter, we'll discuss the differences between simple and complex style sheets, and list the advantages and disadvantages of going complex. We'll also show you how to leverage your simple style sheets when creating more complex style sheets and once again visit a real-life example of a complex style sheet at work.

Beyond Simple: Advanced Style Sheet Components

A style sheet falls into the complex category, not because it is made up of many rules, but because it contains a certain kind of rules. Simple style sheet rules focus on text, background, and margin changes; complex style sheets take rules to the next level by using the box model of page layout, tightly controlling white space, and adding multiple scrolling and fixed backgrounds. A style sheet is also considered complex if it combines inline and external style rules. When two simple style sheets are combined, they create one complex style sheet because they invoke the ever-present cascading guidelines.

Because style sheets are still in their infancy and some properties have only recently begun to be supported by any browser, complex style sheets are few and far between. It's a safe bet that as style sheet acceptance and implementation grows, style sheets will become more complex, just as implementations of HTML have grown more complex with each new set of tags. Web designers have become accustomed to the limitations of HTML, even though many designers have been overcome by creative implementations of tables and other tags. Box properties and white space provide designers with a degree of control over their pages they have never before known. As designers begin to implement and test style sheets, they are creating increasingly complex style sheets that push the limits of technology, demanding more of it, as they have done with HTML.

Is More Always Better?

It's human nature to think that more is always better. But is more better? For style sheets, this question must be answered on a case-by-case basis. As style sheets get more complex and use more properties, they require a great deal of work to implement and maintain. Inheritance can affect the way browsers render pages in ways you didn't expect. This makes debugging your style sheets more difficult because it's hard to find the cause of the problem, much less fix it. If a style sheet is complex because it is a combination of several external style sheets with some inline style thrown in for good measure, cascading becomes an important issue.

We don't want to deter you from the more complex properties of style sheets, because they allow you to take your HTML pages to a new level. However, it is important to have a well-organized way to control, document, and manage the style rules you create and implement. Site- and page-level outlines are essential, and content outlines can help you minimize the final number of rules to create. When mixing inline and external style sheets, it's a good idea to list the styles in each, comparing the elements and their effects to catch any inheritance or cascading problems before they occur.

Once you've set up your style sheets, complex or not, always consider them carefully and review your notes and organizational information before adding any new style rules. The more complex your style rules are, the more elements they may affect. Adding a new rule can send your entire page into a tailspin.

Leveraging Simple Style Sheets

Why reinvent the wheel? Before you make the move from an old, simple style sheet to a new, complex one, first see if the old style sheet can be revamped and added to instead of starting from scratch. If the rules in a simple style sheet work, why change them? Instead, add to them bit-by-bit until you've achieved the look you want. For example, the following style sheet is fairly simple. It creates style rules for a headline, two paragraphs, and bulleted lists.

```
H1        {font: Arial;
          font-size: 36pt;
          color: teal;
          text-align: center;
          }

P.byline {font: Arial;
          font-size:18pt;
          color: navy;
          text-align: right;
          font-style: italic
          }

P.body   {font: Times 12pt;
          color: black;
          text-align: justify;
          margin-left: 5%;
          }

LI        {background: #BC8F8F;
          font: Arial 13pt;
          color: #00009C;
          text-align: justify;
          margin-left: 5%;
          }
```

When combined with the following HTML, it creates the Web page shown in Figure 1.

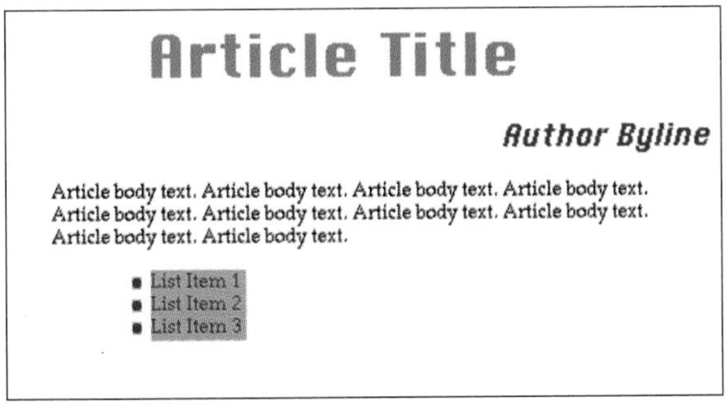

Article Title

Author Byline

Article body text. Article body text. Article body text. Article body text.
Article body text. Article body text. Article body text. Article body text.
Article body text. Article body text.

- List Item 1
- List Item 2
- List Item 3

Figure 1 A simple style sheet can be used to change fonts, text color, margins, and backgrounds.

```
<BODY>

<H1>Article Title</H1>
<P CLASS=BYLINE>Author Byline</P>
<P CLASS=BODY>Article body text. Article body text.
Article body text. Article body text. Article body text.
Article body text. Article body text. Article body text.
Article body text. Article body text.

<UL>
<LI>List Item 1
<LI>List Item 2
<LI>List Item 3
</UL>
</P>

</BODY>
```

Notice that the unordered list is nested within the paragraph of **CLASS BODY**. Both are given a five percent left margin by their style rules. The unordered list items are nested within the paragraph, so they inherit the five percent left margin and then add that to the five percent left margin of their own, causing the entire list to be indented underneath the paragraph.

Things begin to get complicated when we import the following style sheet, using the code **@import "orgstyle"** directly after the **<STYLE>** tag and before the inline style information, which provides site-wide style information to the page that already includes the inline style sheet previously listed.

```
P.body {margin-left: 10%}
H1 {text-align: right}
P.byline {margin-right: 10%}
```

Inline style always takes precedence over linked or imported style sheets. The rules for the **<P CLASS=BODY>** and **<H1>** tags are ignored by the document because inline style includes property/value combinations that are different from those specified in the imported style sheet. The inline style specifies that heading level 1 markup should be centered instead of right-justified as specified by the imported style sheet. The inline style also gives the paragraph of class **BODY** a left margin of 5 percent, which overrides the imported style's specification of 10 percent. The third style rule for paragraphs of style **BYLINE** is not overridden by the inline style information because no margins are specified for this tag. This rule carries through and is combined with the inline rules for **<P.BYLINE>**. Figure 2 shows the results.

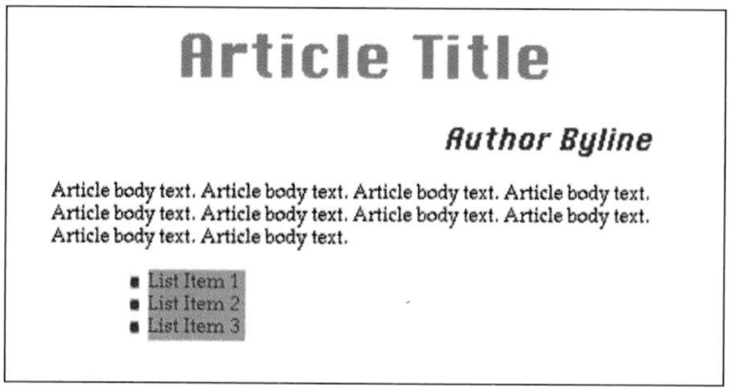

Figure 2   Inline styles override imported styles.

The byline text has been indented 10 percent to the right, unlike the page shown in Figure 1. Although both the imported and inline style sheets are fairly simple, combining the two causes some complex inheritance and cascading issues. In our example, we leveraged two simple style sheets to create one complex set of rules. The organizational style sheet was modified using inline styles to meet the specific needs of the individual page.

A Complex Style Sheet "IRL": The Web Design Group's CSS Reference

John Pozadzides and Liam Quinn of the Web Design Group have put together a remarkable style sheet reference that is a wonderful source of information for anyone using style sheets—

and they fully use style sheets for their Web page design. Found at **http://www.htmlhelp.com/reference/css/**, the CSS reference uses a single style sheet, **style.css**, to provide style rules for all the related pages. This style sheet falls into the complex category because it makes extensive use of inherited margins and has a rule for almost every available HTML element. It is obvious that this style sheet was well thought-out and that each rule was created after careful consideration of how it would affect every other rule. Although we can't show you an implementation of every rule, we do give you a good sampling of how the rules are used throughout the CSS reference as they are needed. The following is a complete listing of the **style.css** code.

```
body {
  background: white none;
  color: black
}

h1 {
  color: #c33;
  background: transparent none;
  font-weight: bold;
  text-align: center
}

h2 {
  color: #00008b;
  background: transparent none;
  margin-left: 2%;
  margin-right: 2%;
  font-weight: bold
}

h3 {
  color: #006400;
  background: transparent none;
  margin-left: 4%;
  margin-right: 4%;
  font-weight: bold
}
```

```
h4 {
  margin-left: 6%;
  margin-right: 6%;
  font-weight: bold
}

h5 {
  margin-left: 6%;
  margin-right: 6%;
  font-weight: bold
}

ul, ol, dl, p, fieldset {
  margin-left: 6%;
  margin-right: 6%
}

fieldset legend {
  margin-left: -2%
}

pre {
  margin-left: 10%;
  white-space: pre
}

table {
  margin-left: 4%;
  margin-right: 4%
}

table caption {
  font-size: larger;
  font-weight: bolder
}

ul ul, ol ol, ul ol, ol ul, table p, table
    ul, table dl,
table ol, ul table, dl table, ol table, ol p,
    ul p, dl p,
dl ul, dl ol, ul dl, ol dl, dl dl, blockquote
p, .note p, .
note ul, .note ol, .note dl,.note table, li
pre, dd pre {
  margin-left: 0;
  margin-right: 0
}

p small { font-size: smaller }
```

```
p.top {
  margin-left: 1%;
  margin-right: 1%
}

blockquote {
  margin-left: 8%;
  margin-right: 8%;
  border: thin ridge #dc143c
}

blockquote pre {
  margin-left: 1%;
  margin-right: 1%
}

dt a {
  font-weight: bold;
  margin-top: .8em
}

a:link {
  color: #00f;
  background: transparent none;
}

a:visited {
  color: #800080;
  background: transparent none;
}

a:active {
  color: green;
  background: #FFD700 none
}

strong.html {
  color: #191970;
  background: transparent none
}

strong.css {
  color: #800000;
  background: transparent none
}

pre code.css {
  color: #800000;
  background: transparent none;
  font-family: Monaco, "Courier New",
monospace
}
```

```
pre code.html {
  color: #191970;
  background: transparent none;
  font-family: Monaco, "Courier New",
monospace
}

pre samp {
  font-family: Monaco, "Courier New",
monospace
}

dfn {
  font-style: normal;
  font-weight: bolder
}

.note {
  font-size: smaller;
  margin-left: 10%
}

.SMA {
  color: fuchsia;
  background: transparent none;
  font-family: Kids, "Comic Sans MS", Jester
}

.oops {
  font-family: Jester, "Comic Sans MS"
}

.author {
  font-style: italic
}

.copyright {
  font-size: smaller;
  text-align: right;
  clear: right
}

.toolbar {
  text-align: center
}

.toolbar IMG {
  float: right
}
```

```
.error {
  color: #DC143C;
  background: transparent none;
  text-decoration: none
}

.warning {
  color: #FF4500;
  background: transparent none;
  text-decoration: none
}

.error strong {
  color: #DC143C;
  background: #FFD700 none;
  text-decoration: none
}

.warning strong {
  color: #FF4500;
  background: #FFD700 none;
  text-decoration: none
}

.warning a:link, .warning a:visited, .warning
a:active {
  color: #FF4500;
  background: transparent none;
  text-decoration: underline
}

.error a:link, .error a:visited, .error
a:active {
  color: #DC143C;
  background: transparent none;
  text-decoration: underline
}

.error strong a:link, .error strong
a:visited, .error
strong a:active {
  color: #DC143C;
  background: #FFD700 none
}

.warning strong a:link, .warning strong
a:visited,
.warning strong a:active {
  color: #FF4500;
  background: #FFD700 none
}
```

Pretty impressive. Even though this style sheet is complex, it is decipherable if analyzed in small chunks. The results of the rules for the body and heading levels 1 through 5, created using the following code and found on the CSS Structure and Rules page at **http://www.htmlhelp.com/reference/css/structure.html**, are shown in Figure 3.

```
h1 {
  color: #c33;
  background: transparent none;
  font-weight: bold;
  text-align: center
}

h2 {
  color: #00008b;
  background: transparent none;
  margin-left: 2%;
  margin-right: 2%;
  font-weight: bold
}

h3 {
  color: #006400;
  background: transparent none;
  margin-left: 4%;
  margin-right: 4%;
  font-weight: bold
}

h4 {
  margin-left: 6%;
  margin-right: 6%;
  font-weight: bold
}

h5 {
  margin-left: 6%;
  margin-right: 6%;
  font-weight: bold
}
```

HTML headings are used to create a visual hierarchy of information. As a heading level number increases, the font size and emphasis decrease.

The whole idea is to provide visual cues to the reader about sets and subsets of information. Even though the CSS reference style sheet alters the appearance of heading levels to include color, size, and margin specifics, the hierarchical information is not lost. Compare Figure 3 with Figure 4. Figure 4 shows the same page from Figure 3, seen in a browser that does not support style sheets. Both renderings of the page clearly indicate that <H1> is a top-level head, while <H5> is lower on the food chain.

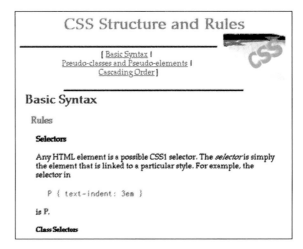

Figure 3 The CSS reference body and heading levels are controlled by style rules.

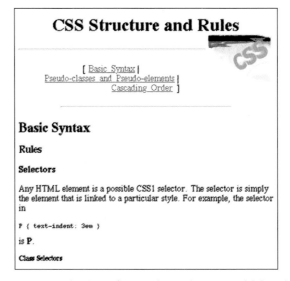

Figure 4 The CSS reference doesn't lose its readability when viewed by a non-CSS browser.

These style sheet rules illustrate an important style sheet design rule: Remember that for every HTML tag there is a purpose and a logic behind the way it renders text. Don't lose sight of that purpose and create rules that violate or inhibit it. The heading levels defined in the CSS reference style sheet stay true to the original intent of the tags they modify.

The CSS reference style sheet also contains a set of rules that specify how CSS and HTML code should be rendered, as shown here:

```
pre code.css {
   color: #800000;
   background: transparent none;
   font-family: Monaco, "Courier New",
monospace
}

pre code.html {
   color: #191970;
   background: transparent none;
   font-family: Monaco, "Courier New",
monospace
}
```

The CSS Structure and Rules page shown in the previous example also incorporates the following HTML affected by these rules:

```
<P>A simple selector can have different
<DFN>classes</DFN>,
thus allowing the same element to have
different styles. For example, an author may
wish to display code in a different color
depending on its language:</P>
<PRE><CODE CLASS=CSS>CODE.HTML
{ color: #191970 }
CODE.CSS { color: #4b0082 }</CODE></PRE>
<P>The above example has created two classes,
```

```
<STRONG CLASS=CSS>CSS</STRONG> and
<STRONG CLASS=CSS>HTML</STRONG>
for use with HTML's <STRONG CLASS=HTML>
CODE</STRONG> element.
The <STRONG CLASS=HTML><A HREF="STYLE
HTML.HTML#CLASS">
CLASS</A></STRONG>
 attribute is used in HTML to indicate the
class of an element,
<I>e.g.</I>,</P>
<PRE><CODE CLASS=HTML>&lt;P
CLASS=WARNING&gt;Only one
class is allowed per selector.
For example, CODE.HTML.proprietary is
invalid.&lt;/p&gt;
</CODE></PRE>
```

The results are shown in Figure 5.

These rules use text color and margins to differentiate between style sheet rules and HTML markup. Because the rules are used consistently throughout the CSS reference, users can tell at a glance what kind of code, HTML, or style sheet they are looking at. This consistency adds value to the information and makes it easier to use. It also illustrates another important style sheet design rule: Once you have established a style for a particular kind of information, be consistent in your use of it or it will lose its effectiveness and may confuse readers.

The remainder of the CSS style rules are used as they are needed. In order to generate such an extensive style sheet, the authors had to think carefully about what styles they would need throughout the site, not just on one page, and consider how those rules would work together and affect each other when combined.

> A simple selector can have different *classes*, thus allowing the same element to have different styles. For example, an author may wish to display code in a different color depending on its language:
>
> ```
> code.html  { color:  #191970 }
> code.css   { color:  #4b0082 }
> ```
>
> The above example has created two classes, css and html for use with HTML's CODE element. The <u>CLASS</u> attribute is used in HTML to indicate the class of an element, *e.g.*,
>
> ```
> <P CLASS=warning>Only one class is allowed per selector.
> For example, code.html.proprietary is invalid.</p>
> ```

Figure 5   The CSS reference style sheet makes use of rules to differentiate between style sheet code and HTML markup.

Looking Ahead

Complex style sheets incorporate advanced box properties, manipulate white space, and use inheritance to control Web pages more tightly than do simple style sheets. Web designers can leverage their simple style sheets to create complex style sheets by combining inline and external style sheets, or by adding rules to existing simple style sheets. In *Do It In Color V*, we'll take a tour of the "Seven Style Sheet Wonders" found on the Web. We'll discuss how style sheets are used effectively on each site, and include both the complete style markup behind the sites and screen shots showing how the style sheets are implemented by a browser that supports CSS1.

GUIDED TOUR OF THE SEVEN STYLE SHEET WONDERS

Throughout this book, we've shown you how real-life Web sites have incorporated style sheets into their designs. In most cases, we've only shown you bits and pieces of the style sheets and HTML as they've related to the topic at hand. *Do It In Color III* and *Do It In Color IV* both included complete style sheets from actual sites to show you how simple and complex style sheets function as parts of Web sites. To give you an even better idea of how style sheets are working in many different ways in a variety of Web sites, we devote this final *Do It In Color* section to a guided tour of what we consider to be the "Seven Style Sheet Wonders" of the Web universe. This section is a true gallery of style sheets in action.

We used several different criteria in choosing the seven sites:

- Extensive use of style sheets throughout the site

- Syntactically correct style rules

- Using style sheets to enhance and promote the delivery of content

- Overall quality of page and site design

Because style sheets are a new technology, we had to choose from a small group of excellent sites,

and the decisions were difficult. Luckily, those site designers who have chosen to forge a path into the territory of this bleeding-edge technology have done so carefully and tastefully. For each site we include two screen shots of pages built using style sheets, a complete sampling of the style sheet code used to create the pages, and a short commentary on how style rules were used to create a certain effect.

You will notice as you visit each site that no two are alike in content or design techniques. Many of the style sheets use similar property and value combinations—margin and text rules abound. However, each site is unique in its use of style sheets, and we believe you can learn a great deal about integrating style sheets into your own Web site by studying the efforts of the designers portrayed throughout this section. We encourage you to visit each of these sites on your own and spend some time wandering their pages. The two screen shots we include only begin to convey the true style and beauty exhibited by each of these sites.

Join us now as we begin our journey through the "Seven Style Sheet Wonders" of the Web.

City Gallery

http://www.webcom.com/cityg/

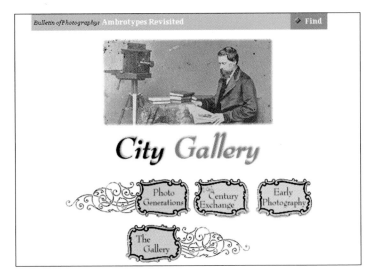

Figure 1 The City Gallery Web site.

The City Gallery site, shown in Figure 1, focuses on nineteenth-century portrait gallery and view photographs. Along with information about preserving pictures from this century, the site also includes several genealogy resources, and hosts a mailing list. The site uses tasteful graphics, in nineteenth-century style, and uses style sheets to define white space, margins, and font specifics.

To create the deep margins, font-type, and color effects shown in Figure 2, and other effects throughout the site, the City Gallery designer relied on the following inline style sheet:

```
body {
    background: #FFFFFF;
    margin-left: 5%;
    margin-right: 5%;
    font-family: Georgia, Times;
    font-size: 100%;
}

a:link {
    color: #804000;
    text-decoration: none;
}
```

```
a:visited {
   color: #807060;
   text-decoration: none;
}

a:active {
   color: red;
}

div.newsbanner {
  margin-left: 0%;
  margin-right: 0%;
}

div.newsbanner td {
   color: #00008B;
   font-size: 10pt;
   font-weight: light;
   font-family: Georgia;
   text-decoration: none;
}

div.newsbanner a:link {
   color: #FFFFF0;
   font-size: 100%;
   font-weight: bold;
   text-decoration: none;
}

div.newsbanner a:visited {
   color: #FFFFF0;
   font-size: 100%;
   font-weight: bold;
   text-decoration: none;
}

div.banner {
  background: #CCCC99;
  margin-left: 0%;
  margin-right: 0%;
  text-align: center;
}

div.banner td {
   color: #00008B;
   font-size: 10pt;
   font-weight: light;
   font-family: Georgia;
   text-decoration: none;
}

div.banner a:link {
   color: #FFFFF0;
   font-size: 100%;
```

```
   font-weight: bold;
   text-decoration: none;
}

strong { font-family: "Century Schoolbook";
font-style: italic; }

blockquote { font-size: 80% }

p.copyright { font-size: 60%; font-family:
Verdana }

hr { color: #CCCC99 }
```

Notice that the body style rule specifies the overall page text as Georgia, with an alternative of Times, and then defines Century Schoolbook and Verdana, respectively, for all strong tags and paragraphs of class copyright. The body rules also set right and left margins of 5 percent to indent the content of the entire page on both sides, while the div.banner rule specifies a division of class banner with a 0 percent margin, creating a banner that spans the width of the entire page. The banner across the top of the page, as shown in Figure 1, is affected by this style rule, so it is not indented like the rest of the page content. This causes the banner to stand out from the rest of the page and catch the reader's attention immediately.

The City Gallery site is well designed and uses correct style and HTML syntax. The style sheet we showed is just one of many incorporated in the City Gallery site. Each page has its own unique style sheet, which is called using the <LINK> tag. To view a complete listing of this excellent collection of style sheets, point your browser at **http:// www.webcom .com/cityg/StyleSheets/** and then click on any style sheet to view its source. If you spend a couple of hours at this site and observe how each style sheet is designed and implemented, you will learn many valuable lessons about creating and implementing style sheets.

City Gallery is dedicated to promoting the history of portrait gallery photographers and view publishers of the nineteenth-century and to the preservation and interpretation of their images, which overflowed family albums and brought the world into every parlor.

city-gallery.com
City Gallery Est. 1995
Steve Knoblock, Prop't

Join *PhotoGen*, the only mailing list devoted exclusively to *photography and genealogy*, bringing together experts in history of photography and archival matters with genealogists to encourage the preservation and interpretation of family photographs. (PhotoGenerations is the homepage of the PhotoGen (Photography and Genealogy mailing list).

The *19th Century Exchange* provides a forum for the sharing of information about nineteenth-century photography and society. Family photo-historians (genealogists) are encouraged to participate.

Figure 2 Margins and font specifics are just two of the page elements set using style rules at the City Gallery Web site.

Marketing Solutions

http://www.engaging.com/

Figure 3 Engaging Media's Marketing Solutions Web site.

In addition to providing a set of tools that includes articles, books, and software related to computing and marketing, Engaging Media created the Marketing Solutions Web site to promote its organization's services. Even though the site incorporates few graphics, it is nonetheless engaging (no pun intended) and visually appealing, due in large part to the use of style sheets.

In addition to an advanced use of tables to create a three-column page, as shown in Figure 3, the site's home page takes advantage of a large collection of style rules, which incorporate specific font types and color, and manipulate font sizes to emphasize text and create a visible information hierarchy. The gray and red text within the page directly follows the color scheme used in the graphical banner at the top of the page.

Subsequent pages, such as the Services page shown in Figure 4, also utilize style rules to create a series of type styles to be used with different kinds of information. Service-related information, such as the Consulting content shown in Figure 4, is rendered in red and black. The page also contains spotlight and comment information. This content, while different from the other infor-mation on the page, is still related to it. To include the two sets of content on the same page, a new style is created for the spotlight and comment headings, and all related text is included in a yellow box, separating it from the rest of the page.

Figure 4   Different styles not only convey like information, but also clearly separate disparate information.

All of the pages on the Marketing Solutions site reference the same external style sheet, enstyles.css:

```
<!-- enstyles.css Copyright 1996-1997 Engaging Media. All
rights reserved. ->

<STYLE TYPE="text/css">
```

```
BODY        {font: 10pt/11pt "Times New
            Roman";
            font-weight:  normal;
            color:        black}
A           {text-decoration: none}
A.ftp       {font: 8pt/11pt "Verdana";
            font-weight: bold;
            color: #009900}
A.home      {font: 8pt/11pt "Verdana";
            font-weight:  bold;
            color:        black}
A.L2        {font: 8pt/11pt "Verdana";
            font-weight:  bold;
            color:        #666666}
A.L3        {font: 8pt/11pt "Verdana";
            font-weight:  bold;
            color:        #CC0000}
A.leave     {color:        #009900}
A.mailto    {font: 8pt/11pt "Courier New";
            color:        #009900}
A.menu      {font: 8pt/8pt "Verdana";
            font-weight:  bold;
            color:        #CC0000}
A.msh       {font:  8pt/8pt "Verdana";
            font-weight:  bold;
            color:        #666666}
B           {font: 10pt/11pt "Times New
            Roman";
            font-weight:  bold;
            color:        black}
B.article   {font: 14pt/14pt "Verdana";
            font-weight:  bold;
            color:        black}
B.artsecthd {font: 13pt/14pt "Verdana";
            font-weight:  bold;
            color:        black}
B.award     {font: 18pt/18pt "Verdana";
            font-weight:  bold;
            color:        black}
B.colhead   {font: 9pt/9pt "Verdana";
            font-weight:  bold;
            color:        black}
B.con1      {font: 24pt/24pt "Verdana";
            font-weight:  bold;
            color:        #0000CC}
B.con2      {font: 18pt/18pt "Verdana";
            font-weight:  bold;
            color:        black}
B.formnum   {font: 18pt/18pt "Verdana";
            font-weight:  bold;
            color:        #0000CC}
B.h3        {font: 18pt/18pt "Verdana"
            font-weight:  bold;
            color:        black}


B.L1        {font: 8pt/11pt "Verdana";
            font-weight:  bold;
            color:        #999999}
B.subtopic  {font: 17pt/19pt "Verdana";
            font-weight:  bold;
            color:        black}
B.topic     {font: 20pt/22pt "Verdana";
            font-weight:  bold;
            color:        #0000CC}
EM.award    {font: 19pt/19pt "Times New
            Roman";
            font-weight:  normal;
            color:        black}
EM.subhead  {font: 21pt/21pt "Times New
            Roman";
            font-weight:  normal;
            color:        black}
H1.masthead {font: 51pt/51pt "Times New
             Roman";
            font-weight:  bold;
            color:        black}
H2          {font: 24pt/24pt "Verdana";
            font-weight:  bold;
            color:        black}
H2.L3       {font: 24pt/24pt "Verdana";
            font-weight:  bold;
            color:        #CC0000}
H3          {font: 18pt/18pt "Verdana";
            font-weight:  bold;
            color:        black}
H3.below    {font: 18pt/18pt "Verdana";
            font-weight:  bold;
            color:        #666666}
P.inside    {font: 40pt/40pt "Verdana";
            font-weight:  normal;
            color:        #999999}
P.menuhd    {font: 15pt/15pt "Verdana";
            font-weight:  normal;
            color:        #999999}
TT          {font: 12pt/13pt "Courier New";
            font-weight:  normal}
TT.screen   {font: 12pt/13pt "Courier New";
            font-weight:  normal;
            color:        #000000}
VAR.menuhd  {font: 18pt/18pt "Verdana";
            font-weight:  normal;
            color:        black}
VAR.small   {font: 9pt/11pt "Times New
            Roman";
            font-weight:  normal;
            color:        black}
</STYLE>
```

Notice that the style sheet is well organized and formatted for easy reading and modification. Because this site uses graphics sparingly, and instead relies on a single, linked style sheet to add color and design elements, the pages download quickly. This site is a prime example of how to incorporate style sheets into a Web site. It is Web design at its best.

Microsoft CSS Gallery

http://www.microsoft.com/typography/css/gallery/extract1.htm

The Microsoft CSS Gallery was created to show how different style sheets can make the same text look completely different. The gallery consists of several different Web pages, each with the exact same content within the <BODY>...</BODY> tags, but with different rules within the <STYLE>...</STYLE> tags. To show you the true impact of the site, we'll deviate from our standard tour format in this particular section to provide more room for screen shots and code, simply because they speak for themselves. Each screen shot is followed by the style sheet used to create it. Comparing style sheets and their final effects dramatizes the difference a style sheet can make when included as part of Web page design.

The following style sheet is used to generate the first exhibit in the Microsoft style sheet gallery:

```
BODY         { background: black;
               color: white;
               font-size: 80%; }
.contrast    { background: cornsilk }
P            { color: black;
               font-size: 80%;
               margin-left: 15%;
               margin-right: 20%;
               font-family: Verdana, Arial, Helvetica, helv,
               sans-serif }
H1, H2, H3 { font-size: 180%;
               margin-left: 10%;
               margin-right: 20%;
               font-weight: medium;
               color: coral;
               font-family: Comic Sans MS, Arial, Helvetica,
               helv, sans-serif }
```

TIPS FROM A DESIGN EXPERT

Kirk Mahoney, the principal at Engaging Media and the designer of this amazing site, offers the following tidbits of advice to Web designers:

- A font's width may vary across platforms for a given browser, as well as between browsers. If you have text that must be of a certain width, you may need to convert that text to an image (e.g., to a low-bit-depth GIF file).

- Help your visitors see your site at its best. Tell them how to get the fonts that your site uses!

- Spread the news about the bandwidth savings of style sheets. Point visitors to sites with CSS info!

```
.descript   { color: silver;           .section2   { margin-right: 10% }
            margin-left: 10%;         H1, H3      { font-size: 120%;
            margin-right: 10%;                    margin-left: 10%;
            font-family: Verdana, Arial,          margin-right: 20%;
            Helvetica, helv, sans-serif }         font-weight: medium;
A:link      { color: coral;                       color: azure;
            font-weight: bold;                    font-family: Impact, Arial,
            text-decoration: none; }              Helvetica, helv, sans-serif }
A:visited   { color: purple;          H2          { font-size: 120%;
            font-weight: bold;                    margin-left: 20%;
            text-decoration: none; }              margin-right: 20%;
.topline    {color: silver;                       font-weight: medium;
            margin-left: 10%;                     color: azure;
            margin-right: 10%;                    font-family: Impact, Arial,
            font-size: 80%;                       Helvetica, helv, sans-serif }
            font-family: Verdana, Arial, A:link    { color: coral;
            Helvetica, helv, sans-serif }         font-weight: bold;
                                                  text-decoration: none; }
                                      A:visited   { color: purple;
                                                  font-weight: bold;
                                                  text-decoration: none; }
                                      .descript   { color: silver;
                                                  font-size: 80%;
                                                  margin-left: 10%;
                                                  margin-right: 20%;
                                                  font-family: Verdana, Arial,
                                                  Helvetica, helv, sans-serif }
                                      .topline    {color: silver;
                                                  margin-left: 10%;
                                                  margin-right: 10%;
                                                  font-size: 80%;
                                                  font-family: Verdana, Arial,
                                                  Helvetica, helv, sans-serif }
```

Figure 5 Microsoft Gallery Exhibit 1.

This style sheet is used to generate the second exhibit in the Microsoft style sheet gallery:

```
BODY        { background: black;
            color: white }
.contrast   { background: darkblue }
P           { color: white;
            font-size: 100%;
            margin-left: 20%;
            margin-right: 20%;
            font-family: Arial, Helvetica,
            helv, sans-serif }
.credit     { margin-left: 10% }
.opening    { margin-left: 10% }
.section3   { margin-left: 10% }
```

Figure 6 Microsoft Gallery Exhibit 2.

This style sheet is used to generate the third exhibit in the Microsoft style sheet gallery:

```
BODY        { background: black;
            color: white }
P           { color: black;
            text-indent: 20%;
            font-family: Comic Sans MS,
            Verdana, Arial, Helvetica, helv,
            sans- serif }
H1 {        color: white;
            margin-left: 5%;
            font-weight: medium;
            font-family: Arial Black, Arial,
            Helvetica, helv, sans-serif }
.contrast   { background: darkorange; }
.opening    { font-size: 55%;
            margin-left: 10%;
            margin-right: 50%; }
H2 {        color: white;
            margin-left: 25%;
            font-weight: medium;
            font-family: Arial Black, Arial,
            Helvetica, helv, sans-serif }
.section2   { font-size: 55%;
            margin-left: 30%;
            margin-right: 30%; }
H3 {        color: white;
            margin-left: 45%;
            font-weight: medium;
            font-family: Arial Black, Arial,
            Helvetica, helv, sans-serif }
.section3   { font-size: 55%;
            margin-left: 50%;
            margin-right: 10%; }
.credit     { margin-top: 5px;
            font-size: 90%;
            font-weight: bold;
            text-indent: 0;
            margin-left: 10%;
            margin-right: 20%; }
.descript   {text-indent: 0;
            color: silver;
            margin-left: 10%;
            margin-right: 20%;
            font-size: 80%;
            font-family: Verdana, Arial,
            Helvetica, helv, sans-serif }
A:link      { color: coral;
            font-weight: bold;
            text-decoration: none; }
```

```
A:visited   { color: purple;
            font-weight: bold;
            text-decoration: none; }
.topline    {color: silver;
            text-indent: 0;
            margin-left: 10%;
            margin-right: 10%;
            font-size: 80%;
            font-family: Verdana, Arial,
            Helvetica, helv, sans-serif }
```

Figure 7 Microsoft Gallery Exhibit 3.

This style sheet is used to generate the fourth exhibit in the Microsoft style sheet gallery:

```
BODY        { background: black;
            color: white; }
.contrast   { background: red }
P           { color: white;
            font-size: 90%;
            text-indent: -5%;
            font-weight: bold;
            font-family: Verdana, Arial,
            Helvetica, helv, sans-serif }
H1, H2, H3 { color: black;
            margin-top: -20px;
            margin-left: 5%;
            font-size: 300%
            font-weight: bold;
            font-style: italic;
            font-family: Times New Roman,
            Times, serif }
I           { background: black }
```

```
.opening    { margin-left: 10%;
              margin-right: 10%; }
.section2   { margin-left: 10%;
              margin-right: 35%; }
.section3   { margin-left: 35%;
              margin-right: 10%; }
.credit     { margin-top: 5px;
              font-size: 90%;
              text-indent: 0;
              margin-left: 10%;
              margin-right: 20%; }
.descript   { margin-top: 5px;
              text-indent: 0;
              color: silver;
              margin-left: 10%;
              margin-right: 20%;
              font-size: 80%;
              font-family: Verdana, Arial,
              Helvetica, helv, sans-serif }
A:link      { color: coral;
              font-weight: bold;
              text-decoration: none; }
A:visited   { color: purple;
              font-weight: bold;
              text-decoration: none; }
.topline    {color: silver;
              font-weight: medium;
              margin-left: 10%;
              margin-right: 10%;
              font-size: 80%;
              font-family: Verdana, Arial,
              Helvetica, helv, sans-serif }
```

Figure 8 Microsoft Gallery Exhibit 4.

This style sheet is used to generate the fifth exhibit in the Microsoft style sheet gallery:

```
BODY        { background: black;
              color: white; }
.contrast   { background: darkgreen }
P           { color: lime;
              font-size: 90%;
              font-weight: bold;
              font-family: Arial, Helvetica,
              helv, sans-serif }
H1          { color: cornsilk;
              margin-left: 10%;
              font-size: 190%
              font-weight: bold;
              font-style: italic;
              font-family: Arial, Helvetica,
              helv, sans-serif }
H2          { color: cornsilk;
              margin-left: 10%;
              font-size: 190%
              font-weight: bold;
              font-style: italic;
              font-family: Arial, Helvetica,
              helv, sans-serif }
H3          { color: cornsilk;
              margin-left: 10%;
              font-size: 190%
              font-weight: bold;
              font-style: italic;
              font-family: Arial, Helvetica,
              helv, sans-serif }
.opening    { text-indent: -20%;
              margin-left: 30%;
              margin-right: 10%; }
.section2   { color: limegreen;
              text-indent: 20%;
              margin-left: 10%;
              margin-right: 10%; }
.section3   { color: lime;
              text-indent: -10%;
              margin-left: 30%;
              margin-right: 10%; }
.credit     { color: limegreen;
              margin-top: -15px;
              font-size: 90%;
              text-indent: 0;
              margin-left: 10%;
              margin-right: 20%; }
```

```
.descript    { margin-top: 5px;
               text-indent: 0;
               color: silver;
               margin-left: 10%;
               margin-right: 20%;
               font-size: 80%;
               font-family: Verdana, Arial,
               Helvetica, helv, sans-serif }
A:link       { color: coral;
               font-weight: bold;
               text-decoration: none; }
A:visited    { color: purple;
               font-weight: bold;
               text-decoration: none; }
.topline     {color: silver;
               font-weight: medium;
               margin-left: 10%;
               margin-right: 10%;
               font-size: 80%;
               font-family: Verdana, Arial,
               Helvetica, helv, sans-serif }
```

Figure 9   Microsoft Gallery Exhibit 5.

This style sheet is used to generate the sixth exhibit
in the Microsoft style sheet gallery:

```
BODY         { background: black;
               color: white; }
.contrast    { background: lightpink }
P            { color: black;
               font-size: 90%;
               margin-left: 20%;
               margin-right: 20%;
```

```
               font-weight: bold;
               font-family: Courier New; fixed-
               pitch }
H1, H2, H3   { color: cornsilk;
               margin-left: 10%;
               font-size: 60px;
               font-weight: bold;
               font-style: italic;
               font-family: Courier New; fixed-
               pitch }
.credit      { color: black;
               font-size: 90%;
               margin-left: 10%;
               margin-right: 20%; }
.descript    { margin-top: 5px;
               text-indent: 0;
               color: silver;
               margin-left: 10%;
               margin-right: 20%;
               font-size: 80%;
               font-family: Verdana, Arial,
               Helvetica, helv, sans-serif }
A:link       { color: coral;
               font-weight: bold;
               text-decoration: none; }
A:visited    { color: purple;
               font-weight: bold;
               text-decoration: none; }
.topline     {color: silver;
               margin-left: 10%;
               margin-right: 10%;
               font-size: 80%;
               font-family: Verdana, Arial,
               Helvetica, helv, sans-serif }
```

Figure 10   Microsoft Gallery Exhibit 6.

The Richmond Review

http://www.demon.co.uk/review/

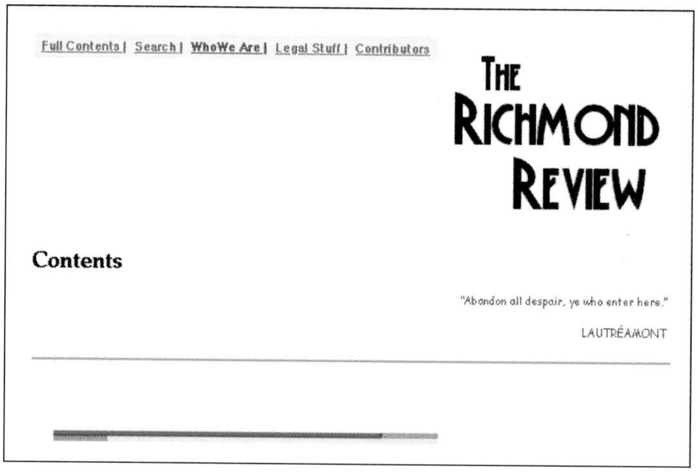

Figure 11   The Richmond Review online literary magazine.

The Richmond Review, created by Steven Kelly, is an online liter-ary magazine based in the U.K. The site's use of style sheets provides an example not only of how style sheets improve page design, but of how a single style sheet can be used to format mate-rials submitted by different authors. All of the site's pages are governed by the same style sheet, images/style0.css, and use both the <LINK> and @import techniques to include the style sheet into the site pages. In addition to this single style sheet, many of the pages, like the home page shown in Figure 11, also include page-specific style embedded between <STYLE> ... </STYLE> tags. The following code from the home page is used to reference the external style sheet and include the page specific styles:

```
<LINK REL=STYLESHEET TYPE="text/css"
      HREF="images/style0.css" TITLE="style0">

    <STYLE TYPE="text/css">

<!--     @import url(images/style0.css);
    H1 { color: blue }
    BODY { background: white }
    TABLE { background: url(images/tabback.gif) repeat
white }
 -->

    </STYLE>
```

All of the site's pages use the same unique hard rule to divide sections of information, and the color scheme and style established on the home page is carried through from page to page. Each page ends with two very nice, tasteful graphics, as shown in Figure 12.

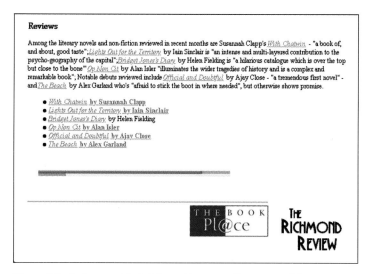

Figure 12   Unique and tasteful graphics grace the pages of the Richmond Review.

Style sheets play a vital role in ensuring consistency from one page to the next within the site. Many different authors and reviewers contribute to the site. Each has his or her own style, and given the opportunity, would most likely create a wide variety of Web pages. Figures 13 and 14 show how the site's general style sheet, whose code follows, helps two different pages created by two authors maintain the site's look and feel.

```
BODY          { font-family: "Times New Roman";
              color: black;
              background: white;
              margin-left: 3%;
              margin-right: 3%
              }

DIV.header    { font-family: "Comic Sans MS";
              color: #8B008B;
              background: transparent
              }
```

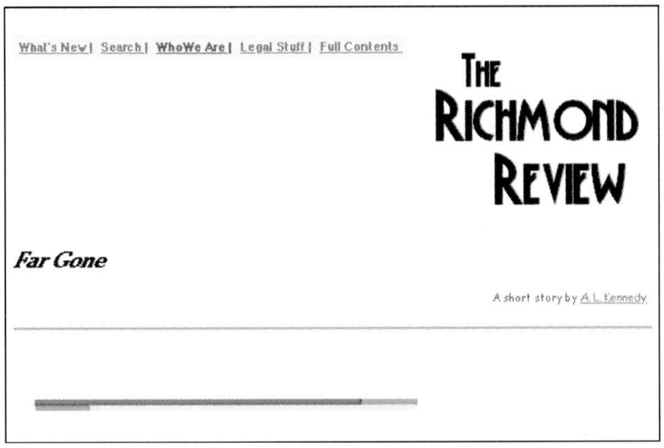

Figure 13

Figure 14

These two pages from the Richmond Review contain different content but still conform to the site's overall look and feel.

```
DIV.content    { font-family: "Times New
               Roman";
               color: black;
               background: transparent
               }

CITE.edit      { font-weight: bold;
               color: black;
               background: transparent }

HR             { color: #FF8C00;
               background: transparent
               }

HR.sub         { color: #6495ED;
               background: transparent
               }

A:link         { color: #7B68EE;
               background: transparent;
               font-weight: bold
               }

A:visited      { color: #B22222;
               background: transparent
               }

H1, H2, H3, H4   { color: black;
               background: transparent;
               font-family: Futurist
               }
```

```
SPAN.mailto    { color: #3CB371;
               background: transparent
               }

SPAN.isbn      { font-weight: bold
               }

TABLE          { font-family: Helvetica;
               background: url(tabback.gif)
               repeat
               }

.author        { font-weight: bold;
               color: black;
               background: transparent
               }
```

Not only are the stories and reviews at the Richmond Review intriguing and a good read, but an appropriate and well-implemented style sheet enhances the content while maintaining a consistent reading environment.

The Department Of Typography And Graphic Communication, The University of Reading

http://www.rdg.ac.uk/AcaDepts/lt/web/msie/index.htm

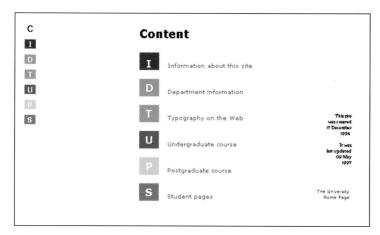

Figure 15   The Department of Typography and Graphic Communication at the University of Reading's Web site.

Believe it or not, the entire Web page pictured in Figures 15 and 16 consists of text rendered using style rules. No images were used to create this very graphical layout. The Department of Typography and Graphic Communication at the University of Reading uses the following advanced style sheet to create blocks of color and closely control the positioning of elements within the page.

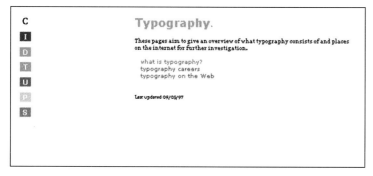

Figure 16   The site's color scheme is maintained by both the navigation tool and textual headings.

```
A.normal      {
        margin-right: 10pt;
        margin-left: 00pt;
        font-weight: normal;
        font-style: normal;
        font-size: 10pt;
        line-height: 12pt;
        font-family: Georgia, serif;
        }
A.normalsmall      {
        margin-right: 10pt;
        margin-left: 0pt;
        font-weight: normal;
        font-style: normal;
        font-size: 8pt;
        line-height: 10pt;
        font-family: Georgia, serif;
        }
A.content      {
        margin-right: 10pt;
        margin-left: 30pt;
        font-weight: normal;
        font-style: normal;
        font-size: 12pt;
        line-height: 16pt;
        font-family: Georgia, serif;
        }
A.link      {
        margin-right: 10pt;
        margin-left: 10pt;
        text-decoration: none;
        font-weight: normal;
        font-style: normal;
        font-size: 10pt;
        line-height: 12pt;
        font-family: Verdana, sans-serif;
        }
A.smalllink      {
        margin-right: 10pt;
        margin-left: 10pt;
        text-decoration: none;
        font-weight: normal;
        font-style: normal;
        font-size: 10pt;
        line-height: 12pt;
        font-family: Verdana, sans-serif;
        }
A.vsmalllink      {
        margin-right: 10pt;
        margin-left: 10pt;
        text-decoration: none;
        font-weight: normal;
        font-style: normal;
        font-size: 8pt;
        line-height: 10pt;
        font-family: Verdana, sans-serif;
        }
A.linktext      {
        margin-right: 10pt;
        margin-left: 0pt;
        text-decoration: none;
        font-weight: normal;
        font-style: normal;
        font-size: 10pt;
        line-height: 12pt;
        font-family: Verdana, sans-serif;
        }
A.Address      {
        text-decoration: none;
        margin-right: 20pt;
        margin-left: 20pt;
        font-weight: normal;
        font-style: normal;
        font-size: 10pt;
        line-height: 14pt;
        font-family: Verdana, sans-serif;
        }
A.H5      {
        margin-right: 10pt;
        margin-left: 0pt;
        font-weight: bold;
        font-style: normal;
        font-size: 12pt;
        line-height: 20pt;
        font-family: Verdana, sans-serif;
        }
A.H6      {
        font-weight: bold;
        font-style: normal;
        font-size: 10pt;
        line-height: 14pt;
        font-family: Verdana, sans-serif;
        }
A.maptitle      {
        font-weight: bold;
        font-style: normal;
        font-size: 8pt;
        line-height: 10pt;
        font-family: Verdana, sans-serif;
        }
A.navtitle      {
```

```
        margin-right: 20pt;
        margin-left: 0pt;
        color: black;
        text-decoration: none;
        font-weight: bold;
        font-style: normal;
        font-size: 13pt;
        line-height: 17pt;
        font-family: Verdana, sans-serif;
    }
H2    {
        text-decoration: none;
        margin-right: 10pt;
        margin-left: 0pt;
        font-weight: normal;
        font-style: normal;
        font-size: 15pt;
        line-height: 17pt;
        font-family: Verdana, sans-serif;
    }
H3    {
        text-decoration: none;
        margin-right: 10pt;
        margin-left: 0pt;
        font-weight: normal;
        font-style: normal;
        font-size: 12pt;
        line-height: 14pt;
        font-family: Verdana, sans-serif;
    }
H1    {
        text-decoration: none;
        margin-right: 10pt;
        margin-left: 00pt;
        font-weight: normal;
        font-style: normal;
        font-size: 20pt;
        line-height: 24pt;
        font-family: Verdana, sans-serif;
    }
A.header    {
        text-decoration: none;
        margin-right: 10pt;
        margin-left: 0pt;
        font-weight: bold;
        font-style: normal;
        font-size: 20pt;
        line-height: 24pt;
        font-family: Verdana, sans-serif;
    }
```

```
A.contentT    {
        text-decoration: none;
        margin-right: 50pt;
        margin-left: 10pt;
        font-weight: normal;
        font-style: normal;
        font-size: 10pt;
        line-height: 10pt;
        font-family: Georgia, serif;
    }
A.cap    {
        text-decoration: none;
        color: white;
        font-weight: bold;
        font-style: normal;
        font-size: 18 pt;
        line-height: 20pt;
        font-family: Verdana, sans-serif;
    }
A.navcap    {
        text-decoration: none;
        color: white;
        font-weight: bold;
        font-style: normal;
        font-size: 13 pt;
        font-family: Verdana, sans-serif;
    }
A.navcapC    {
        text-decoration: none;
        color: black;
        font-weight: bold;
        font-style: normal;
        font-size: 15 pt;
        font-family: Verdana, sans-serif;
    }
```

The site uses tables and frames to create a clean and easily navigable layout. All of the pages within the site, such as the Typography top page, shown back in Figure 16, use this external style sheet, main.css, to ensure a consistent look and feel. The color scheme established at the home page and continually displayed in the navigation bar in the left frame of the screen is carried through the entire site. The typography block is orange, so all headings associated with typography are orange as well. Thanks to the color cues, users never have to wonder what section they are in.

As well as being a fine example of how good style rules are written and implemented, this site shows how style sheets provide for unique text displays without resorting to needless graphics and image maps.

Virtually Boston

http://www.vboston.com/vb-about.htm

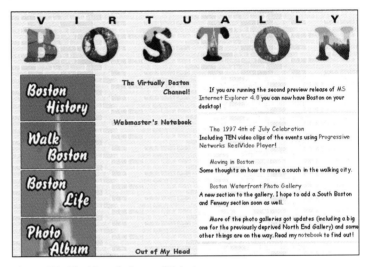

Figure 17 The Virtually Boston Web site.

Virtually Boston, shown in Figure 17, is a site dedicated to all things Bostonian. Although the content is regionally focused, the site style and style sheets provide valuable lessons to any Web designer, regardless of the content they have to convey. The site makes excellent use of white space and a charming but unobtrusive background to focus the reader's attention. The site's graphics are cohesive and obviously designed to complement one another as well as the site's content.

Style rules are used to set margins and specify font type and color. The following external style sheet is referenced by all the site's pages using the **<LINK>** tag:

```
body        {font: 10pt Comic Sans MS;
            font-weight: normal;
            text-decoration: none}
```

```
p               {font-size: 10pt}
p.indent               {font-size: 10pt;
                        text-indent: 0.25in}

p.bold                 {font-size: 10pt;
                        font-weight: bold}
p.boldindent           {font-size: 10pt;
                        font-weight: bold;
                        text-indent: 0.25in}

p.quote                {font-size: 12pt}

p.quoteindent          {font-size: 12pt;
                        text-indent: 0.25in}
dt                     {font-size: 12pt}

dd                     {font-size: 10pt}

dt.small               {font-size: 10pt}

dd.small               {font-size: 9pt}

h1                     {font-size: 17pt}

h2                     {font-size: 15pt}

h3                     {font-size: 12pt}

h4                     {font-size: 10pt}

li                     {font-size: 10pt}
```

This style sheet, although shorter and less complex than many we've seen in this section, completes the site's design by adding the necessary font and margin rules. This proves that a style sheet doesn't have to be long and complicated to be effective. Because all of the pages in the site use this style sheet, the site's look and feel is carried through each page, including the "About Virtually Boston" page shown in Figure 18.

Note that about midway through the page is a list of the tools the site uses, what software is necessary to make use of the site, and links to related sources. At the bottom of the "About" page is a short paragraph explaining how to use the Comic Sans font and pointing users to where they can download the font for free. Both of these information blocks are excellent examples of how to make your style sheet-enhanced pages more accessible to your readers without hitting them over the head with "download this" messages on every page.

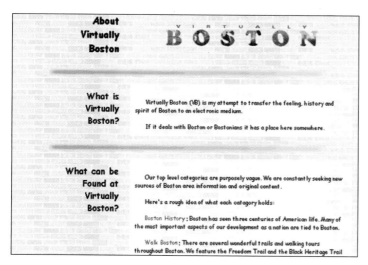

Figure 18 Style sheets allow siets' look and feel to be easily maintained.

The World Wide Web Consortium (W3C) Style Sheets Pages

http://www.w3.org/Style/

We've visited this site many times already, but we would be remiss if we didn't also include it in this section. This site is truly a style sheet wonder, if not *the* style sheet wonder. Not only is it well designed, and makes copious use of style sheets in the design, but it is also the leading repository for the latest information on all things style-related. We've commented often enough on the site, and the full listing of its code is available in Chapter 4. However, we haven't had a chance to show it to you in full color, and that's at least half the fun of it. So, to close this color section, we offer these two final screen shots of style sheets in action—found at the home of style sheets themselves.

W3C
Web Style Sheets
What's new?
What are style sheets?
Press clippings
Styled software
CSS

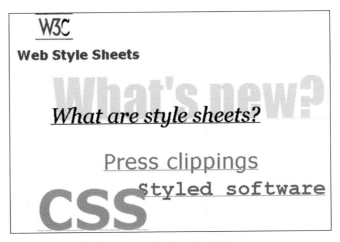

Figure 19 Style sheet examples from the W3C.

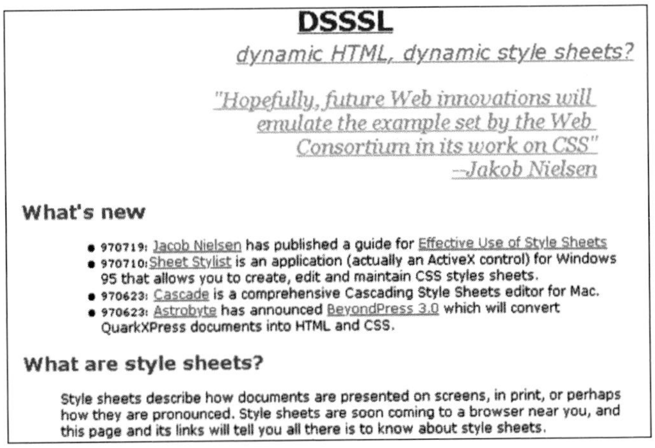

DSSSL
dynamic HTML, dynamic style sheets?
"Hopefully, future Web innovations will emulate the example set by the Web Consortium in its work on CSS"
--Jakob Nielsen
What's new
970719: Jacob Nielsen has published a guide for Effective Use of Style Sheets
970710: Sheet Stylist is an application (actually an ActiveX control) for Windows 95 that allows you to create, edit and maintain CSS styles sheets.
970623: Cascade is a comprehensive Cascading Style Sheets editor for Mac.
970623: Astrobyte has announced BeyondPress 3.0 which will convert QuarkXPress documents into HTML and CSS.
What are style sheets?
Style sheets describe how documents are presented on screens, in print, or perhaps how they are pronounced. Style sheets are soon coming to a browser near you, and this page and its links will tell you all there is to know about style sheets.

Figure 20 The W3C style sheets pages.

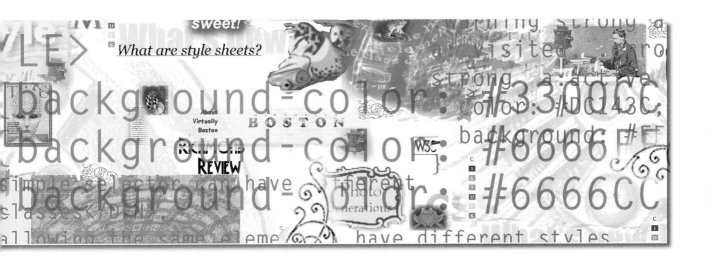

MANAGING

FONT

PROPERTIES

8

In this chapter:

- **The many faces of fonts**

- **Adding style to fonts**

- **Regulating font weight**

- **Font variances**

A standard dictionary defines a font as the complete set of type of one size and face. Using this definition, Times Roman 10-point is a font and Times Roman 12-point is a different font. However, the modern vernacular of computing defines a font by its typeface, not size. Therefore, Times Roman, Times Roman Bold, Times Roman Italic, and Courier are all different fonts. However, Times Roman 12 and Times Roman 18 are not considered different fonts.

CSS1 specifies five font properties you can set—**font family**, **font style**, **font variant**, **font weight**, and **font size**. In addition, the **font** property lets you specify the family, size, style, variant, and line-height in a single line of code. With these properties, you can specify virtually every aspect of the fonts you want your Web site to display. Of course, the user can instruct his or her browser to override your font specifications, but at least you can design your site's text to look the way you desire.

Beyond Times And Courier

The Times font is probably the most commonly used font in newspapers around the world written in languages using Arabic letters. It was designed to be easily read in a variety of sizes. Courier was used for decades as the primary font of manual and electric typewriters. It is still widely used today as the main nonproportionally spaced font in many word processing programs. The following two lines show samples of the Times New Roman and Courier fonts:

This is an example of the Times New Roman font.

```
This is an example of the Courier font.
```

The following HTML code shows the use of the **font family** and **font style** properties to accomplish the font displayed in Figure 8.1. As you can see, it's quite simple.

```
<HTML>
<HEAD>
<STYLE TYPE ="text/css">
BODY { font-family: Times }
em { font-family: Courier }
em {font-style: normal }
</Style>
</HEAD>
<BODY>

This is an example of the Times font.<p>

<em>This is an example of the Courier font.</em>

</BODY>
</HTML>
```

Properties

For the vast majority of Web sites, the most useful style sheet
property is the ability to set font properties. Unfortunately, no
standard set of font names or terms to describe fonts exists. For
example, *italic* is commonly used to describe a font style in which
the text is slanted from left to right. However the terms, *oblique,
slanted, incline*, and *cursive* may also be applied to the same
slanted text. For this reason, reliably mapping font selection
properties to a specific font is virtually impossible. CSS1 attempts
to use the **font family**, **font style**, **font variant**, and **font weight**
properties to describe a font well enough to enable your viewer's
browser to display the text on your Web site in the font you

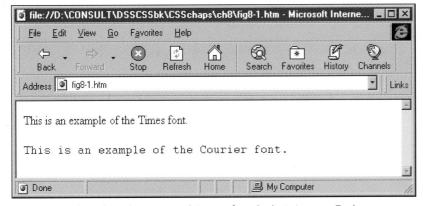

Figure 8.1 This is how the Times and Courier fonts look via Internet Explorer.

specify, if the user's system contains the font; or in a font reasonably close to the one you have in mind. In this case, close counts. So, read on to learn how to use style sheets to accomplish this font magic...er, matching.

Font Matching

Lacking a universal font description system, CSS1 proceeds in a strictly defined order when attempting to match the font you describe with the fonts available on your viewer's Web browser. This process is detailed in the CSS1 section 5.2.1, "Font Matching." Following is a brief summary of the steps it takes:

1. The browser creates a database of the CSS1 properties of all the fonts it can find on the user's computer system. It then checks the properties of the characters in each element that it tries to display in order to arrive at a font family to use for that particular element.

2. It tries **font style**.

3. It tries **font variant**.

4. It tries **font weight**, which never fails because it is a relative scale value.

5. It tries **font size**, which must match within a margin of error set by the browser.

So much for the fly-by look at how the browser attempts to carry out your orders. The following sections show you how to give these orders to the browser via your HTML and style sheets, and how your orders may be displayed by a browser, Internet Explorer in this case.

Font Family

You can assign font families by using the specific font name or by referring to the generic font family. Of course, you won't match a specific font as easily as a generic font family. However, you can assign multiple families in the same statement, separated by commas, so that if the specific font is not available, a close match will be made by the generic family. A simple font family declaration to set the body text font to Times New Roman, Times, or any serif font would look like this:

```
P { font-family: "Times New Roman", Times, serif }
```

The first two assignments are specific type faces. Place all font names containing white space within quotation marks. The generic *serif* font family is listed last, in the event that the user's browser does not have access to either of the other font families. You may also use the **font family** property within the **font** property.

The initial value for each font is determined by the user's browser and applies to all elements, except replaced elements. The **font family** property is inherited. Any specific font name is allowed. The following generic font families are recognized by the **font family** property: serif, sans serif, monospace, cursive, and fantasy.

```
<HTML>
<HEAD>
</HEAD>
<BODY>

<H1> Heading 1 </H1>
<H2> Heading 2 </H2>
<H3> Heading 3 </H3>
<H4> Heading 4 </H4>
<H5> Heading 5 </H5>

</BODY>
</HTML>
```

The following HTML code shows the use of standard headings to accomplish the display in Figure 8.2.

The following HTML code shows the use of the **font family** property to enhance the fonts used in the headings in the display in Figure 8.3.

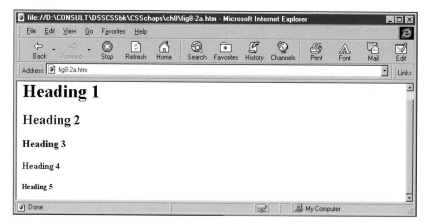

Figure 8.2 This is how standard headings look via Internet Explorer.

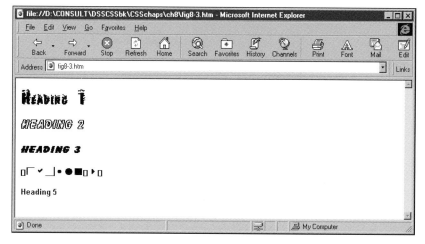

Figure 8.3 This is how the headings look with different font families via Internet Explorer.

```
<HTML>
<HEAD>
<STYLE TYPE ="text/css">
H1 { font-family:    crackling}
H2 { font-family:   "Cartoon hollow"}
H3 { font-family:   "Cartoon wide"}
H4 { font-family:    fantasy}
H5 { font-family:    Helvetica, sans-serif}</Style>
</HEAD>
<BODY>

<H1> Heading 1 </H1>
<H2> Heading 2 </H2>
<H3> Heading 3 </H3>
<H4> Heading 4 </H4>
<H5> Heading 5 </H5>
```

```
</BODY>
</HTML>
```

The difference is striking, even in this small example. Notice that H4 uses a generic fantasy font family that lacks a character set useful for standard text. This should be a reminder to you that if you want your Web site to be widely viewed, always test your style sheets on several different computers.

Although choosing an appropriate font family for your style sheet will go a long way toward making your Web site more exciting, you can also use the **font style** property to add even more interest to your text.

Font Style

Use the **font style** property to define a font as *normal, italic,* or *oblique*. Most of us can't differentiate between italic and oblique fonts unless they are next to one another. They both slant to the right (top to the right). However, in the wonderful non-classification system, some fonts are grouped in the generic style of *italic* or *cursive* while others are called *oblique, slanted,* or *inclined*.

To further confuse the situation, if your style sheet requests the italic font style, you will get italic if it is available or oblique if the font family doesn't have an italic style. However, if you request oblique and the font family doesn't have an oblique style available, you will not get the italic style. Instead, you will get the next closest family with an oblique style. Got that? To be safe, always use italic when you want a slanted style and you'll have a higher probability of getting what you asked for, or something close within the same font family.

The initial value of the **font style** property is *normal*. It applies to all elements and is inherited. The format of a sample style sheet with font style declarations will look similar to this:

```
<HTML>
<HEAD>
<STYLE TYPE ="text/css">
```

```
H1 { font-family: Helvetica, sans-serif}
H1 { font-style: italic}
BODY { font-family: "Times New Roman", Times, serif}
Body { font-style: normal}
em { font-family: "Times New Roman", Times, serif}
em {font-style: italic}
</Style>
</HEAD>
<BODY>

<H1> This heading uses the italic font style
   with the Helvetica font family.</H1>

This text is an example of the Times New Roman font
family
   using normal font style.<p>

<em>This text is an example of the Times New Roman font
family
   using italic font style.</em>
</BODY>
</HTML >
```

The HTML code in the preceding example shows the use of the **font style** property to accomplish the font display in Figure 8.4.

Font Variant

The **font variant** property lets you display a font in small caps within its font family. Small caps look like capital letters that have been reduced to 75 percent to 80 percent of their normal size. However, they are actually quite different. Simply reducing

Figure 8.4 This is how the font styles in the preceding sample code look via Internet Explorer.

capital letters tends to produce thin-looking characters, and it is time-consuming to define in HTML. Using the small caps **font variant** property in your style sheets is a quick and easy way to produce the desired effect, providing you choose an appropriate font family. The initial value of font variant is *normal.* It applies to all elements and is inherited.

Small caps are particularly useful in headings, as shown in the following example:

```
<HTML>
<HEAD>
<STYLE TYPE ="text/css">
H1 H2 H3 body {font-variant: small-caps}
</Style>
</HEAD>
<BODY>
Headings and body text in small caps.
<H1> Heading 1 </H1>
<H2> Heading 2 </H2>
<H3> Heading 3 </H3>
</BODY>
</HTML >
```

The HTML code in the preceding example shows the use of the **font** variant property to accomplish the font display in Figure 8.5.

Not all font families contain a small caps variant, nor do all browsers respond to the **font variant** property. You would be wise to think twice before using this widely. Although the font variant

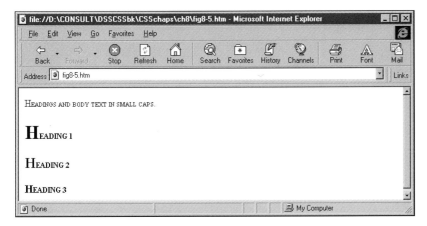

Figure 8.5   This is how the font styles in the preceding sample code look via Internet Explorer.

of small caps is useful in special instances, the **font weight** property will come in handy for making gradient darkness changes in your text.

Font Weight

The **font weight** property is great when you want to specify the weight (degree of darkness) of the font family you are using. This property allows the use of nine numeric values (100 to 900), two familiar values (normal = 400 and bold = 700), and two relative values (lighter and bolder). Not all font families contain nine possible weights; therefore, some browsers use the nearest available weight, with the 100 to 300 weights replacing lighter first, and the 600 to 900 weights replacing darker first.

The initial value of font weight is *normal.* It applies to all elements and is inherited. The following code shows an example of several different font weights and how they can help perk up your Web site:

```
<HTML>
<HEAD>
<STYLE TYPE ="text/css">
em {font-weight: 100}
b {font-weight: 700}
strong{font-weight: 900}
</Style>
</HEAD>
<BODY>
This is standard body text.<p>
<em>This is font-weight 100.</em><p>
<b>This is font-weight 700 (aka bold).</b><p>
<strong>This is font-weight 900.</strong>
</BODY>
</HTML>
```

The HTML code in the preceding example shows the use of the **font weight** property to accomplish the font display in Figure 8.6.

You can couple the **font weight** property with the **font size** property to produce many different effects within the same font family.

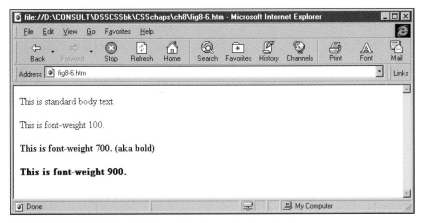

Figure 8.6 This is how the font styles in the preceding sample code look via Internet Explorer.

Font Size

The **font size** property gives you four options for value types in changing the size of your displayed font. You can use an *absolute size*, a *relative size*, a *length*, or a *percentage* to set the **font size** property. Each of these font size values accepts a number or set of keywords as subvalues. The initial value is *medium*. It is applied to all elements and is inherited. When using percentages, remember that they are calculated relative to the parent's font size.

Absolute Size Value

The seven recognized values for absolute size—xx-small, x-small, small, medium, large, x-large, and xx-large—are based on the medium version of each font, with a factor of up to 1.5 times the previous size. The browser calculates a table of absolute size values based on the available sizes for a given font family, then applies the corresponding size when you use x-small, large, and so on. You can include these in your style sheets in a manner similar to the following example:

```
<HTML>
<HEAD>
<STYLE TYPE ="text/css">
H1{font-size: xx-large}
body {font-size: large}
H2 {font-size: x-large}
```

```
</Style>
</HEAD>
<BODY>
<H1>This is xx-large H1.</H1>
This is large size body text.
<H2>This is x-large H2.</H2>
</body>
</HTML>
```

The HTML code in the preceding example shows the use of the absolute size value of the **font size** property to accomplish the font display in Figure 8.7.

Relative Size Value

The relative size value allows you to set the font size relative to the element's parent size. You can do this using one of two allowed key words, *larger* or *smaller*. The amount of *larger* or *smaller* is determined by the absolute size table set up by the browser. Therefore, if the parent element is *body* and the body size is *medium*, the larger setting will be *large* and the smaller setting will

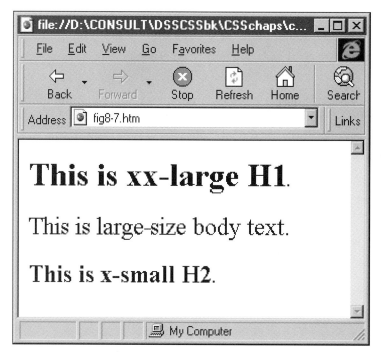

Figure 8.7 This is how the font styles in the preceding sample code look via Internet Explorer.

be *small*. These are one value larger and one value smaller than the parent size of the body element. The relative size value is useful for ensuring that certain elements in your HTML document remain larger or smaller than their parent elements, thereby keeping the proportions of your document the same, regardless of the font size:

```
<HTML>
<HEAD>
<STYLE TYPE ="text/css">
H3{font-size: larger}
body {font-size: medium}
H4 {font-size: smaller}
</Style>
</HEAD>
<BODY>
<H3>This H3 is larger relative size.</H3>
This is the parent body element of medium size.
<H4>This H4 is smaller relative size.</H4>
</body>
</HTML>
```

The HTML code in the preceding example shows the use of the relative size value of the **font size** property to accomplish the font display in Figure 8.8. Figure 8.9 shows what the three lines of HTML look like under normal circumstances.

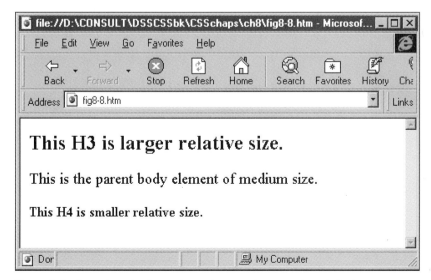

Figure 8.8   This is how the font styles in the preceding sample code look via Internet Explorer.

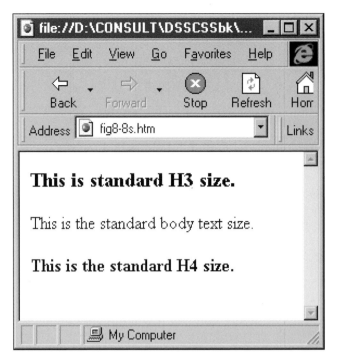

Figure 8.9 This is how the three lines in the preceding sample code are normally displayed via Internet Explorer.

Length Value

The length value allows you to set the font size as a numeric value in units of points, millimeters, centimeters, inches, or possibly others. Following is an example of this use of length:

```
<HTML>
<HEAD>
<STYLE TYPE ="text/css">
body {font-size: 14pt}
</Style>
</HEAD>
<BODY>
This is 14-point body text.
</body>
</HTML>
```

The HTML code in the preceding example shows the use of the length value of the **font size** property to accomplish the font display in Figure 8.10.

The length value may seem like a familiar tool to anyone who has used a modern word-processing program with font size in

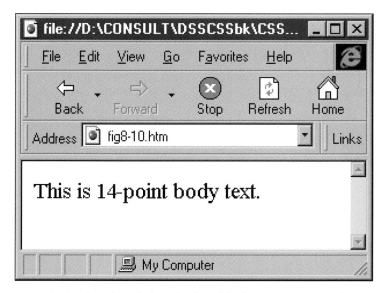

Figure 8.10 This is how the length value of the font size property in the preceding sample code displays via Internet Explorer.

points, cm, and so on. However, using a numeric length in a Web document creates problems when the document is scaled on monitors of different sizes or resolutions. Also, the exact font size you specify may not be available on a user's browser. Therefore, you are much better off using any of the relative size values.

Percentage Value

Percentage value sets the font size as a percentage of the parent element's font size. You can specify any percentage, but remember that the resulting font size may not match one available to the user's browser. It is generally a better idea to use the relative size value instead of the percentage value whenever possible. The following example shows how to format the percentage value:

```
<HTML>
<HEAD>
<STYLE TYPE ="text/css">
H3 {font-size: 150%}
body {font-size: medium}
H4 {font-size: 75%}
</Style>
</HEAD>
<BODY>
<H3>This H3 is 150% of the body text.</H3>
```

```
This is the parent body element of medium size.
<H4>This H4 is 75% of the body text.</H4>
</body>
</HTML>
```

The HTML code in the preceding example shows the use of the percentage value of the **font size** property to accomplish the font display in Figure 8.11.

Font

The **font** property lets you put it all together in a single statement. With this property, you can set all five font properties (family, style, variant, weight, and size) and line height, too. Just remember to separate each property. For example, rather than using each one separately, as in

```
<STYLE TYPE ="text/css">
body {
font-style: italic;
font-variant: normal;
font-weight: bold;
font-size: 14pt;
line-height: 16pt}
font-family: "cartoon wide", fantasy
</Style>
```

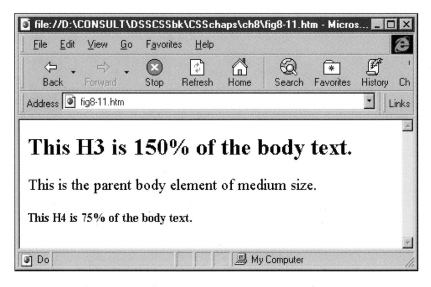

Figure 8.11 This is how the font styles in the preceding sample code look via Internet Explorer.

you can shorten this to a single font statement in your style sheet:

```
<STYLE TYPE ="text/css">
body {font: italic bold 14pt/16pt "cartoon wide",
fantasy}
</Style>
```

The HTML code in the preceding example shows the use of the **font** property to accomplish the font display in Figure 8.12.

The **font** property uses the initial values of the individual parts it controls, and accepts all values for each of its parts. Notice how font size and font weight are abbreviated using the slash (12pt/14pt).

Style Sheet Design Guide: Using Fonts For Flair

It's easy to get excited about being able to individualize every aspect of the text on your Web site using font properties. But font properties can also make your site a big mess. Unless you're trying to win the "Most-Fonts-Used-in-a-Single-Page" award, follow the advice of newspaper and magazine editors: Use no more than three, maybe four, fonts on the same page.

You can use color, font families, and sizes to enliven your text without cluttering your page. As you can see in this book, few

FAMILY MATTERS

List the font family last in the font properties to make sure it will work with the largest number of browsers.

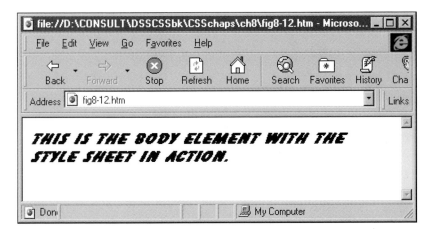

Figure 8.12   This is how the font styles in the preceding sample code look via Internet Explorer.

pages contain more than four fonts. Of course, you'll see many Web pages with a multitude of fonts used. Make sure you really want your Web page to look like these before you set your style sheets to use several fonts.

When you do set your fonts, keep them compatible with the overall tone and style of your site. Make sure they add to the look you're trying to achieve. By all means, look at the source of the Web pages you like the most to see how they set their font properties. Then, try a few properties on your Web site to see what you like.

Before you finalize your fonts, though, remember to test your pages with several browsers on different types of computers if you're serious about trying to use font families that aren't widely distributed. Also, ask your Web site users what they think about the fonts you used. There's nothing like user feedback to help you find and correct problems. Now, on to text properties for even more fun on your site.

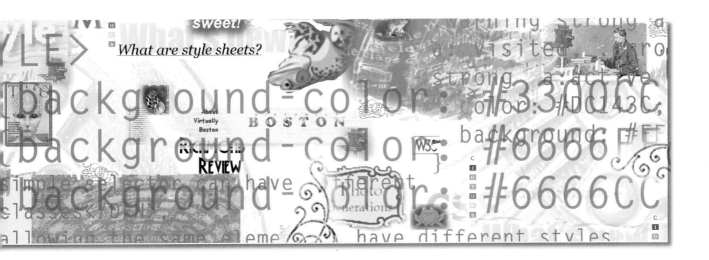

TEXTURING

TEXT

PROPERTIES

9

In this chapter:

- **Controlling text with style sheets**

- **Setting letter and word spacing**

- **Defining line height**

- **Adding flair and decoration to text**

- **Specifying vertical and horizontal alignment**

A picture may be worth 1,000 words, but just try telling a 5,000-word story with only five pictures. Something may be lost in the translation. Yes, the Internet was awakened by the Web's capability to display pictures. But the lowly word still reigns as king over true communication on the Web.

```
You wouldn't think of using only the courier
font family on your Web site. If you did, all
your text would look like this. Exciting,
isn't it?
```

Font properties were discussed in the previous chapter. Ah, yes, this chapter is about what you can do with your text after you choose your font properties. CSS1 gives you eight properties for customizing the display of your lines and paragraphs of text. The first six we cover here let you suggest how users' browsers should display the space within paragraphs. The first three—**text-alignment**, **text-indention**, and **line-height**—are used most frequently because they affect the overall look of large blocks of text. The second three—**word-spacing**, **letter-spacing**, and **vertical-align**—are best used for creating dramatic effects with a few words of text. Add to these the **text-decoration** and **text-transformation** properties (underline, strike-through, uppercase, and so forth) and you can create just about any text look you can imagine—more than you will probably ever use.

Text-Align

The **text-align** property is the one you know from your word processing program as the align, or justify, function. Most text is left-justified, or, more properly, left-aligned. You probably center titles and seldom use the right-align or justify (both sides aligned) function. Although newspapers and many books use justified text, ragged-right (left-aligned) text is easier and faster to read because our vision picks up the different line lengths, thereby making it easier to drop down only one line at a time when reading the paragraph. Keep this in mind when you're tempted to set up justified columns on your Web site.

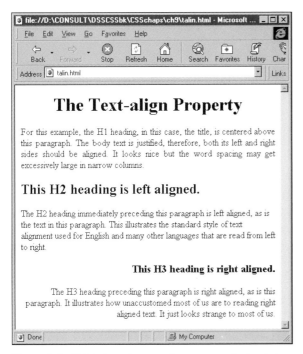

Figure 9.1 This is how the text-align property looks via Internet Explorer.

Also keep in mind that text alignment is relative to the width of the element in which it is used, not the width of the frame or computer screen. This is most noticeable when you center text in a frame without borders. Make sure you check your use of this property with several browsers and display resolutions.

The **text-align** property works with block-level elements (body, P, headings, and so forth) with values of **left**, **right**, **center**, and **justify**. Its function is similar to the HTML align attribute when used on paragraphs, headings, and divisions. Its initial value is set by the browser. This property is inherited.

The following HTML code shows the use of the **text-align** property to accomplish the display in Figure 9.1.

```
<HTML>
<HEAD>
<STYLE TYPE ="text/css">
H1 {text-align: center}
H2 {text-align: left}
H3 {text-align: right}
```

```
BODY {text-align: justify}
</Style>
</HEAD>
<BODY>
<H1>The Text Align Property</H1>
For this example, the H1 heading (in this case, the title) is
centered above this paragraph. The body text is justified;
therefore, both its left and right sides should be aligned.
It looks nice, but the spacing between words may get
excessively large in narrow columns.
<H2>This H2 heading is left-aligned.</H2>
<P STYLE="text-align: left"> The H2 heading immediately
preceding this paragraph is left-aligned, as is the text in this
paragraph. This illustrates the standard style of text alignment
used for English and many other languages that are read from
left to right.</P>
<H3>This H3 heading is right-aligned.</H3>
<P STYLE="text-align: right"> The H3 heading preceding this
paragraph is right-aligned, as is this paragraph. It illustrates
how unaccustomed most of us are to reading right-aligned text.
It just looks strange to most of us.</P>
</BODY>
</HTML>
```

Justified text is somewhat of a special case because it affects and is affected by the **letter-spacing** and **word-spacing** properties. Because CSS1 does not explicitly specify how text should be justified, browsers use different methods. One may stretch the space between words, another may stretch the space between letters and words to simultaneously align the left and right text boundaries. Some may even compress letter or word spacing to squeeze a word onto a line. To keep text from being stretched too thinly, the hyphen was invented. However, CSS1 does not hyphenate. And because the size of the browser window and the resolution of the user's display screen together determine how many characters of a certain size can be displayed on a single line, it is useless to attempt manual hyphenation of long words. Although HTML lets you enter the soft hyphen tag ­ in a word at the hyphenation position, some browsers erroneously insert a hyphen when the word doesn't need it. This will probably be rectified in future versions of the browsers, so give it a try if you must use long words and justified text.

Text-Indent

Use the **text-indent** property in block-level elements (P, H, and so forth) to set the amount of indentation the browser will give the first line of a paragraph.

The value may be a length or a percentage of the width of the paragraph (parent element).

Text-indent is inherited, but only the computed value is passed on to the child elements. The value is based on the size of the element, which is determined by its font size. Therefore, when a text indent value of 5 em is applied to an element with a font size of 10 pt, 50 pt indention is passed on to all child elements regardless of their font sizes.

Negative values are allowed and can be used for dramatic effects when the browser supports them. They are especially useful when combined with the **vertical-align** property to create initial dropped capitals.

Figure 9.2 illustrates the values of the **text-indent** property. It also shows the need to extend the left margin when using a negative text indent; otherwise, the negatively indented line will extend past the left boundary of the page.

The following HTML code shows the use of the text indent property to accomplish the display in Figure 9.2.

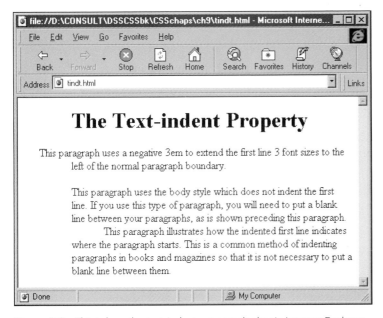

Figure 9.2   This is how the text-indent property looks via Internet Explorer.

```
<HEAD>
<STYLE TYPE ="text/css">
BODY {margin-left: 5em}
</Style>
</HEAD>
<BODY>
<H1>The Text Indent Property</H1>
<DIV STYLE="text-indent: -3em"> This paragraph uses a negative
 3em to extend the first line three font sizes to the left of
the normal paragraph boundary.</P>
This paragraph uses the body style, which does not indent the
first line. If you use this type of paragraph, you will need to
put a blank line between paragraphs, as shown preceding this
paragraph.
<DIV STYLE="text-indent: 3em"> This paragraph illustrates how
the indented first line indicates where the paragraph starts.
This is a common method of indenting paragraphs in books and
magazines, so it is not necessary to put a blank line between
them.</DIV>
</BODY>
</HTML>
```

One other aspect of the **text-indent** property is that it may not function properly when the first line of text of an element is inside another element that overrides it. For example, the text-indent setting in a <**DIV**> will be overridden by the text-indent value within a <**P**> element inside the <**DIV**>. Also, the text-indent value works only on the first line of a paragraph. What may look like several paragraphs may actually be a single paragraph split by other elements; <**BR**>, for example.

Line-Height

Use the **line-height** property with a number, length, or percentage value to set the minimum spacing between baselines of text. You can use this property to create what is commonly referred to as *double-spaced* text—text with twice the normal line height. Values given as a percentage or length (1.1 em, 11 pt., and so forth) are relative to the element's font size. When the value is a number, line height is calculated by multiplying the element's font size by the number. Negative values are not permitted, and the CSS1 specification suggests that the initial value of **normal** be defined by the browser at between 1.0 em and 1.2 em. This results in the most easily readable paragraphs of text.

Using a number value has one important difference in comparison with the length or percentage. For the **line-height** property, the number value is

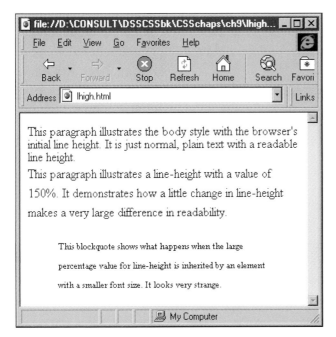

Figure 9.3 This is how the line-height property looks via Internet Explorer.

inherited and calculated separately for each child element based on the child element's font size, whereas length and percentage values are calculated only for the parent element, and the resulting line height is used for all child elements, regardless of their font sizes. Length and percentage values always work this way. The number value departs from the norm in this property.

These two modes of creating line height give you a great deal of flexibility in setting the line height of your paragraphs.

The following HTML code shows the use of the line height property to accomplish the display in Figure 9.3.

```
<HEAD>
<STYLE TYPE ="text/css">
BODY {line-height: 150%}
BLOCKQUOTE {font-size: 8pt}
</Style>
</HEAD>
<BODY>
<DIV STYLE="line-height:100%">
This paragraph illustrates the body style with the browser's
line height. It is normal plain text with a readable line height.</
DIV>
```

```
This paragraph illustrates a line height with a value of 150%.
It demonstrates how a little change in line height makes a big
difference in readability.
<BLOCKQUOTE>This blockquote shows what happens when
the large percentage value for line height is inherited by an
element with a smaller font size. It looks strange.
</BLOCKQUOTE>
</BODY>
</HTML>
```

Because the line height property sets the *minimum* distance between the baselines of each line of text, the actual distance between lines may be greater when the font size is greater or an inline image causes the user's browser to increase the distance. As with the other text properties, you can only *suggest* the way you want the text to be displayed.

Word-Spacing

The **word-spacing** property allows you to increase or decrease the amount of space between words. More precisely, it allows you to add space to or subtract space from the word spacing provided, by setting the property to a positive or negative value. This property can have a value of **normal** or a given length.

The value must be in length format, but it can be an absolute value (1.2 mm), a relative value (1.2 em), or a device-dependent value (12 px). The two relative types of values will have a similar effect on the parent element because they are based on the font size. However, when the amount of word spacing is computed from the length value, only the *result* is inherited. It is not computed again for any child elements based on the child elements' font sizes. Therefore, if a word-spacing value of 1.2 em is applied to a 12 pt parent font, the resulting word spacing of 1.4 (14 pt) will be inherited by a child element, regardless of the child element's font size. This may create an undesirable effect.

A setting of 0 (zero) is the same as the normal word spacing. Using negative word-spacing produces the expected results unless the total spacing is negative. This happens if, for example, the normal word spacing is 10 pt and the value of the word spacing is 12 em, resulting in a 2 pt spacing. Browsers generally ignore the negative and treat it as "normal" word spacing. However, some browsers take it literally and overlap the words. Check your work using the browsers that your site's viewers are likely to use.

Word spacing should be changed only for creative purposes, and even then should usually be applied in small increments to body text. The spacing of headings and other words or phrases you wish to stand out can be more exaggerated.

None of the major PC browsers implement word spacing; therefore, the examples shown in Figures 9.4 and 9.5 were created using the word processor, and merely illustrate the effects of word spacing.

Using greater word spacing in a title can be very effective though, as shown in Figure 9.4.

> The words in this paragraph are spaced by 2 ems rather than the standard 1 em. As you can plainly see, it looks somewhat strange and is more difficult to read.

Figure 9.4 This is how the word-spacing property looks with larger spaces on standard text.

The following HTML code shows how to use the **word-spacing** property for headings and paragraphs. It should work when you use a browser that implements the **word-spacing** property.

```
<HTML>
<HEAD>
<STYLE TYPE ="text/css">
H1 {word-spacing: 3em}
P {word-spacing: -.5em}
</Style>
</HEAD>
<BODY>
<H1>This H1 heading has 3em word spacing</H1>
This is standard body text with its standard browser
spacing.
It reads quite well.
<P> The words in this paragraph are squeezed together by
a word
spacing of negative 0.5em. It looks quite crowded.</P>
</BODY>
</HTML>
```

Welcome to Cascading Style Sheets

Figure 9.5 This is how the word-spacing property looks on large headings and titles.

Letter-Spacing

The **letter-spacing** property lets you increase or decrease the amount of space between characters. This property works the same way as the **word-spacing** property, except that it affects spacing between each character. It accepts values of **normal** or a length; the length value can be negative. This property applies to all elements, defaults to **normal**, and is inherited. Set letter spacing to zero to prevent justification.

The value must be in length format, but it can be an absolute value (1.2 mm), a relative value (1.2 em), or a device-dependent value (12 px). The two relative types of values will have a similar effect on the parent element because they are based on the font size. However, when the amount of letter spacing is computed from the length value, only the *result* is inherited. It is not computed again for any child elements based on the child elements' font sizes. Therefore, if a letter-spacing value of 0.2 em is applied to a 10 pt parent font, the resulting letter spacing of 2 pt will be inherited by a child element regardless of the child element's font size. This may not create the effect you desire, especially if the child element has a larger font size than the parent.

Although the letter-spacing value can be negative, the resulting total letter-spacing for a given element cannot be negative (less than zero and therefore undefined) or the results will be erratic. Some browsers treat negative total letter-spacing as zero; others may overlap the characters.

The following HTML code shows the use of the **letter-spacing** property to accomplish the display in Figure 9.6.

```
<HTML>
<HEAD>
<STYLE TYPE ="text/css">
H1 {letter-spacing: 0.5em}
DIV {letter-spacing: 0.5em}
P {letter-spacing: -0.1em}
</Style>
</HEAD>
```

```
<BODY>
<H1>This H1 heading has 0.5em letter spacing</H1>
The H1 heading still looks relatively good with the expanded
spacing. This paragraph is standard body text with its standard
browser spacing. It reads quite well.
<DIV>
The letters in the words in this paragraph are expanded by 0.5em
letter spacing. Notice how much more obvious this spacing is in
normal text than it is in the heading.</DIV>
<P> The letters in the words in this paragraph are compressed
by a negative 0.1em letter spacing. The words look very
compressed and the text is difficult to read.</P>
</BODY>
</HTML>
```

If the **word-spacing** property is difficult to use effectively in body text, the **letter-spacing** property is almost impossible to use in body text. Why? Although both word spacing and letter spacing are based on the font size of the element, letter spacing is highly font-specific. Each proportional font has been carefully designed with the best spacing already built-in for each character in the font—*best* meaning most legible. After all, when we combine letters into words, the words should be easily discernable to ensure that readers understand the idea we're trying to present. Avoid anything that interferes with this. For

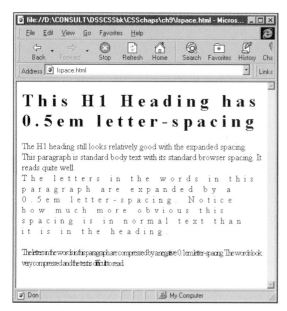

Figure 9.6   This is how the letter-spacing property looks via Internet Explorer.

this reason, changing font family, font color, or font size is generally more appropriate than changing the letter spacing in most of your Web text.

Using the **letter-spacing** property can be useful when you want to present a small amount of text in a unique or dramatic manner. Combining letter-spacing with word-spacing allows you to produce text so dramatic it rivals a graphic image, but is still text.

Vertical-Align

Ah, yes! Superscript and subscript letters are finally possible as a class. You can use the **vertical-align** property to position an inline element (character, word, and so forth) above or below its parent element or the rest of the line of text, depending on the value. For this property, an inline element is defined as having no line break before and after it (for example, <IMG>, <EM>, <A>, and so forth). The possible values for the **vertical-align** property are:

- **baseline** (the initial value)
- **sub**
- **super**
- **top**
- **text-top**
- **middle**
- **bottom**
- **text-bottom**
- a percentage (which may be negative)

When you use a percentage value, it is calculated based on the element's **line-height** property and is applied relative to the element's baseline. The baseline is the imaginary line on which all letters of the same line sit, regardless of their font, size,

and so forth. Therefore, negative percentages cause the element to display below the parent's baseline, as does the **sub** value.

The **vertical-align** property understands several keyword values. These keywords provide a quick way to set an element's vertical alignment without calculating percentages. And you don't have to worry about it being unreadable, because the degree of change achieved by using a keyword depends on its parent element's positioning and size, or the font size and line height of the line of text in which the element resides. However, remember that **vertical-align** is not inherited, so you will need to set it for the elements you want altered.

The following values for the **vertical-align** property are applied relative to the parent element:

- **baseline**. Aligns the element's baseline with the parent's baseline. This is the initial value.

- **middle**. Aligns the element's vertical midpoint with the baseline plus 1/2 of the x-height (font height) of the parent element (usually the lowercase letters). This centers the element 1/2 ex above the parent element's baseline.

- **super**. An old favorite, the superscript. It aligns the element with the font's or browser's suggested position for superscripts. Generally, the element is centered on top of the parent's uppercase letters.

- **sub**. Another old favorite, the subscript. It aligns the element with the font's or browser's suggested position for subscripts. Generally, the element is centered on the parent's baseline.

- **text-top**. Aligns the top of the element with the top of the parent element's tallest letter.

This produces a superscript-like look without increasing the line height or crowding lines of text.

- **text-bottom**. Aligns the bottom of the element with the bottom of the parent element's font, thereby making it sit on the baseline.

The **top** and **bottom** values for the **vertical-align** property are applied relative to the line of text and elements within the line in which the affected element resides. You should use these, along with the **middle** keyword, to position images within your text. Be careful when you use these keywords because they align the element relative to the highest or lowest element on that line. You can get into a catch-22 situation if you specify top alignment for one element and bottom alignment for another on the same line in which both these elements are larger than the line's text. Because both elements are taller and extend lower than the text, the browser will try to align each with the other's line. The easiest way to avoid this conundrum is to refrain from specifying both top and bottom alignment within the same line, or by using elements that are not taller than, and do not extend lower than, the surrounding text.

- **top**. Aligns the top of the element with the top of the tallest element on the line.

- **bottom**. Aligns the bottom of the element with the bottom of the lowest element on the line.

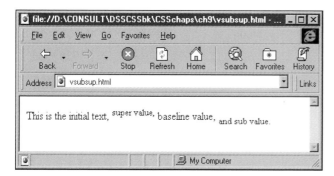

Figure 9.7   This is how the vertical-align property with super and sub values looks in Internet Explorer.

As of mid-1997, only the **super** and **sub** values for vertical-align are implemented on Netscape Navigator and Internet Explorer.

The following HTML code shows the use of the **vertical-align** property with **super** and **sub** values to accomplish the display in Figure 9.7.

```
<HTML>
<HEAD>
<STYLE TYPE="text/css">
</Style>
</HEAD>
<BODY>
This is the initial text,
<SPAN STYLE="vertical-align: super">
 super value,</SPAN>
<SPAN STYLE="vertical-align: baseline">
 baseline value, </SPAN>
<SPAN STYLE="vertical-align: sub">
 and sub value.</SPAN>
</BODY>
</HTML>
```

Because no PC browser will display it, we simulated how the percentage value looks in Figure 9.8.

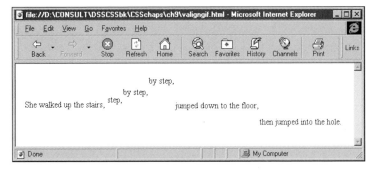

Figure 9.8   This is how the vertical-align property looks when implemented with percentage values in Internet Explorer.

The following HTML code shows the use of the **vertical-align** property with percentage values to accomplish the display in Figure 9.8.

```
<HTML>
<HEAD>
```

```
<STYLE TYPE="text/css">
</Style>
</HEAD>
<BODY>
She walked up the three stairs,
<SPAN STYLE="vertical-align: 33%">
 step,</SPAN>
<SPAN STYLE="vertical-align: 67%">
 by step, </SPAN>
<SPAN STYLE="vertical-align: 100%">
 by step, </SPAN>
<SPAN STYLE="vertical-align: 0%">
 jumped down to the floor,</SPAN>
<SPAN STYLE="vertical-align: -100%">
 then jumped into the hole.</SPAN>
</BODY>
</HTML>
```

Text-Decoration

You can use the **text-decoration** property to underline, overline, or line-through (strike out) text; or make text blink. All these values, as well as **none**, are accepted. However, the **blink** value is optional in the CSS1 specification, so not all browsers will implement it. In addition, as of August 1997, no major PC browser properly implements the **overline** value. The **text-decoration** property applies to all elements, but is not inherited.

Although it is not technically inherited, when you decorate a parent element, the child element continues the same decoration even though it may contain its own decoration. This includes the color property. This ensures that, for example, when you underline a passage containing several different elements, the underline looks the same throughout the passage. This doesn't make a big difference in the current values for text-decoration, but future values may need this semi-inheritance to function properly. Refer to Chapter 10 for more on the technicalities of inheritance.

When you use text-decoration, make sure you have a good reason. Keep in mind that underlining was developed during the days of the manual typewriter, or maybe even prior to that, as an easy way to emphasize a word or passage of text. It was also used (and sometimes still is by typewriter users) to indicate the title of a published work. You could type the text and then underline it without changing any other properties. Back then, writers didn't have easy access to colors, fonts, style sheets, or many of the other elegant properties that we have now. Text-decoration values have their place, but don't use them unless you're sure you can't accomplish the same effect using your properties.

Figure 9.9 shows the **underline** and **line-through** values and the nonfunctioning **overline**. We can't say it's missed because we can't think of a good use for **overline**. Of course, we can't show you the **blink** function on paper, and we suggest you not use it on your Web site. In surveys of Web users, the second most annoying thing on the Web was blinking text—right behind spam email.

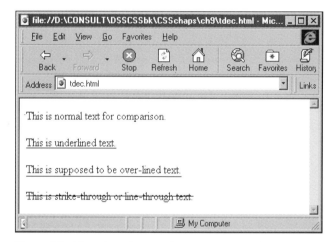

Figure 9.9 This is how the text-decoration property looks via Internet Explorer.

The following HTML code shows the use of the **text-decoration** property to accomplish the display in Figure 9.9.

```
<HTML>
<HEAD>
<STYLE TYPE="text/css">
</Style>
</HEAD>
<BODY>
This is normal text for comparison.<P>
<SPAN STYLE="text-decoration: underline">
This is underlined text.</SPAN><P>
```

```
<SPAN STYLE="text-decoration: overline">
 This is supposed to be overlined text.</SPAN><P>
<SPAN STYLE="text-decoration: line-through">
 This is strike-through or line-through text.</SPAN><P>
<SPAN STYLE="text-decoration: underline">
</BODY>
</HTML>
```

Text-Transform

With the **text-transform** property, you can literally transform your text by changing the case. It has values of **capitalize, uppercase, lowercase,** and **none.** Text-transform defaults to **none** for all elements. It is inherited.

The three active values effect the following actions:

- Capitalize—capitalizes (uses the uppercase variant of the element's font) only the first character of each word in the element.

- Uppercase—capitalizes (uses the uppercase variant of the element's font) all characters within each word in the element.

- Lowercase—sets the characters of each word in the element to the lowercase variant of the element's font.

Figure 9.10 shows examples of using the **capitalize, uppercase,** and **lowercase** values for **text-transform:**

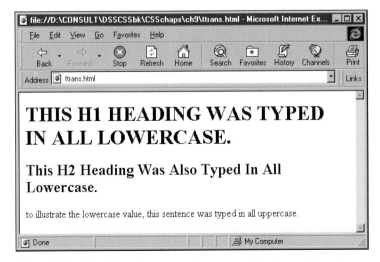

Figure 9.10 This is how the text-transform property looks via Internet Explorer.

The following HTML code shows the use of the **text-transform** property to accomplish the display in Figure 9.10.

```
<HTML>
<HEAD>
<STYLE TYPE="text/css">
H1 {text-transform: uppercase}
H2 {text-transform: capitalize}
BODY {text-transform: lowercase}
</Style>
</HEAD>
<BODY>
<H1>this h1 heading was typed in all
lowercase</H1>
<H2>this h2 heading was also typed in all
lowercase</H2>
TO ILLUSTRATE THE LOWERCASE VALUE, THIS
SENTENCE WAS
TYPED IN ALL UPPERCASE.
</BODY>
</HTML>
```

As you can see in the previous example, unless you really want all the letters in each word in uppercase or lowercase, or you want the first letter of **every** word capitalized, you shouldn't use the **text-transform** property. Also, because the **text-transform** property depends on the font you are using for a specific element, you should take care not to get tangled in the web of transforming a unique font just because it looks great on your browser. CSS1 allows browsers to ignore the **text-transform** property for characters that are not from the Latin-1 group and for elements in languages with different case-conversion tables. The bottom line is to use **text-transform** sparingly for dramatic effect if the standard text still communicates your message when viewed via non-compliant browsers.

A Style Sheet Design Guide: Taking Advantage Of Text

Use the **text-align**, **text-indent**, and **line-height** properties to arrange the overall look of paragraphs on your Web page. Use the **word-spacing**, **letter-spacing**, and **vertical-align** properties sparingly and carefully to enhance the readability of your text and to better communicate your message. Use the **text-decoration** and **text-transform** properties to emphasize or dramatize titles or headings.

If your Web site contains scientific information, use of **vertical align: sub**, and **super** throughout your text may be quite appropriate for your equations and chemical formulas. These will also come in handy if your Web site is devoted to demonstrating what you can do with text properties of style sheets or is an online magazine with mostly images using stylized titles and captions. Otherwise, you will have only limited need for many of the text properties discussed in this chapter. If you apply text properties to your Web documents without an overall plan, you'll probably end up with a visually fragmented and unappealing site.

Include text properties as well as the other style sheet properties when planning your site to ensure a consistent overall tone and look. Design the forest by making appropriate use of the different types of trees. But don't get trapped, staring at only the types of bark on the trees. Our final words on text properties are: Don't change them from the browser's defaults unless you have a well-planned approach in which your text changes enhance the overall communication and effectiveness of your Web site.

PART 3

STYLE
SHEETS
AND YOUR
WEB PAGES

LINKING TO AND USING STYLE SHEETS IN YOUR WEB PAGES

10

In the many style rule examples you've seen so far, we've given you a bit of a preview of how to include and reference style information within your HTML pages. And that's just the beginning. There is more than one way to skin this particular cat, and we'll show them all to you in this chapter.

Right In The Page: Inline Style Sheets

This example from Chapter 6 illustrates how style information can be included directly within an HTML page:

```
<HTML>
<HEAD>
<STYLE TYPE="text/css">
DIV.sample1 {margin-left: 10%}

DIV.sample2 {margin-right: 20%}

DIV.sample3 {margin-top: 15%}

DIV.sample4 {margin-bottom: 35px}

DIV.sample5 {margin-left: 100px;
        margin-right: 50px;
            }

DIV.sample6 {margin-top: 25px;
        margin-bottom: 100px;
            }

</STYLE>
</HEAD>
```

It's that simple. **<STYLE>... </STYLE>** tags contain the style rules, and they appear within the **<HEAD>... </HEAD>** markup. We've also included the attribute **TYPE="text/css"** within the **<STYLE>** tag to let the browser know that the information is written using the CSS1 rules and syntax. These inline style sheets are placed within the header tags for two reasons. First, this is page-related information—just like title or meta information—that is relevant to the content of the page, but isn't part of the actual displayed document.

Second, those early versions of browsers that don't support style sheets or recognize style information will not display your style code as part of the page if it is included within the <HEAD>... </HEAD> tags. If the style information is placed elsewhere in the page—within the body, for example—these browsers will treat it as regular text and include it as part of the page users see. To be on the safe side and make sure your underthings—the style rules—aren't hung out to dry for everyone to see, you can include comment tags around your style information. Figure 10.1 shows what readers would see if your style information were to be displayed as part of the page.

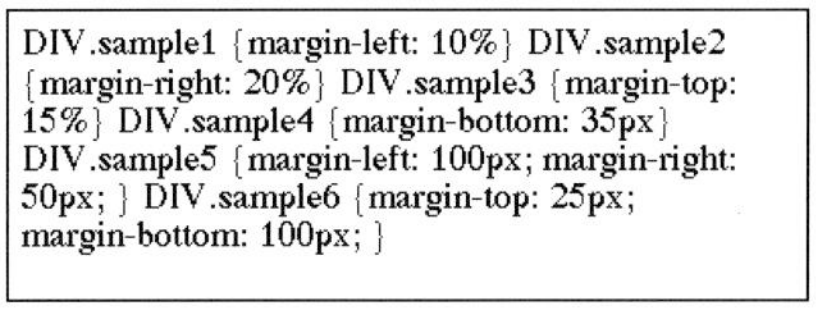

If we add comment tags to the code from the previous example, not much will change, but there is a noticeable difference:

```
<HTML>
<HEAD>
<STYLE TYPE="text/css">
<!-- DIV.sample1 {margin-left: 10%}

DIV.sample2 {margin-right: 20%}

DIV.sample3 {margin-top: 15%}

DIV.sample4 {margin-bottom: 35px}

DIV.sample5 {margin-left: 100px;
             margin-right: 50px;
             }

DIV.sample6 {margin-top: 25px;
             margin-bottom: 100px;
             }
                 -->
</STYLE>
</HEAD>
```

Note that the comment tags, <!—... —>, are nested within the <STYLE>... </STYLE> tags. They don't prevent a browser that supports style sheets from implementing your inline style rules, but they do ensure that a nonsupporting browser won't display your code.

That's it for inline style information. Once the rules are written and included within that style markup, you are ready to create the

DIV.sample1 {margin-left: 10%} DIV.sample2 {margin-right: 20%} DIV.sample3 {margin-top: 15%} DIV.sample4 {margin-bottom: 35px} DIV.sample5 {margin-left: 100px; margin-right: 50px; } DIV.sample6 {margin-top: 25px; margin-bottom: 100px; }

Figure 10.1 Without comment tags around style information, some browsers will display style rules as page content. Not a pretty site.

HTML that references them. The only drawback in referencing style information in this way is that the style sheet only governs the individual HTML page that contains it. If you want to use the style sheet again, you must copy and paste it into another HTML document. You could also create an external style sheet that can be referenced by many pages at once. How? Read on.

Write Once, Use Often: External Style Sheets

Before you panic, we'll tell you this: Regardless of how a Web page references a style sheet, it is written in the same way. The only two differences are where the information is stored and what HTML is used to reference it. Creating an external style sheet is simple. To show you how, we'll convert the inline style sheet we've been working with in our first example to an external style sheet.

To do so, we'll first copy all of the style rules, minus any HTML markup, to a new text file. Our new file now contains the following style information:

```
DIV.sample1 {margin-left: 10%}

DIV.sample2 {margin-right: 20%}

DIV.sample3 {margin-top: 15%}

DIV.sample4 {margin-bottom: 35px}

DIV.sample5 {margin-left: 100px;
        margin-right: 50px;
        }

DIV.sample6 {margin-top: 25px;
        margin-bottom: 100px;
        }
```

Notice that the style rules are identical to the inline version. If we wanted to create this file from scratch instead of from a previously existing style sheet, we would simply type the style rules into a new text file, without all the HTML, of course.

For the second and last step of the process, we save the plain text file as margins.css. We include the suffix ".css" to remind ourselves that the file is a style sheet and not an HTML file.

That's all there is to it. We've just created a new style sheet entitled *margins.css* and it's ready to be referenced by as many HTML pages as our hearts desire. We can accomplish this linkage in one of two ways.

Linking Up Style Sheets With <LINK>

Linking to external style sheets using the <LINK> tag is just as easy as writing style rules right into your HTML page. To include the style sheet we just created, *margins.css*, in a separate HTML page, we use this single line of code:

```
<LINK REL=STYLESHEET HREF="margins.css".>
```

<LINK> is a singleton tag, so it can't contain any other text or HTML markup. The attribute/value pair **REL=STYLESHEET** alerts the browser that the linked file is a style sheet and should be treated accordingly. **HREF="margins.css"** provides the name and location of the style sheet. In this case, the style sheet file is stored in the same folder as the linking HTML page. If we placed all of our style sheets in a folder named "style," we would reference it using the attribute/value pair **HREF="style/margins.css"**. Absolute and relative

addressing rules apply to links to external style sheets just as they do to links to Web pages.

You can use multiple **<LINK>** tags to reference multiple style sheets within one HTML page. If we want to link to a style sheet named colors.css, in addition to margins.css, we simply add another tag, making the code look like this:

```
<LINK REL=STYLESHEET HREF="margins.css".>
<LINK REL=STYLESHEET HREF="colors.css">
```

Because margins.css is linked to first, it is the default style sheet. Later in the chapter, in "Mixing and Matching," we'll discuss combining external style sheets with inline style sheets, as well as how to resolve conflicts between multiple style sheets.

Importing Style Information Using <STYLE>

At the beginning of the chapter, we showed you how to include style rules directly within your HTML pages using the **<STYLE>**... **</STYLE>** markup tags. You can also use these tags to import information from an external style sheet, or sheets, into a Web page. The key to this method of referencing style is the **@import** property. This referencing mechanism is written like a style rule, with **@import** as the property and the style sheet's name as the value.

If we want to import our margins.css style sheet, rather than linking to it, we would use this code:

```
<STYLE TYPE="text/css">
    @import "margins.css";
</STYLE>
```

Using this same notation, we can also link to the colors.css style sheet:

```
<STYLE TYPE="text/css">
    @import "margins.css";
    @import "colors.css";
</STYLE>
```

FILE NAMING

You can name your style sheets anything you like, as long as you comply with your Web server's naming conventions; you don't have to include the ".css" suffix. We include it to help us better manage the documents on our site.

We can reference multiple external style sheets in this way. The style sheets are assigned priority based on their place in the list, so in the previous example, margins.css has priority over colors.css because it is listed first.

Both linking and importing mechanisms allow you to create multiple external style sheets that can be referenced in any combination by a large group of documents. The argument for utilizing external style sheets is a strong one. If one style sheet governs a sizable group of documents and is included in each document, modifying or adding to the style sheet will be a time-consuming task. Each page has to be changed, and even with a strong search-and-replace tool, this is not a simple task. If all of the pages reference a single external style sheet, you can make the change once and it will affect all of the documents. This is not to say that you should never use inline style sheets. If you are creating a few simple style rules that apply only to an individual page, it is much faster and easier to include them directly within that page.

Obviously, both inline and external style sheets have appropriate uses, and the CSS1 specification was written to provide mechanisms for both types for this very reason. But what if you have a global style that you apply to all Web pages in a document collection, and need to include page-specific styles as well? This too can be done.

Mixing And Matching

You can include both inline and externally referenced style sheets in two ways by combining inline style rules and one of the two external style sheet referencing mechanisms. One option is to use the `<LINK>` tag to call an external style sheet and then create page-specific style rules within the `<STYLE>`... `</STYLE>` tags, as this code does:

```
<HEAD>
<LINK REL=STYLESHEET HREF="margins.css">
<STYLE TYPE="text/css">
P.booktitle {Font: 24pt Arial navy};
P.author {Font: 18pt Arial teal};
</STYLE>
</HEAD>
```

Your second option is to include an import statement within style markup, as well as page-specific style markup. Using this method, the previous code now looks like this:

```
<HEAD>
<STYLE TYPE="text/css">
@import "margins.css";
P.booktitle {Font: 24pt Arial navy};
P.author {Font: 18pt Arial teal};
</STYLE>
</HEAD>
```

If you use the link method of combining style sheets, the inline style sheet is the default style sheet and the linked style sheet is an option users can choose (when browsers make it possible for users to choose from a selection of style sheets). This means that the linked style sheet is an alternative to the inline style sheet, not an addition. However, if you use the import method, the imported external style sheet becomes a part of the inline style sheet and they work together to create one style sheet for the entire document. Pretty nifty, eh?

When Conflicts Arise

Linking to multiple external style sheets and combining external and inline styles can lead to rule conflicts. For example, suppose your global style sheet defines <H1> as 36-point teal Garamond, and your local inline style sheet defines it as 38-point blue Arial. You've used the import method to combine them both within a single document. Which style rule will prevail? Local rules have priority over imported rules, so the inline style rule defining <H1> as 38-point blue Arial prevails.

In another situation, suppose you import three different external style sheets, each with different rules for the selector **P.byline**. Which rule will the browser choose? Whichever style sheet you import first takes priority, so the declaration for **P.byline** found in the first style sheet listed prevails.

The rules of conflict have evolved quite a bit since CSS1 was first created, and probably will continue to do so. Our suggestion is that you carefully compose your style sheets, both external and inline, and try to avoid conflicts in your designs. Because you have control over your style sheets, you can prevent conflicts from the outset.

The conflicts you can't control are between the user's browser style preferences and the styles you define for your Web pages. If a user has his or her browser font set to white 18-point Times with a blue background, and your style sheets define blue 12-point Helvetica on a white background, what will the browser display? In general, the user's preferences win out, simply because they were designed to let users control their own environments. Don't be dismayed, however. Most users have their browsers set to allow designer-defined styles to show through. In a worst-case scenario, the styles affected are font size as well as family, background, and text and link colors. Your pages

may not look as pretty in some users' browsers, but at least the information will be there.

So Many Choices

Style sheets were created to be versatile and to provide Web designers with more tools for Web page design. This versatility also gives you multiple mechanisms for imposing style rules on your HTML pages. As we've described each method of including or referencing style sheets, we've given you an indication of when you want to use one method instead of another. As with all things Web, practice and play provide enlightenment. The more you work with style sheets and your Web content, the better your implementations will be. Because no two Web pages or sites are alike, there are no hard-and-fast style sheet inclusion rules. Use the combination of inline and external style sheets that works best for you.

Looking Ahead

We've finally come to the end of our discussion of Cascading Style Sheets, their rules, and their syntax. But, as we said earlier, there is always more than one way to skin a cat. In Chapter 11, we'll introduce you to yet another bleeding-edge technology. Dynamic HTML was created to alleviate the static nature of Web pages in favor of a more active, user-responsive, means of communication.

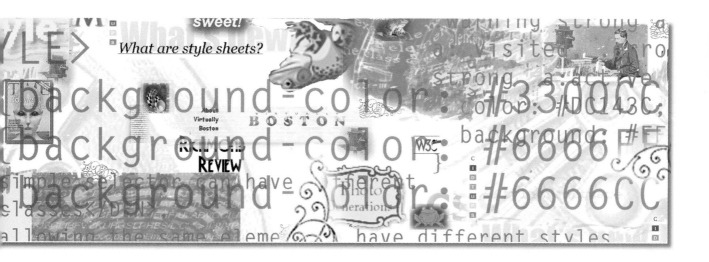

DYNAMIC HTML 11

In this chapter:

- **Dynamic HTML defined and explained**

- **Competing visions: Microsoft, Netscape, and the W3C**

- **The Document Object Model (DOM)**

- **CSS1 can be Dynamic, too!**

Of all the new HTML technologies to be introduced and debated in the context of the emerging HTML 4.0 standard (in a reasonably solid draft form as this chapter is being written), none has engendered as much controversy, furor, or enthusiasm as dynamic HTML. Starting with dueling proposals from Microsoft and Netscape, and continuing with some radically different ideas about what the "dynamic" part of dynamic HTML really means, this topic has been a bone of contention since it was initially introduced.

The basic concept behind dynamic HTML is fairly straightforward, no matter which interpretation you are inclined to follow: Making existing page content mutable—so that its appearance can change after it has been downloaded—relieves Web servers of the burden of generating and delivering new versions of a document every time minor changes occur. This lets the client handle making such changes (as long as it knows how), and relieves the server of carrying the burden of dynamism, on top of everything else it has to do.

Of course, the details are considerably more complex than this brief overview might suggest. In this chapter, you'll learn more about those details and the competing points of view that drive them, along with where emerging standards for dynamic HTML are headed. Better yet, you'll be able to understand the true value of dynamic HTML to Web page authors and users alike, and why this capability may be one of the most interesting innovations to hit HTML since interactive forms in HTML 2.0.

When used in tandem with CSS, dynamic HTML offers capabilities that permit Web documents to display the kind of interactive behavior that has previously been limited to those with the time and money to spend buying and learning Java-based, object-oriented Web authoring environments. By the end of this chapter, you should have a pretty good idea of what this nascent technology means to your own Web pages.

A Matter Of Definitions

By the end of the first quarter of 1997, both Microsoft and Netscape had begun to use the term "dynamic HTML" freely in their list of upcoming technologies for Internet Explorer and Navigator, respectively. By that point, it was clear that both companies felt strongly about this technology and that key aspects of their future directions hinged on its capabilities.

At the same time, it became clear that the battling browser behemoths used the same name to describe different approaches to making HTML documents dynamic, and that the differences were in many ways incompatible. At about this juncture, the W3C began to take an active interest to forestall too much controversy, and a set of standards and descriptions for what dynamic HTML might mean began to be forged. The following sections delineate the broad outlines of Microsoft's and Netscape's visions for dynamic HTML, followed by a description of the W3C's emerging interpretation of the term.

Because both companies have vowed to conform to whatever standard results from the W3C process, it's just a matter of time before these two visions converge. But their differing viewpoints are more than merely technically interesting; both speak directly to the development directions for each company, and attest to the importance of dynamic HTML, whatever it may ultimately become.

Microsoft's "Dynamic HTML"

In Microsoft's view, Dynamic HTML (notice the initial capital "D" on Dynamic—they've trade-marked the name "Dynamic HTML") consists of four primary components:

- An HTML document object model

- A method for controlling element positioning on a page

- A set of multimedia controls for animation, channel filtering, and other uses

- The ability to bind sets of data to an HTML page

In addition, Internet Explorer supports a Scripting Object Model, which means—at least theoretically—that developers can use whatever scripting language they prefer for controlling page elements within the browser. At present, however, Microsoft ships only components for Jscript (its own implementation of JavaScript) and for Visual Basic, Scripting edition (usually called VBScript), along with Internet Explorer 4.0 (IE4) preview versions.

The IE4 object model stores HTML elements that appear in any given document in a collection object named "all." This object takes the form of a variant array, which can store multiple values in multiple formats in a single array structure. Developers can traverse this object hierarchy—which is built as the browser parses an HTML document—and address and alter the contents of any element within that hierarchy. For instance, to point to the fifth level-two heading in a document, the reference would be specified as follows:

```
document.all.tags.("H3").item(4)
```

Note that all items are numbered starting with zero, so the fifth element appears as item (4) in the reference. To change the font family associated with that same element, the syntax looks like this:

```
document.all.tags.("H3").item(4).font.family
= "Baskerville";
```

Microsoft's Dynamic HTML also supports some useful concepts of events. Simply put, user actions like mousedown (when an object is highlighted and the user clicks on the mouse) or mouseover (when the cursor moves across an object) can cause automatic behavior when objects with specific event-handlers respond to these events. This behavior can be as simple as provoking pop-up, context-sensitive help messages about buttons and controls, or as complex as opening a new window for text input or dynamically rebuilding forms on the fly, based on user input and menu selections.

For Microsoft, the object model provides the power and the flexibility necessary to locate all elements of a certain class, or individual instances of elements within a document. In its "Dynamic HTML White Paper" it describes Dynamic HTML succinctly, as follows:

> "Dynamic HTML extends HTML with an object model allowing scripts or programs to change styles and attributes of page elements (or objects), or even to replace existing elements (or objects) with new ones. Other additions include multimedia and database features."
>
> **http://www.microsoft.com/workshop/prog/**
> **aplatfrm/dynhtml.htm**, page 2

Fortunately, the model used for controlling element positioning is drawn straight from the work done at the W3C for addressing page positioning within the context of CSS1, so it's right in keeping with what has already been covered in Chapters 5 through 7.

The key elements of this specification include the ability to precisely position objects on a page, in terms of a variety of units; and the ability to organize and address information in layers, so that objects may be referenced in terms of x, y, and z coordinates. Likewise, objects have associated ordering, transparency, and clipping attributes so that the display of overlapping elements can be controlled explicitly. Those interested in consulting this specific reference can read the W3C's draft specification, "Positioning HTML Elements with Cascading Style Sheets" (sometimes called CSS-P for short) at **http://www.w3.org/TR/WD-positioning**.

The multimedia effects that Microsoft considers part of Dynamic HTML—at least until the W3C makes its pronouncements on the subject—include all kinds of capabilities. These cover a range of complex visual effects that include moving sprites; animated color washes and textures; font and screen transition effects (such as wipes, dissolves, morphs, bleeds, and so on); and support for vector graphics for compact, scalable images. On the audio side, Microsoft provides support for dynamic multichannel audio mixing, so that characteristic sounds or commentary can overlap, and user-driven transitions can trigger corresponding audio effects.

Microsoft's built-in database support, *data binding*, permits Web designers to build pages that can organize data either when loaded or on demand. All such data-handling occurs on the client side of the Web interaction, so that users can organize and reorganize data locally, without having to reload a new page from the server. Under the hood, however, this requires access to a data-handling tool, be it an Excel spreadsheet or Access database of some kind. But it means that users can sort tables by one index for one use, and then by another index later. Thus, a table of stock reports could be indexed for one viewing by purchase date, and for another by rate of return, without requiring any further server interaction once the data is made local.

The uses to which Microsoft and its followers have already put this technology are nothing less than amazing. Modest, but especially effective, uses include cascading menus, in which making a higher-level menu selection provokes the next menu level to appear. Because the data is already local—it's just not visible until called—lower-level menus pop up without noticeable delay. Likewise, because a document's object hierarchy can be scanned, categorized, and organized on the fly, it's possible to construct automatic tables of contents, graphical site maps, and all kinds of other interesting infrastructure elements without coding them in advance (or by hand, as is so often the case for old-fashioned, static HTML).

Dynamic HTML has been used to implement games like Tetris and Battleship, to create fully interactive, self-modifying screen forms, and even to build self-calculating expense reports, purchase orders, and the like. It does indeed appear to offer rich interactivity for Web pages.

In short, much of the enthusiasm for Dynamic HTML in the Microsoft camp appears well-intentioned and may even be well-deserved. In fact, you'll see many more echoes of Microsoft's approach in the W3C's work on Dynamic HTML than Netscape's.

Netscape's "dynamic HTML"

In Netscape's view, dynamic HTML consists of three elements:

- HTML, including Netscape extensions—especially those for addressing document <**LAYER**>s and dynamic font controls

- Java and JavaScript, to be used in tandem with JavaScript-Accessible Style Sheets (JASS)

- An object model for HTML documents, which differs from Microsoft's

The most significant difference in perspective between the Microsoft and Netscape approaches to dynamic HTML is Microsoft's dependence on CSS1 specifications and terminology, especially for positioning and style information; and Netscape's reliance on proprietary tags and terminology. Despite claims you may see on Netscape's site to the contrary, Navigator's conformance with the CSS1 specification lags considerably behind Microsoft's. For instance, if you examine the first paragraph after the numbered list on Netscape's "Dynamic HTML" page at **http://home.netscape .com/comprod/products/communicator/features/Dynamic_HTML.html** you'll see some "corporate hyperbole" at work!

Netscape's <**LAYER**> tag provides the mechanism used to organize content into layers with strict orders of precedence, transparence, and visibility on a page. They also provide support for x, y, and z coordinates that support precise positioning of elements on a Web page. These layers work quite a bit like the layer model implemented in Adobe Photoshop; if you're already familiar with it, you'll be well-equipped to understand Netscape's in a hurry. Interesting <**LAYER**> attributes include:

- **NAME**—reference in scripts and in controlling layer movement and access

- **WIDTH**—right margin text-wrap controls

- **CLIP**—specifies a viewable region

- **VISIBILITY**—indicates whether layer is visible or invisible at any given moment

Furthermore, **BGCOLOR** and **BACKGROUND** are used just as in the <**BODY**> tag to set a background color or image on any <**LAYER**>.

JASS is an interesting technology that permits access to any object with a NAME attribute while a page is loading. It currently works only with JavaScript or programs that generate JavaScript output. Also, JASS doesn't permit dynamic changes to page content or structure after a page has finished loading, unlike Microsoft's Document Object Model. But otherwise, JASS does permit programmatic manipulation of content, styles, and document structures on the fly.

Unfortunately, because of these differences, dynamic HTML on IE requires different markup on Navigator to achieve some, if not all, of the same effects. To address the issue of handling Navigator and IE users gracefully with dynamic HTML, Shelley Powers wrote an article for *NetscapeWorld* entitled "Writing dynamic pages that look and work great in both Navigator and IE" that explains how to build pages that provide a similar look, feel, and functionality to users with either browser. Check it out at **http://www.netscapeworld.com/netscapeworld/nw-03-1997/nw-03-coin.html**.

You may have heard that building multiple versions of code for different browsers involves considerably more effort. If it communicates nothing else, Powers' article delivers this message quite forcefully!

The W3C's Dynamic HTML Activities

At present, the World Wide Web Consortium operates under the aegis of a number of activity domains. HTML, Cascading Style Sheets, and the Document Object Model, all fall under the User Interface (UI) domain. The bulk of ongoing activity on dynamic HTML, which bridges all of these areas, falls into this domain as well.

As this chapter is being written, all of the W3C's important documentation on dynamic HTML appears under the heading for the Document Object Model. As the topic that follows next here, suffice it to say that the W3C is strongly inclined to support a complete and thorough object model for documents, along with requiring sufficient generality to support not just HTML and CSS, but also the eXtensible Markup Language (XML). This is quite general indeed, because XML is emerging as an intermediate step between HTML and SGML as an open-ended markup language that goes well beyond what's possible with HTML without embracing all of the power and generality of SGML.

The Document Object Model (DOM)

As of mid-1997, the DOM specification is still a Working Draft. This means it's far from complete, and will probably undergo two or more rounds of significant revision before attaining Draft Specification status, and then at least one more round thereafter before reaching full-blown Recommendation or Specification status. The W3C places a standard disclaimer in the head of all such working documents, which is probably worth repeating here:

> "Please remember this is subject to change at any time, and may be updated, replaced, or obsoleted by other documents at any time. It is inappropriate to use W3C Working Drafts as reference material or to cite them as other than work in progress."

So consider yourselves warned: What you are about to read is subject to change and is more an indication of tendencies and proclivities where the DOM in particular, and dynamic HTML in general, are concerned. Given the W3C's caveats, there's enough interesting material in here to make it worth reviewing and discussing. For the complete Document Object Model Working Draft, please visit **http://www.w3.org/MarkUp/DOM/drafts/requirements.html**.

General Requirements

The document begins with a set of requirements for DOM, which are unlikely to change. These show a strong inclination in some of the same directions as some of the more significant parts of Microsoft's Dynamic HTML vision. They are paraphrased here for brevity.

To all intents, DOM must be:

- Language-neutral and platform-independent
- Endowed with a common core of concepts and terminology that applies equally to HTML, CSS, and XML, but with each language's constructs driving its own specific DOM

- Supportive of external user agents and internal scripts

- Consistent throughout in its naming conventions

- Indifferent, to user interfaces, since a visual user interface may not appear in all conforming implementations (think agents, search engines, 'bots)

- Consistent, so that a document read in from an external source and a version of the same document saved to disk are structured identically

- Secure, able to produce only valid documents as output, and designed to avoid multiuser data consistency or integrity problems

- Open to other document manipulation tools, methods, or techniques

Interesting DOM Properties

The remainder of the working draft is broken into numerous sections, each of which addresses a variety of topics. Rather than reviewing it in its entirety, we'll cover only those elements that pertain directly to dynamic HTML, largely in order of appearance.

One key aspect of the DOM is its ability to address and manipulate any element of a document that conforms to its requirements. This means that programs can access and manipulate any aspect of a document's content, including all elements and their associated attributes, by name or by class. Because this applies equally to HTML documents and style sheets, content, presentation, and structure information are accessible and can be changed at will. Furthermore, the specification requires that a set of primitive operations to fetch and manipulate document elements and their attributes (get first, get next, and so on) be defined to facilitate access to document content and structure information.

The DOM also includes an event model designed to facilitate interaction, including the ability to respond to actions related to a document as it's presented to the user. This implies that some user interface must be involved in signaling events as they occur. Furthermore, any element must be able to generate an event, where events constitute some kind of interaction with, or an update or change to, a document's content. Responses to user interactions must appear in the event model as well, with the ability to assign defaults, and overrides to default behavior, when necessary. (Translation: DOM-based applications can include branching and conditional instructions.)

In the DOM, events may sometimes climb up the structural hierarchy of a document (the working draft uses the term "bubble up," which, like Microsoft's own term, means that an event that affects a child element can propagate upward and affect parent elements, where appropriate). In order to provide unambiguous event handling, events are assumed to be synchronous, which means they must be handled in the order in which they arrive.

For generality, events are explicitly required to be both platform-independent and language-neutral. Finally, the document states that some interface

will be provided to permit binding to events, so that particular named events can automatically provoke certain behaviors (such as binding a mouseover event to automatically deliver associated help text, for example).

When it comes to style sheets, many of the same characteristics that pertain to dynamic HTML also pertain to dynamic behavior in style sheets. Especially important is an ability to add, remove, or change selectors, rules, and properties in style sheets. Likewise, it's stated that any cascading style elements must be accessible—this means that any linked, imported, or alternative style sheets can be accessed consistently, whether local or remote. In the same vein, CSS pseudo-classes and pseudo-elements; contextual selectors; and inline styles may also be similarly manipulated. What's really described by all of this access information is a set of operations to manipulate style information, wherever it originates.

At the Document Type Definition (DTD) level, the presence of a governing DTD will be detectable through the DOM. If a DTD is available, it too will be subject to additions, deletions, or changes. Validity checks on documents are ensured by a stipulation that a mechanism to test all or part of any document for conformance to a DTD also be provided. This gives the SGML-savvy an opportunity to redefine document markup and structure to their hearts' content.

To handle errors, the DOM supports document-wide error logging and reporting, where errors take the form of exception messages (when results are not forthcoming; syntactic errors are detected;

or semantic problems manifest themselves at runtime). The DOM must also maintain current error status information so that a document's "error state" can be checked at any time. This should permit a more graceful handling of errors than is currently available in HTML or CSS1 implementations.

A variety of security-related information is to be included in the scope of the DOM, but it's not terribly germane to this discussion. For details, please consult the original document. Suffice it to say that these requirements are intended to control access to some documents (or elements within those documents); to control navigation within or among documents; and to respect a site's need for multiuser consistency, data integrity, and information boundaries such as firewalls.

The DOM tries to ensure that descriptive information about documents is also available, by stating that documents must provide metadata (data about themselves). In this case, metadata includes source attribution, creation date, and associated cookies, where applicable. Likewise, the DOM tries to ensure smooth user interaction by expecting automatic delivery of information about any user's browser and display environment. At the same time, the DOM requests checks on MIME types supported, to facilitate delivery of usable data.

The most significant element of these W3C requirements demands complete access to document contents, structure, and properties, plus on-the-fly alterations to elements. Because it responds to events and the interest in user interaction, this model is powerful. Your authors envision a brave new world in which HTML documents transform themselves to respond fluidly to user input, and make it natural for developers to build many more "one version fits all users" Web pages than is currently possible.

Another significant W3C credo is an unrelenting demand for platform independence and language neutrality. Both Microsoft and Netscape grabbed for a share of the market by forcing allegiance to certain operating systems, Web servers, APIs, and scripting languages. In keeping with the open and neutral heritage of the Web as we know it, the W3C remains adamant that partisan efforts have no place in their standards.

Style Sheets And Dynamic HTML

Cascading Style Sheets appear poised to play an important role in dynamic HTML. For one thing, it's evident that the W3C advocates controlling document presentation through style sheet objects, elements, and properties. It's also readily apparent that the W3C wants it to be as easy for scripts or programs to manipulate style sheets as it is easy for intrepid developers to manipulate HTML directly with Microsoft's beta technologies today. For that reason, the DOM addresses both HTML and style sheets equally. This suggests that content be managed through dynamic HTML, and that presentation information be managed through *dynamic CSS* (to coin a phrase for programmatic manipulation of Cascading Style Sheets).

For example, it might be more user-friendly to enlarge font sizes when a mouse moves over any document heading. By addressing this kind of dynamic behavior through the mouseover event, it's much easier to redraw documents to reflect user activity than by individually altering every instance of each element. Likewise, changing background colors or images on any object's mouseover or mousedown event may be generalized more effectively in style sheets than in individual documents.

The guiding principle is a belief that general changes to a document's appearance are best handled through style sheets. Anything else requires outright content changes, which means using dynamic HTML to change the document itself, not a style sheet that governs its appearance. Unfortunately, this tendency toward content, and away from style, applies to most of the dramatic uses of dynamic HTML, including context-sensitive mouseover help; cascading menus; interactive, self-modifying screen forms; and more.

Dynamic CSS may suddenly sound like much ado about nothing. But in an online universe where many Web sites undergo facelifts or makeovers every six to twelve months, programmatic changes to style sheets can be a real boon. Once you've gone through the exercise of defining style sheets to create a consistent look and feel for your site, be comforted by knowing that dealing with changes involves less work ever afterward.

A Dynamic HTML Sampler

Although dynamic landscapes are by definition ever-changing, many stunning examples of dynamic HTML are worth a visit. If nothing else, they will sharpen your appreciation for what dynamic

HTML and CSS are all about, and what they might do for your Web site. To begin, run nothing older than Internet Explorer 4.0 or Netscape Navigator 4.0. The 3.x versions of these redoubtable browsers won't display the essence of this dynamic behavior. Because of compatibility issues covered earlier in this chapter, both hotlists are distinguished by browser type, to help you experience these sites at their peak powers. Tables 11.1 and 11.2 cover Web sites aimed at Netscape Navigator and Internet Explorer, respectively.

Infant Standard Or Enfant Terrible? The Future Of Dynamic HTML

Even with a set of requirements well in hand, there's still a lot of work to do to develop a draft specification for the Document Object Model (and by implication, for dynamic HTML). At this point, speculation is about as close as anyone can get to asserting what final forms this technology may take.

But given the strong manifestations of some of the W3C's ideas in its Document Object Model and in its beta implementation of dynamic HTML in IE 4.0 Preview 2, several broad outcomes appear likely:

- The "dot notation" used to access document objects, with their hierarchical ability to access component elements by class or by specific instance, looks like a winning naming convention.

- The ability to change documents on the client side, based on substitution of new style and content information for old, followed by redrawing changed documents on screen, makes too much sense to ignore.

Table 11.1 Nifty Netscape dynamic HTML sites.

Category	Description	URL
Advertisements	Online fashion mall	www.fashionmall.com
	Premiere Technologies Layers demo	http://www.premierecomm.com/layers/
Animations	WebMonkey Star Wars Parody	http://www.hotwired.com/webmonkey/ webmonkey/html/97/03/monkeyboy.html
	Taboca ArtworK	http://www.taboca.com/layer/
	Sinfomic Layers Demo	http://www.sinfomic.fr/Demo/
Games	Mix-a-Pol	http://www.xnet.com/~april/mix/
	Ridge Layer	http://www1.nisiq.net/~jimmeans/ridge/
	Space Fire	http://www1.nisiq.net/~jimmeans/harrier2/
Dynamic Fonts	StockWatch	http://home.netscape.com/comprod/products/ communicator/fonts/ stockwatch_demo/index.html
Canvas Mode	Stella Chelsea Demo	http://home.netscape.com/comprod/products/ communicator/user_agent.html
Style sheets	Royal Newsletter Demo	http://home.netscape.com/comprod/products/ communicator/user_agent_style.html
	Web Design Group Tutorial	http://www.htmlhelp.com/reference/css/

Table 11.2 Excellent Internet Explorer Dynamic HTML sites.

Category	Description	URL
Overview	Dynamic HTML home page	http://www.microsoft.com/workshop/author/ dhtml/default.htm
	Overview document	http://www.microsoft.com/workshop/author/ dhtml/default.htm
	Event Handling in IE 4.0	http://www.microsoft.com/sitebuilder/features/ ie4event.asp
Examples	Microsoft's Dynamic HTML Gallery	http://www.microsoft.com/gallery/files/html/

- Precise positioning as described in the CSS-P draft looks like a slam dunk.

- The proliferation of dynamic buttons, menus, navigation tools, and "layered animation" is a sure bet.

Even more interesting are some less likely possibilities that the DOM and dynamic HTML proffer:

- Systematic alteration of style sheets may appear in tool form, ready to help automate Web site maintenance and renovation.

- Self-modifying surveys, questionnaires, tests, and input forms will become popular, and give "filling in the blanks" new zest.

- HTML and CSS document validation, as part of the DOM, will become part of the routine of building Web pages.

- Web designers will begin to think more in terms of "page logic," rather than "site logic," as complex, built-in interactive behavior on fewer multifunction pages begins to replace simple, hand-built interactive behavior on many more single-function pages.

- New visual scripting tools for the dynamic HTML environment will bring to page design what tools like Visual Café or Latte bring to Java applet design.

But before anyone can be sure which of these possibilities will manifest themselves, and what shapes they will take, more work will be required among the members of the User Interface Domain at the W3C. Because this group includes vigorous representation from both Microsoft and Netscape, among others, discussion is sure to be detailed, partisan, and passionate. It will be interesting to see which of these potential boons or banes survives the process, and to learn the details of how the related markup really works. That's why it's absolutely imperative to keep in touch with current developments in this area—our next, and final, topic in this chapter.

Investigation Beats Speculation

Because the areas of dynamic HTML, CSS, and the underlying Document Object Model remain

so fluid, it's important to check this material regularly to learn about the shape of things to come. The potential benefits of using these technologies appear large enough to warrant the effort of keeping up with them. Table 11.3 recaps various URLs you'll want to visit, both inside and outside the confines of the W3C.

All the resources outside the W3C generally go stale with time; likewise, the W3C site will go through changes. But all of the root URLs that appear here should still warrant further investigation, because they should continue to deal with Dynamic HTML and the Document Object Model for the foreseeable future.

Beyond Style, Then What?

This discussion also ends the chapter portion of the book. We hope it has led you to the information you need to help you design your Web site and to exploit the formidable capabilities inherent in Cascading Style Sheets. Better yet, we hope you've found this information useful and know where to look for enlightenment beyond these pages. Especially where dynamic HTML is concerned, but for CSS as well, these areas are still in the throes of heated development. Even though the shape of the next version of HTML appears to be finalized at this point, you've learned enough history to know that further changes are inevitable.

If you need additional information on the topics covered in the book, please consult the *Do It In Color* sections in the middle, and the appendices at the end. Be sure to check out the CD-ROM packaged with the book as well—it includes all the code that appeared herein, plus a variety of

Table 11.3 Late-breaking resources on Dynamic HTML, Dynamic CSS, and the DOM.

Category	Description	URL
W3 resources	CSS Home page	http://www.w3.org/Style/
	User Domain Activities page	http://www.w3.org/UI/#Activities
	Technical Reports & Pubs	http://www.w3.org/TR/
Microsoft	Microsoft vs. Netscape:	http://www.microsoft.com/workshop/author/dhtml/dhtml.htm
Dynamic HTML	Dynamic HTML FAQ	http://www.microsoft.com/workshop/author/dhtml/dhtmlqa.htm
	ClNet's Browser Playground	http://cnet.com/Content/Features/Techno/Playground/index.html
	ActiveIE	http://www.activeie.com/ie4.html
	Web Review: Web Coder	http://webreview.com/97/06/27/coder/index2.html
	LogOn Internet Solutions	http://log.on.ca/dhtml/index.htm
	Joel's IE 4.0 Info Center	http://www.icomnet.com/~jcarley/dynamic.htm
Netscape	Third-party review of HTML 4.0 including Dynamic HTML NetscapeWorld: D-HTML	http://www.netscapeworld.com/common/nw.tags.html http://www.netscapeworld.com/netscapeworld/nw-06-1997/nw-06-animated.html
Good Articles	HotWired's Webmonkey on Dynamic HTML (in four parts)	http://www.hotwired.com/webmonkey/97/13/position.html
	Computer Shopper's Erik Sherman "Microsoft Pushes Dynamic HTML"	http://www5.zdnet.com/cshopper/content/9706/cshp0087.html
	WebWeeks' Nate Zelnik does a 3-parter on Dynamic HTML	http://www.webweek.com/97Apr21/software/brewing.html http://www.webweek.com/97Apr28/software/builds.html http://www.webweek.com/97May5/software/document.html
	Web Review's Dale Dougherty interviews Microsoft's lead CSS developer, Chris Wilson, in depth	http://www.webreview.com/97/05/30/feature/wilson.html

hotlists and pointers to resources online, and some CSS-related demonstration and evaluation software to play with.

If you have specific feedback for the authors, or wish to share your opinions about any of the material covered—or omitted—in the book, please send email to the address listed in the introduction. All feedback is acknowledged and appreciated.

CASCADING STYLE SHEETS 1 REFERENCE

For this appendix, we've gathered all of the Cascading Style Sheets Level 1 (CSS1) properties discussed throughout the book into one all-inclusive reference. Grouped into the same families as in the book, each CSS1 property includes the following: the specific syntax, a complete list of associated values, the default value, the inheritance state, and a listing of applicable HTML elements. Although the book discusses each property family in detail, complete with example and design tips, this appendix will serve as a reference tool as you work with style sheets.

Before we dive into the property reference, it's important that you are able to translate and understand the methods that describe the syntax used in the property definition. Table A.1 serves as the key to this markup, showing a sample of each syntax, an explanation of what the syntax represents, and an example of that syntax in use.

Sample Property Definition

In addition to the syntax key, we'd also like to provide you with a sample property definition. Each of the definitions in this appendix takes the following form:

Background-Image

Description:
Use this property to define the location of a background graphic to be included with an HTML element.

The property name and description provide you with an identifying name for a property and a general description of its purpose and use.

Property Syntax:
```
background-image: <value>
```

The property syntax code shows you the exact code used to call the property and what kind of values the property takes. If a property is followed by the generic **<value>** syntax, refer to the

Table A.1 Property definition syntax.

Value	Description	Example
<type>	Identifies a specific type of value.	<absolute-size>; <value>
Keyword	Identifies a keyword that must appear exactly as it is listed in the definition.	background-image
X | Y	The value of X or Y must be used (selection not limited to two values).	normal | italic | oblique
X || Y	The value of X or Y or both must be used.	<font-style> || <font-variant> || <font-weight>
[Items]	Items with brackets are a group.	[<family-name> | <generic-family>]
Value*	Asterisk indicates that the value is repeated zero or more times.	[[<family-name> | <generic-family>],]*
Value?	The value is optional.	[<font-style> || <font-variant> || <font-weight>]?
Value{X,Y}	The value must occur at least X times; at the most, Y times.	[<length> | <percentage> | auto]{1,4}

following possible values to see which values you can assign to the property.

Values:

`<url> | none`

The values section provides you with a list of the values any given property can take.

Default Value:

`None`

The default value is the value automatically assigned to the property.

Inherited:

No

The inherited section lets you know whether or not a property is inherited by any child elements.

HTML Elements:

All

HTML Elements lists those HTML tags that can successfully be affected by the property.

Now that you know how to use this reference, let's move on to the property definitions.

Box Properties

Top Margin

Description:

Specifies the size of an element's top margin.

Property Syntax:

`margin-top: <value>`

Values:

`<length> | <percentage> | auto`

Default Value:

`0`

Inherited:

No

HTML Elements:

All

Right Margin

Description:

Specifies the size of an element's right margin.

Property Syntax:

`margin-right: <value>`

Values:

`<length> | <percentage> | auto`

Default Value:

`0`

Inherited:

No

HTML Elements:

All

Bottom Margin:

Description:

Specifies the size of an element's bottom margin.

Property Syntax:

`margin-bottom: <value>`

Values:

`<length> | <percentage> | auto`

Default Value:

0

Inherited:

No

HTML Elements:

All

Left Margin

Description:

Specifies the size of an element's left margin.

Property Syntax:

`margin-left: <value>`

Values:

`<length> | <percentage> | auto`

Default Value:

0

HTML Elements:

All

Inherited:

No

Margin

Description:

Shorthand notation that defines the size of all four of an element's margins at one time.

Property Syntax:

```
margin: <value>
```

Values:

```
[ <length> | <percentage> | auto]{1,4}
```

Default Value:

Undefined

Inherited:

No

HTML Elements:

All

Top Padding

Description:

Specifies the amount of space between an element's contents and its top border.

Property Syntax:

```
padding-top: <value>
```

Values:

```
<length> | <percentage>
```

Default Value:

0

Inherited:

No

HTML Elements:

All

Right Padding

Description:

Specifies the amount of space between an element's contents and its right border.

Property Syntax:

```
padding-right: <value>
```

Values:
`<length> | <percentage>`

Default Value:
`0`

Inherited:
No

HTML Elements:
All

Bottom Padding

Description:
Specifies the amount of space between an element's contents and its bottom border.

Property Syntax:
`padding-bottom: <value>`

Values:
`<length> | <percentage>`

Default Value:
`0`

Inherited:
No

HTML Elements:
All

Left Padding

Description:
Specifies the amount of space between an element's contents and its left border.

Property Syntax:
`padding-left: <value>`

Values:
`<length> | <percentage>`

Default Value:

0

Inherited:

No

HTML Elements:

All

Padding

Description:

Shorthand notation that sets the padding size for all sides of an element at one time.

Property Syntax:

padding: <value>

Values:

[<length> | <percentage>]{1,4}

Default Value:

0

Inherited:

No

HTML Elements:

All

Top Border Width

Description:

Specifies the width of an element's top border.

Property Syntax:

border-top-width: <value>

Values:

thin | medium | thick | <length>

Default Value:

Medium

Inherited:

No

HTML Elements:

All

Right Border Width

Description:

Specifies the width of an element's right border.

Property Syntax:

```
border-right-width: <value>
```

Values:

```
thin | medium | thick | <length>
```

Default Value:

```
Medium
```

Inherited:

```
No
```

HTML Elements:

All

Bottom Border Width

Description:

Specifies the width of an element's left border.

Property Syntax:

```
border-bottom-width: <value>
```

Values:

```
thin | medium | thick | <length>
```

Default Value:

```
Medium
```

Inherited:

No

HTML Elements:

All

Left Border Width

Description:

Specifies the width of an element's left border.

Property Syntax:
```
border-left-width: <value>
```

Values:
```
thin | medium | thick | <length>
```

Default Value:
```
Medium
```

Inherited:
No

HTML Elements:
All

Border Width

Description:
Shorthand notation that sets the width of all four of an element's borders at one time.

Property Syntax:
```
border-width: <value>
```

Values:
```
[ thin | medium | thick | <length>]{1,4}
```

Default Value:
Undefined

Inherited:
No

HTML Elements:
All

Border Color

Description:
Defines the color for all four sides of an element's border.

Property Syntax:
```
border-color: <value>
```

Values:
```
<color>{1,4}
```

Default Value:

The value assigned to the color property.

Inherited:

No

HTML Elements:

All

Border Style

Description:

Specifies the style for all four sides of an element's border.

Property Syntax:

```
border-style: <value>
```

Values:

```
[ none | dotted | dashed | solid | double | groove |
ridge | inset |
outset]{1,4}
```

Default Value:

```
None
```

Inherited:

No

HTML Elements:

All

Top Border

Description:

Shorthand notation that sets the width, color, and style of an element's top border.

Property Syntax:

```
border-top: <value>
```

Values:

```
<border-top-width> || <border-style> || <color>
```

Default Value:

Undefined

Inherited:

No

HTML Elements:

All

Right Border

Description:

Shorthand notation that sets the width, color, and style of an element's right border.

Property Syntax:
```
border-right: <value>
```

Values:
```
<border-right-width> || <border-style> || <color>
```

Default Value:

Undefined

Inherited:

No

HTML Elements:

All

Bottom Border

Description:

Shorthand notation that sets the width, color, and style of an element's bottom border.

Property Syntax:
```
border-bottom: <value>
```

Values:
```
<border-bottom-width> || <border-style> || <color>
```

Default Value:

Undefined

Inherited:

No

HTML Elements:

All

Left Border

Description:

Shorthand notation that sets the width, color, and style of an element's left border.

Property Syntax:

`border-left: <value>`

Values:

`<border-left-width> || <border-style> || <color>`

Default Value:

Undefined

Inherited:

No

HTML Elements:

All

Border

Description:

Shorthand notation that sets the width, color, and style for all of an element's borders.

Property Syntax:

`border: <value>`

Values:

`<border-width> || <border-style> || <color>`

Default Value:

Undefined

Inherited:

No

HTML Elements:

All

Width

Description:

Defines an element's width.

Property Syntax:

`width: <value>`

Values:

`<length> | <percentage> | auto`

Default Value:

`Auto`

Inherited:

No

HTML Elements:

Replaced and block-level elements

Height

Description:

Defines an element's height.

Property Syntax:

`height: <value>`

Values:

`<length> | auto`

Default Value:

`Auto`

Inherited:

No

HTML Elements:

Replaced and block-level elements

Float

Description:

Allows text to be wrapped around an element.

Property Syntax:

`float: <value>`

Values:
left | right | none

Default Value:
None

Inherited:
No

HTML Elements:
All

Clear

Description:
Specifies to which sides text can be wrapped around an element.

Property Syntax:
clear: <value>

Values:
none | left | right | both

Default Value:
None

Inherited:
No

HTML Elements:
All

Classification Properties

Display

Description:
Specifies if an element should be displayed as inline, a block, a
list-item, or none of these.

Property Syntax:
display: <value>

Values:
block | inline | list-item | none

Default Value:
Block

Inherited:
No

HTML Elements:
All

Whitespace

Description:

Specifies how white space within an element should be rendered.

Property Syntax:
white-space: <value>

Values:
normal | pre | nowrap

Default Value:
Normal

Inherited:
Yes

HTML Elements:
Block-level elements only

List Style Type

Definition: Defines the type of marker to be used within a list.

Property Syntax:
list-style-type: <value>

Values:
disc | circle | square | decimal | lower-roman | upper-roman | lower-alpha | upper-alpha | none

Default Value:
Disc

Inherited:
Yes

HTML Elements:

Elements with a display type of list-item and HTML list markup.

List Style Image

Description:

Defines an image to be used as a list-item marker.

Property Syntax:

`list-style-image: <value>`

Values:

`<url> | none`

Default Value:

`None`

Inherited:

Yes

HTML Elements:

Elements with a display type of list-item and HTML list markup.

List Style Position

Description:

Specifies whether text in a list should be displayed inside or outside of the list-item marker.

Property Syntax:

`list-style-position: <value>`

Values:

`inside | outside`

Default Value:

`Outside`

Inherited:

Yes

HTML Elements:

Elements with a display type of list-item and HTML list markup.

List Style

Description:

Shorthand notation that defines the list-style type, position, and marker image URL at one time.

Property Syntax:

```
list-style: <value>
```

Values:

```
<list-style-type> || <list-style-position> || <url>
```

Default Value:

Undefined

Inherited:

Yes

HTML Elements:

Elements with a display type of list-item and HTML list markup.

Color And Background Properties

Color

Description:

Sets an element's color.

Property Syntax:

```
color: <color>
```

Default Value:

Specified by browser

Inherited:

Yes

Background Color

Description:

Sets an element's background color.

Property Syntax:

```
background-color: <value>
```

Values:
```
<color> | transparent
```

Default Value:
```
Transparent
```

Inherited:

No

HTML Elements:

All

Background Image

Description:

Attaches a background image to an element.

Property Syntax:
```
background-image: <value>
```

Values:
```
<url> | none
```

Default Value:
```
None
```

Inherited:

No

HTML Elements:

All

Background Repeat

Description:

Specifies how an element's background image should be repeated.

Property Syntax:
```
background-repeat: <value>
```

Values:
```
repeat | repeat-x | repeat-y | no-repeat
```

Default Value:
```
Repeat
```

Inherited:

No

HTML Elements:

All

Background Attachment

Description:

Specifies whether an element's background image is fixed in the browser window or scrolls with the element.

Property Syntax:

```
background-attachment: <value>
```

Values:

```
scroll | fixed
```

Default Value:

```
Scroll
```

Inherited:

No

HTML Elements:

All

Background Position

Description:

Defines the position of an element's background image in relation to the element.

Property Syntax:

```
background-position: <value>
```

Values:

```
[<percentage> | <length>]{1,2} | [top | center | bottom]
|| [left | center | right]
```

Default Value:

```
0% 0%
```

HTML Elements:

Replaced and block-level elements only

Inherited:

No

Background

Description:

Shorthand notation that defines an element's background color and image, as well as how the image repeats, its attachment, and its position.

Property Syntax:

```
background: <value>
```

Values:

```
<background-color> || <background-image> || <background-
repeat> || <background-attachment>
|| <background-position>
```

Default Value:

Undefined

HTML Elements:

All elements

Inherited:

No

Font Properties

Font Family

Description:

This property specifies the font in which the text affected by the style rule should be displayed.

Property Syntax

```
font-family: [[<family-name> | <generic-family>],]*
[<family-name> | <generic-family>]
```

Values

```
<family-name>
<generic-family>
```
- serif (ex: "Century Schoolbook")
- sans-serif (ex: Helvetica)
- monospace (ex: Courier)
- cursive (ex: Zapf-Chancery)
- fantasy (ex: Western)

Default Value:

Specified by browser

Inherited:

Yes

HTML Elements:

All

Font Size

Description:

Sets the size of text using either absolute or relative measurements.

Property Syntax:

```
font-size: <absolute-size> | <relative-size> | <length> |
<percentage>
```

Values:

```
<absolute-size>
xx-small | x-small | small | medium | large | x-large |
xx-large
<relative-size>
larger | smaller
<length>
<percentage>
```

Default Value:

```
Medium
```

Inherited:

Yes

HTML Elements:

All

Font Style

Description:

This property defines how the text affected by the property should be styled.

Property Syntax:

```
font-style: <value>
```

Values:

```
normal | italic | oblique
```

Default Value:

```
Normal
```

Inherited:

Yes

HTML Elements:

All

Font Variant

Description:

This property causes the affected text to be rendered as normal text or in small caps.

Property Syntax:

```
font-variant <value>
```

Values:

```
normal | small-caps
```

Default Value:

Normal

Inherited:

Yes

HTML Elements:

All

Font Weight

Description:

Use this property to define how dark or light text should be.

Property Syntax:

```
font-weight: <value>
```

Values:

```
normal | bold | bolder | lighter | 100 | 200 | 300 | 400
| 500 | 600 | 700 | 800 | 900
```

Default Value:

Normal

Inherited:

Yes

HTML Elements:

All

Font

Description:

Shorthand notation that combines all of the font properties into one property-value set.

Property Syntax:

font: <value>

Values:

[<font-style> || <font-variant> || <font-weight>]?
<font-size>
[/<line-height>]? <font-family>

Default Value:

Undefined

Inherited:

Yes

HTML Elements:

All

Text Properties

Word Spacing

Description:

Sets the amount of space between the words within an element.

Property Syntax:

word-spacing: <value>

Values:

normal | <length>

Default Value:

Normal

Inherited:

Yes

HTML Elements:

All

Letter Spacing

Description:

Sets the amount of space between the letters within an element.

Property Syntax:

letter-spacing: <value>

Values:

normal | <length>

Default Value:

Normal

Inherited:

Yes

HTML Elements:

All

Text Decoration

Description:

Specifies how the text within an element should be decorated.

Property Syntax:

text-decoration: <value>

Values:

none | [underline || overline || line-through || blink]

Default Value:

None

Inherited:

No

HTML Elements:

All

Vertical Alignment

Description:

Specifies how an inline element should be positioned relative to its parent element.

Property Syntax:

`vertical-align: <value>`

Values:

`baseline | sub | super | top | text-top | middle | bottom | text-bottom | <percentage>`

Default Value:

`Baseline`

Inherited:

No

HTML Elements:

Inline elements only

Text Transformation

Description:

Specifies in what case the text within an element should be rendered, regardless of the case it is typed in.

Property Syntax:

`text-transform: <value>`

Values:

`none | capitalize | uppercase | lowercase`

Default Value:

`None`

HTML Elements:

All

Inherited:

Yes

Text Alignment

Description:

Specifies how text within an element should be aligned relative to its parent element and the page.

Property Syntax:

```
text-align: <value>
```

Values:

```
left | right | center | justify
```

Default Value:

Specified by browser

Inherited:

Yes

HTML Elements:

Block-level elements only

Text Indentation

Description:

Specifies how much the first line of a block-level element should be indented.

Property Syntax:

```
text-indent: <value>
```

Values:

```
<length> | <percentage>
```

Default Value:

```
0
```

Inherited:

Yes

HTML Elements:

Block-level elements only

Line Height

Description:

Defines the amount of space between lines in an element.

Property Syntax:

`line-height: <value>`

Values:

`normal | <number> | <length> | <percentage>`

Default Value:

`Normal`

Inherited:

Yes

HTML Elements:

All

ABOUT THE B CD-ROM

In creating the CD-ROM, we put together a set of resources that will help you as you develop your own style sheets. You'll find three different kinds of materials on the CD-ROM:

- **Web Pages.** The Web itself houses some of the best style sheet resources. Throughout the book, we've referred you to site after quality site. To make it easy as a click of the mouse button for you to visit those sites, we've created a hotlist of all the URLs mentioned in the book. In addition, we did some more surfin' of our own to bring you hotlists of the best style sheet Web resources. The Web pages also include links to style sheet and dynamic HTML-aware software, and an about the authors section that allows you to mail any of the authors directly.

- **Sample Code.** In many of the book's chapters, we included sample style sheet code to show you how the properties and values can be combined to create style rules. The Sample Code section of the CD-ROM includes copies of all of these code samples saved as plain text so you can incorporate them into your own Web pages.

- **Styled Software.** The makers of Web publishing tools are quickly beginning to realize what an important role style sheets are going to play in the future of HTML. Some have already begun to incorporate style sheet tools and support into their software packages to make creating and maintaining style sheets easier. We've gathered up many of these styled software packages and included evaluation versions on the CD-ROM for you to try. A quality tool can make all the difference when you're designing quality Web pages. The ones included on the CD-ROM are some of the best.

The rest of the appendix provides you with a detailed listing of the resources available on the CD-ROM. Enjoy!

How To Use The CD-ROM

The CD-ROM has been designed to make navigating its contents and resources simple. Regardless of the platform or operating system you are running on your computer, you will be able to use the CD-ROM and access its materials. To do so, simply launch the

CD-ROM and follow the instructions on the screen. The contents will be installed locally onto your computer for quick access. Some of the software packages only run on one platform, but only those that match your platform and OS will be installed on your computer. Once the files are installed, you can browse the Web pages with any Web browser, and the code files may be opened and manipulated with any program that supports plain text.

All of the CD-ROM's files are mirrored on the LANWrights Web site. If you have problems accessing the CD-ROM, point your Web browser at **http://www.lanw.com/HTMLStyle/** to download the files.

The Web Pages

All of the Web pages can be accessed from home.html, shown in Figure B.1, which serves as the Web page collection's "home page."

The resources are divided into four different categories including:

- URLs from the book. A complete listing of the book's URLs, organized by chapter.

Figure B.1 The CD-ROM Web page collection home page.

- Other online resources. A hotlist whose resources point to many different style sheet-related Web resources.

- Links to software. A hotlist whose resources point to style sheet and dynamic HTML-aware software packages.

- About the authors. Biographical information about the authors and email hyperlinks to help you contact each of us.

All of these resources can be accessed from the home page by clicking on its corresponding hyperlink, as shown in Figure B.2.

Be sure to read the User Caveat section for information on broken or changed links.

The Code Samples

We went back through the chapters of the book to provide you with electronic versions of the many style sheet code samples included in the book. If a sample was only one line long, or came from someone else's Web page, we didn't include it. We trust you can type a line of code in less time than it would take you to locate and open a text file. For copyright reasons, we couldn't include the code from the sites we highlighted throughout the book. To view those style sheets, simply view the source of the HTML file in your Web browser, and if the style sheet isn't included directly within the page, use the file information in the

Figure B.2 Access all of the other Web resources from the home page.

document's <LINK> tag to locate and view the source of an external style sheet.

The code sample files are named ch*N*ex*N*.txt, where *N* is a number between 0 and 9 and represent the chapter number and sample number. For example, ch4ex2.txt is code sample two from chapter four. Table B.1 provides a rundown of the file names and a description of the style code included in each one. This should help you correlate the text files with the examples printed in the book.

Table B.1 Code sample file names and descriptions.

File Name	Description
ch1ex1.txt	A CSS style rule similar to a style set up in Microsoft Word
ch1ex2.txt	A style rule that specifies square bullets for a list item
ch3ex1.txt	Four different ways to include style information in an HTML page
ch4ex1.txt	The basic HTML structure for a document that includes inline style information
ch4ex2.txt	The basic HTML structure of a document with a style rule that defines a white background for the document
ch4ex3.txt	Grouping selectors from four rules with identical declarations into one style rule
ch4ex4.txt	Grouping declarations from four rules with identical selectors into one style rule
ch4ex5.txt	Creating a single style rule using the shorthand notation for the font properties
ch4ex6.txt	Adding class to selectors
ch4ex7.txt	Adding context requirements to a selector
ch4ex8.txt	An example of inherited style
ch5ex1.txt	Setting line height as a number
ch5ex2.txt	Setting line height as a percentage
ch6ex1.txt	Creating and referencing margin style rules
ch6ex2.txt	Creating and referencing padding style rules
ch6ex3.txt	A style rule for a double border 20 pixels wide
ch6ex4.txt	A style rule for a solid teal border 20 pixels wide
ch6ex5.txt	A style rule that creates a different kind of border on each side of an element
ch6ex6.txt	A style rule that creates a division 200x600 pixels in size
ch6ex7.txt	Floating elements to the left or right of an object
ch6ex8.txt	Style rules and HTML take the place of table markup
ch7ex1.txt	Creating an inline display

(continued)

Table B.1 Code sample file names and descriptions (*continued*).

File Name	Description
ch7ex2.txt	Specifying bullet and number types for list items
ch7ex3.txt	Using the pre value with the white-space property
ch7ex4.txt	Specifying an image as a list item marker
ch8ex1.txt	Using style rules to specify text fonts
ch8ex2.txt	Assigning a different font to each heading level
ch8ex3.txt	Setting font style
ch8ex4.txt	Using the small-caps font style
ch8ex5.txt	Setting font weight
ch8ex6.txt	Setting font size using absolute size
ch8ex7.txt	Setting font size using relative size
ch8ex8.txt	Setting font size using length
ch8ex9.txt	Setting font size using percentage
ch8ex10.txt	Creating a style rule using the font shorthand notation
ch9ex1.txt	Setting text alignment
ch9ex2.txt	Setting text indent
ch9ex3.txt	Setting line height
ch9ex4.txt	Setting word spacing
ch9ex5.txt	Setting letter spacing
ch9ex6.txt	Setting vertical alignment, subscript, and superscript
ch9ex7.txt	Setting vertical alignment using percentages
ch9ex8.txt	Specifying text decoration
ch9ex9.txt	Specifying text transformation
ch10ex1.txt	Linking to multiple external style sheets
ch10ex2.txt	Importing one or more external style sheets
ch10ex3.txt	Mixing linked style sheets with inline style rules
ch10ex4.txt	Mixing imported style sheets with inline style rules
clr2ex1.txt	Specifying that text within <FONT CLASS=teal> tags will be teal
clr2ex2.txt	Embedding HTML tags with different font color styles
clr2ex3.txt	Combining font properties notation and other style rules to create a heading style
clr2ex4.txt	Using the background-color property
clr2ex5.txt	Embedding HTML tags with different background color styles
clr2ex6.txt	Defining a background image that is fixed on the page

(*continued*)

Table B.1   Code sample file names and descriptions (*continued*).

File Name	Description
clr2ex7.txt	Defining a background image and specifying its position
clr2ex8.txt	Creating a shorthand version of the background properties
clr3ex1.txt	The style sheet for an elementary school frog habitat Web page
clr3ex2.txt	The style sheet for a college level frog habitat Web page
clr4ex1.txt	A simple style sheet that governs fonts, text color, and backgrounds

Only those chapters that contain sample code that meets the criteria listed above will have corresponding sets of code samples.

Styled Software

A good set of tools is as important to a Webmaster's success as his or her own knowledge. Quality tools make it easier to design pages, as well as manage and maintain them. Because style sheet technology is still on the bleeding edge, only a small fraction of the available HTML design packages support style sheets. We've included evaluation versions of six of these packages for you to install and try at your leisure. They are all designed to assist you in your Web page development, and include advanced page layout and site management tools as well. The fact that their developers have incorporated style sheet support into them so quickly indicates that the developers are quick to recognize hot technologies and can implement them in a hurry. This speaks volumes about the high quality of the software and its developer's commitment to keeping up with the rapid changes in HTML and Web technologies.

The following listings include the package name, developer information, a URL for more information, and operating system information for each of the six software packages.

Sheet Stylist

Developer

http://www.tcp.co.uk/~drarh/Stylist/

THE SKINNY ON EVALUATION VERSIONS

Evaluation versions are just that, versions of a software package made available to you to evaluate. If you choose to continue using the package after its evaluation period expires (usually between 60 and 90 days), you should pay for it. If you keep the software and don't pay for it, the developers who invested the knowledge, talents, and sleepless nights spent in the creation of the package won't be compensated. By installing the evaluation versions of the software onto your hard disk, you are automatically agreeing to the developer's licensing agreement. Each is different, so make sure to read the documentation included with each evaluation version, and if you have questions, visit the developer's Web site for more information. It is important that we pay for the software we use. This helps keep smaller developers in business and supports the continued development of quality software tools and utilities.

Operating Systems Supported

Windows 95

Windows NT

Cascade

Developer

Media Design in * Progress

http://interaction.in-progress.com/cascade/index.html

Operating Systems Supported

Macintosh

StyleMaker

Developer

Danere Group

http://danere.com/StyleMaker/

Operating Systems Supported

Windows 95

Hot Dog

Developer

Sausage Software

http://www.sausage.com/

Operating Systems Supported

Windows 95

Windows NT

HomeSite

Developer

Allaire

http://www.allaire.com/products/homesite/
overview.cfm?tbsection=Overview

Operating Systems Supported

Windows 95

Windows NT

QuickSite 2.0

Developer

DeltaPoint

http://www.deltapoint.com/qsdeved/index.htm

Operating Systems Supported

Windows 3.1x

Windows 95

GLOSSARY

API (Application Programming Interface) Software used by an application program to request and carry out computer system services, or services from other subsystems outside an application's control.

ASCII (American Standard Code For Information Exchange) A character encoding technique that translates letters, numbers, and symbols into digital form.

background properties This term refers to the features of the area behind text and graphics.

bitmapped A graphic image that is depicted as an array of binary values. These images are typically converted from some other graphics format.

Box properties In CSS, this term describes the use of the box page design model to define borders, margins, and other rules for boxed areas of text and graphics.

browser service A utility that maintains a list of network resources within a domain, and provides lists of these domains, servers, and resource objects to any Explorer-type interface that requests it (e.g., browse lists).

cell padding The amount of space in a cell between an element and its margin or its border.

CERN (Conseil Europeen pour la Recherche Nucleaire) A high-energy particle physics laboratory. The place where the World Wide Web began, located in Geneva, Switzerland.

class A way of designating type information for an object; for CSS1, class permits an instance of a particular tag to be assigned a named type, so that multiple instances of the same tag may be distinguished by their class.

classification properties They control the basic way in which browsers display HTML by giving you more control of the spacing and list displays.

color property The declaration of a color value in a CSS1 style tag consists of the property name color, followed by a colon, followed either by a color name or the RGB numeric value for some particular color combination (for example {color:aqua} is valid, as is {color:102030}).

computer display devices A tool used to show the information produced on a computer; such as cathode-ray terminals (CRTs) and liquid crystal displays (LCDs), among others.

conversion factors The numerical values applied to absolute or relative measurements to systematically manipulate the size and shape of objects, or the boxes in which they are placed.

corporate identity The establishment of a unique perception of your company internally and to the public.

CRT (cathode-ray terminal) A term that refers to a monitor that uses a vacuum tube as a display screen.

CSS (Cascading Style Sheets) the collection of specifications that comprise the current prevailing standard for HTML-based Style Sheets.

CSS1-aware browsers *See* CSS1-compliant browser.

CSS1-compliant browser A Web browser that is capable of inter-preting and rendering CSS1-based style tags, and of interpreting external style sheets for the Web documents to which they're attached.

D-HTML(Dynamic HTML) A form of HTML that includes the ability for a document's on-screen display, to be changed on the fly, in response to user-generated events, or script-driven pro-grammatic instructions.

descriptor A word or phrase used to describe how a text or an object is to appear within HTML.

DIV (abbreviation for Division) An HTML markup tag used to separate individual sections of a document, each of which may have its own separate styles, backgrounds, and so forth.

DOM (Document Object Model) A definition of a Web document that permits each entity it contains to be addressed and manipulated individually, by tag, by class, or by specific instance.

domain name A name that is used on the Internet to translate physical addresses to computer names and computer names into physical addresses.

dpi (dots per inch) The measurement used for printer resolution.

DSSSL (Document Style Semantics and Specification Language) An International Standard (ISO/IEC 10179:1995) specifying document transformation and formatting, that is intended to be neutral to both the computing platform and the software in use.

DTD (Document Type Definition) The SGML document that defines a particular kind of document, and includes its named markup elements, predefined entities, and rules for how elements must be rendered.

dynamic CSS Like Dynamic HTML, dynamic CSS refers to Cascading Style Sheet documents built around the W3C DOM that can be altered on the fly, in response to user-generated events, or by manipulation from embedded scripts.

em value The numeric value, in terms of some unit of measure, of the width of the "m" character for some particular font and point size.

email (electronic mail) A method used by users on networked systems to exchange information.

event handling The code that "recognizes" that a particular user action has taken place (such as moving the mouse, clicking a mouse button, and so forth) and takes appropriate action, or code that recognizes more generic events (document completed download, images displayed, and so forth) and reacts to them.

EXtensible Markup Language (XML) A markup language that is emerging as an intermediate step between HTML and SGML as an open-ended markup language that goes well beyond what's possible with HTML without embracing all of the power and generality of SGML.

external style sheet A CSS document defined as a standalone file, referenced within the context of an HTML or XML document.

firewall A barrier between two networks made of software and/or hardware that permits only authorized communication to pass.

font family A named collection of identical fonts, of different point sizes (Baskerville, Arial, Times Roman, and so forth).

font properties The kinds of attributes, and their associated values, that describe a particular display font (such properties include font family, point size, em width, x height, and font treatment).

font treatment The manner in which characters for a font are to be rendered (for example, plain text, italic, bold, and so forth).

font variant Permits designer to specify a small-caps style (where capital letters from a smaller point size are used to act as lower-case characters for a larger font) for a particular font family.

font weight The stroke weight of a particular font, relative to other forms it may take (for example, a bold font may be demi-bold, bold, or ultra bold, which indicates progressively "heavier" versions of the same underlying font).

FTP (File Transfer Protocol) A protocol that transfers files to and from a local hard drive to an FTP server located elsewhere on another TCP/IP-based network (such as the Internet).

GIF (Graphics Interface Format) A graphics format that is used in Web documents to encode images into bits so that a computer can "read" the GIF file and display the picture on a computer screen. GIFs only support 256 colors, which compresses it and makes it easier to transfer across phone lines.

gopher A service that provides text-only information over the Internet, most suited to large documents with little or no formatting or images.

GUI (Graphic User Interface) A computer interface that uses graphics, windows, and a trackball or mouse as the method of interaction with the computer.

HDL (Hypertext Delivery Language) version of Hewlett-Packard's Semantic Delivery Language (SDL) tailored specifically for HTML.

hexadecimal values A collection of ten numbers that represent a variety of colors.

hotlist A list of links to a related topic located on a Web page.

HTML (HyperText Markup Language) Based on SGML, it is the markup language used to create Web pages.

HTTP (HyperText Transfer Protocol) This is the World Wide Web protocol that allows for the transfer of HTML documents over the Internet or intranets that respond to actions like a user clicking on hypertext links.

hypertext A way of organizing data, so when you click on a name or graphic, it links you to another area.

inline style sheet A collection of CSS1 style tags and properties that define styles for an HTML document, and that are embedded directly within the document itself.

Internet Explorer The Microsoft Web browser that runs under the Windows 95 and Windows NT operating systems.

Internet Media Type Any of a named set of recognized internet media, which can include things such as ASCII text, HTML, XML, SGML, and other, more complex media types.

ISO Latin-1 character set A term that defines the character and numeric entities for non-Roman and special ASCII characters, along with the metacharacters used to bracket HTML markup itself.

Java A programming language used for the World Wide Web and intranet applications.

JavaScript A scripting language used to write Web pages. It is easier than Java and is supported by Netscape 2.0 and higher.

LAYER tag A tag supported by Netscape that provides the mechanism used to organize content into layers with strict orders of precedence, transparence, and visibility on a page.

LCD display (Liquid Crystal Display) A type of computer display that uses individually addressable LCD elements to control how images are rendered on screen.

LINK tag An HTML tag that provides information about links from the current document to other documents or URL resources, including named relationships such as next, previous, help, index, toc, and so forth.

Lynx A character-mode Web browser commonly used through UNIX hosts that remains quite common today, despite the prevalence of graphical-mode browsers like Netscape Navigator and Internet Explorer.

metacharacters Characters used in HTML to indicate special handling. The angle brackets (<>), pound sign (#), ampersand(&), and semicolon (;) are metacharacters in HTML.

metadata Information that describes other information.

MIME (Multipurpose Internet Mail Extension) types Any of a collection of predefined document types, used by electronic mail software and HTTP-based services to identify the documents that are transported across a TCP/IP network.

monospaced font A font in which every character is the same width.

mousedown When an object is highlighted and the user clicks on the mouse.

mouseover When the cursor moves across an object.

multichannel Making a common channel into more than one channel by either splitting the frequency band of that channel into many thinner bands or by designating portions of the whole channel.

navigation On the World Wide Web, navigation is the movement between HTML documents and Web resources by the use of hyperlinks.

Netscape extensions A series of proprietary HTML tags, or proprietary attributes for standard tags, that are unique to Netscape Navigator and Communicator, which may not be supported by most other browsers.

Netscape Navigator One of the most popular Web browsers, built and maintained by Netscape Communications, Inc.

newsgroup A group of Usenet users that discuss well-defined topics.

NNTP (Network News Transfer Protocol) An extension of TCP/IP that is used to connect Usenet groups on the Internet.

nowrap One of the three values of the white space property. The value displays carriage returns, linefeeds, and multiple spaces as a single space.

operating system (OS) A software program that controls the operations of a computer system.

pica When referring to word processing, it is a monospaced font that prints 10 characters per inch. When referring to typography, it is about 1/6th of an inch or 12 points.

pixel (picture element) In a video screen image, it is the smallest unit of area. Pixels can be turned on and off and varied in intensity.

point A typographical unit of measure commonly used to state font sizes, equal to approximately 1/72nd of an inch.

property A named attribute of a class tag, each property usually has an associated value as well. Properties give CSS tags their specific values, and define individual instances of style information.

pseudo-class a special extension to the normal values associated with attributes for Style tags, pseudo-classes permit definition and specification of particular typographic effects, including status colors for hyperlinks (one color can indicate a tag that's never been followed, another a tag that's been followed before).

pseudo-element Permits style to be set only on a part of an element's content, so that, for instance, the first character in a paragraph can be "tagged" for special treatment (usually in the form of a drop cap, where the font size is many times that of the rest of the body), or the first line of a paragraph can be set in a large point size, while remaining lines use whatever point size is defined in the general style definitions.

RGB (Red Green Blue) The computer graphics color model derived from variations of Red, Green, and Blue.

RRGGBB A 6-digit notation that expresses relative values for R(ed) G(reen) and B(lue) color saturation in numeric format.

sans-serif font A font that does not have the horizontal lines at the tops and bottoms of letters. Helvetica and Arial are two popular sans-serif fonts.

scripting language A programming language that uses English statements in the coding.

Scripting Object Model A model for defining how scripts operate, and how scripts can address internal or document-based objects while they're executing.

selector One of the parts of a one-rule style sheet.

serif font A font that has horizontal lines at the tops and bottoms of letters. Times Roman is a serif font.

SGML (Standard Generalized Markup Language) An ISO standard text-based language that defines, specifies, and creates documents.

singleton tag A tag that stands alone, and supports no closing tag.

specification A formal statement of the requirements and capabilities of a particular set of notation, a program, or a technology.

style rule Applying a selector and declaration to an element so that it appears constant throughout the style sheet.

Telnet A terminal emulation utility used to interact with remote computers.

typography The process of making and laying out typewritten materials to print.

Unix An interactive time-sharing operating system developed in 1969 by a hacker to play games. This system developed into the most widely used industrial-strength computer in the world and ultimately supported the birth of the Internet.

URL (Uniform Resource Locator) The name of the addresses on the World Wide Web. URLs define what protocols to use, the domain name of the resource's Web server, the communication port address, and the directory path used to find the named Web file or resource.

Usenet The Internet service and protocol that gives users access to newsgroups.

User Interface Domain A group of members at the W3C.

Vector graphics In computer graphics, vector graphics are images that are represented as lines and points.

VGA (Video Graphics Array) A PC display standard of 640x480 pixels, 16 colors, and a 4:3 aspect ratio.

Visual Basic Microsoft's version of the BASIC programming language, used to develop Windows applications.

Visual Cafe A Java development environment, often used to create applets for use in Web pages, designed and maintained by Symantec Corporation.

W3C (World Wide Web Consortium) A consortium based in Cambridge, MA that develops the standards for the World Wide Web.

WAIS (Wide Area Information Server) A powerful system that looks up information on databases across the Internet.

Wayfinding Tool Kit A set of instructions on a Web page that instructs visitors how to find their way around the Web site in which they appear.

Web browser Client side software that allows you to search for information on the Internet.

Web server A computer that contains and distributes Web resources when it receives a request from a Web browser.

Web site An addressed location that allows users to access a set of Web pages that correspond to a site's URL.

white space The area of a page that is not occupied by text or graphics. Spaces and paragraph marks usually render white space.

INDEX

A

Absolute value
   size, 123
   word spacing, 138
Acender, 74
Adobe Photoshop, 163
Alignment, 132
   headings, 134
   sample code, 133
   syntax, 199
   vertical, 198
Allaire, 208
Anchor tags, 58
Andreesen, Mark, 18
APIs, 212
Application style sheets, 9
ASCII, 212

B

Background
   attachment, 192
   color definition, 190
   images, 174, 191
   position, 192
   properties, 212
   repeating, 191
   syntax, 193
Baseline, 74
   vertical alignment, 142
Bubble up, 166
Berners-Lee, Tim, 16
Bitmap, 212
   fonts, 18
Blink, 146
Block-level elements
   body, 133
   display value, 103
   DIV, 59
   margins, 85

span, 51
   value sample, 105
BLOCKQUOTE, 103
Borders, 38, 78
   adding color, 92, 182
   defining style, 91, 180, 183
   padding, 84
   properties, 90
   setting width, 90
   specifying entire border, 93
   specifying individual sides, 92
   width, 182
Bos, Bert, 22, 30
Bosak, Jon, 21, 23
Bottom margin, 177
Box properties, 78, 176, 212
   borders, 90, 180
   clear, 94
   margins, 83, 176
   padding, 88, 178
   size, 93
   width, 186
Browsers
   controlling display, 101–112
   font matching, 116
   font sizes, 123
   graphical browsers, 18
   Internet Explorer, 18
   Lynx, 17
   Mosaic, 18
   Netscape Navigator, 18
   overriding styles, 37
   resolving style conflicts, 159
   support for dynamic HTML, 168
   vertical-align support, 145
   word spacing support, 139

C

Capitalize, 148
Carriage returns

X

Digital Camera Design Guide
Peter Aitken
1-57610-184-3 • $45.00/$64.00 (US/CAN)
Available Now

NetObjects Fusion 2 Design Guide
Dan Shafer and Ed Smith
1-57610-212-2 • $44.99/$62.00 (US/CAN)
Available Now

HTML Style Sheets Design Guide
Pitts, Tittel, James
1-57610-211-4 • $39.99/$55.99 (US/CAN)
Available Now

Softimage 3D Design Guide
Barry Ruff and Gene Bodio
1-57610-147-9 • $39.99/$55.99 (US/CAN)
November 1997

COMING SOON!
**3D Studio MAX 2 Clay Sculpture, Digitizing, &
Facial Animation Guide**
Stephanie Reese
1-57610-150-9 • $49.99/$69.99 (US/CAN)

Geared towards art and design professionals who work with electronic graphics tools, Design Guides present original and diverse techniques developed by a team of professional artists and graphics designers.

The Design Guide Series includes highly visual and practical books with detailed step-by-step techniques. Computer-accomplished graphics professionals can learn to create cutting-edge, commercial quality graphics for games, Web presentations, VRML, video, and numerous other uses.

DESIGN GUIDE SERIES

Guides for Today's Creative Professionals

CORIOLIS GROUP BOOKS

An International Thomson Publishing Company   I T P

Prices and availability dates are subject to change without notice.

(800) 410-0192 • International Callers (602) 483-0192 • Fax (602) 483-0193 • www.coriolis.com

Dynamic HTML
Black Book

Includes techiques for creating interactive Web pages using multimedia effects on text, colors, graphics and more.

Only $49.99

1-57610-188-6

Call 800-410-0192

Fax 602-483-0193

Outside U.S. 602-483-0192

Dynamic HTML Black Book contains everything a Web professional needs to know about utilizing the creative features available with Dynamic HTML. This book contains complete coverage of HTML (version 3.2) and the nearly standard extension of Dynamic HTML put forth by Microsoft, Netscape, and the W3C. Developers will learn how to build simple cascading style sheets (CSS) and Dynamic HTML content, and how the two interact. The book also contains complete examples of HTML documents transformed into Dynamic HTML environments.

CORIOLIS GROUP BOOKS

http://www.coriolis.com

NetObjects Fusion 2 Design Guide

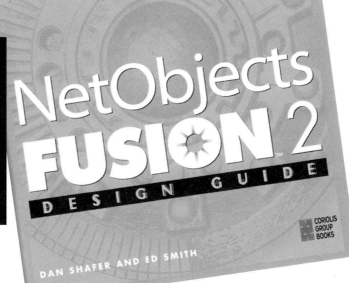

Lists "inside design tips" and shortcuts that make NetObjects Fusion 2 even more powerful and easier to use.

Only $44.99

1-57610-212-2

Call 800-410-0192

Fax 602-483-0193

Outside U.S. 602-483-0192

NetObjects Fusion 2 Design Guide shows Web designers and graphics artists how to create award-winning Web pages and Web sites. Using the numerous projects in this book, Web publishers can create sites without HTML coding using NetObjects Fusion 2, a Windows-based visual design application. Net Objects Fusion 2 supports popular Web browsers, sound, graphics, Java, ActiveX, Shockwave, and advanced JavaScript and VBScript controls.

CORIOLIS GROUP BOOKS

http://www.coriolis.com

• JAVA • VB • VC++ • DELPHI • SOFTWARE COMPONENTS • OCX, DLL •

CLIENT/SERVER • HTML • VRML • JAVA • VB • VC++ • DELPHI • SOFTWARE COMPONENTS

SOFTWARE COMPONENTS • DELPHI • VC++ • VB • JAVA • VRML • HTML • CLIENT/SERVER

magazine

Give Yourself the Visual Edge

Don't Lose Your Competitve Edge Act Now!

1 Year $21.95
(6 issues)

2 Years $37.95
(12 issues)

($53.95 Canada; $73.95 Elsewhere)
Please allow 4-6 weeks for delivery
All disk orders must be pre-paid

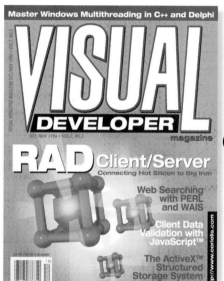

The first magazine dedicated to the Visual Revolution

Join Jeff Duntemann and his crew of master authors for a tour of the visual software development universe. Peter Aitken, Al Williams, Ray Konopka, David Gerrold, Michael Covington, Tom Campbell, and all your favorites share their insights into rapid application design and programming, software component development, and content creation for the desktop, client/server, and online worlds. The whole visual world will be yours, six times per year: Windows 95 and NT, Multimedia, VRML, Java, HTML, Delphi, VC++, VB, and more. *Seeing is succeeding!*

1-800-410-0192

See *Visual Developer* on the Web! http://www.coriolis.com

14455 N. Hayden Rd. Suite 220 • Scottsdale, Arizona 85260

• WEB • CGI • JAVA • VB • VC++ • DELPHI • SOFTWARE COMPONENTS •